JOSSEY-BASS
A Wiley Imprint
www.josseybass.com

Designing Your Organization

Using the Star Model
to Solve 5 Critical
Design Challenges

Amy Kates
Jay R. Galbraith

BICENTENNIAL
1807
WILEY
2007
BICENTENNIAL

John Wiley & Sons, Inc.

Published by Jossey-Bass
A Wiley Imprint
989 Market Street, San Francisco, CA 94103-1741—www.josseybass.com

Wiley Bicentennial logo: Richard J. Pacifico

Jossey-Bass books and products are available through most bookstores. To contact Jossey-Bass directly call our Customer Care Department within the U.S. at 800-956-7739, outside the U.S. at 317-572-3986 or fax 317-572-4002.

Jossey-Bass also publishes its books in a variety of electronic formats. Some content that appears in print may not be available in electronic books.

Library of Congress Cataloging-in-Publication Data

Kates, Amy.
    Designing your organization: using the star model to solve 5 critical design challenges/Amy Kates, Jay R. Galbraith. — 1st ed.
        p. cm.
    Includes bibliographical references and index.
    ISBN-13: 978-0-7879-9494-5
    1. Organizational change.   2. Organizational effectiveness.   I. Galbraith, Jay R.   II. Title.
HD58.8.K3774 2007
658.4′02—dc22
                                                                                            2007026558

Printed in the United States of America
FIRST EDITION

PB Printing 10 9 8 7 6 5 4 3 2

The Jossey-Bass Business & Management Series

Contents

Decision Tools Included on the CD-ROM

Introduction

IN THEIR CLASSIC 1972 work on the structure of multinational corporations, Stopford and Wells noted, "Management has rarely gone through the steps of stating its strategy explicitly and of weighting the contributions and costs associated with alternative organizational structures. . . . Our analysis has imposed an elaborate rational framework on what is largely an intuitive decision process of the businessman" (p. 171). In the intervening thirty-five years, business leaders have become much more aware of the need for a structured, rather than intuitive, approach to making decisions about organization design. Our previous book together, *Designing Dynamic Organizations*, written with Amy Kates's late business partner, Diane Downey, sought to provide that structured, step-by-step process. In that book, which has enjoyed a positive reaction from the business community, we laid out the concepts and process of organization design in the form of a how-to guide in order to provide a clear and explicit framework for decision making and practical application (Galbraith, Downey, and Kates, 2002).

Over the past few years, however, we have noticed five specific organization design challenges that seem to confront a majority of the organizations that we work with, read about, and observe. Our clients have asked us to provide them guidance in dealing with these more complex issues using the same clear step-wise approach. That has been the impetus for this book. Following the first chapter, "Fundamentals of Organization Design," which reviews key concepts and design principles, the remainder of the book is organized around the following five challenges:

- *Designing around the customer.* The growing number of global customers, the increased buying power and access to information that all customers have, and the difficulty in keeping up in the race to create products that stand out in a crowded marketplace are all factors driving many companies to search for ways to deliver integrated interfaces, customized products, and high-value solutions. Such firms are finding that this is impossible without completely rethinking the way in which the components of their organizations work together internally. Chapter Two defines customer-centric strategies and provides guidance on designing three levels of customer-centric organizations.

• *Organizing across borders.* Increasing levels of foreign direct investment, the liberalization of trade within and between countries, and growing markets in emerging economies are motivating more companies to seek nondomestic opportunities and build global organizations. Chapter Three addresses different types of global strategies, focusing on building geographically based organizations and multinational product and customer networks.

• *Making a matrix work.* In response to strategies that require increased collaboration across customer, geographic, function, and product dimensions, many companies are using a matrix to formally connect the disparate elements of their organizations. Despite advances in communication technology, formidable challenges of coordinating work across organizational boundaries remain. Chapter Four presents what we have learned about overcoming these challenges to make the matrix an effective coordinating mechanism.

• *Solving the centralization—decentralization dilemma.* As an organization grows, it has the opportunity to leverage its size and scale. But consolidating decisions can result in a loss of speed and responsiveness. Many companies oscillate between the extremes of centralization and decentralization, never finding a happy medium. Chapter Five explains how an understanding of the business portfolio determines the design of the corporate center and offers an analysis of which decisions are best centralized and which are best left at the business unit level and how to get the benefits of both centralization and decentralization without having to choose between the two.

• *Organizing for innovation.* The final challenge we address is how to design the organization to support organic growth, particularly the breakthrough innovations and new business launches that require a delicate balance between separating from the core business while taking advantage of the parent company's assets. Chapter Six discusses the range of innovation strategies and the design considerations to support them.

This book does not aim to present new research or theory. It draws from Jay Galbraith's writing, particularly his two most recent books, *Designing the Customer-Centric Organization* (2005) and *Designing the Global Corporation* (2000), as well as many other authors' contributions to organization design theory. We expect this book to be helpful to leaders and managers who make choices about their organizations' structures as well as to human resource and organization design and development practitioners who guide and influence those decisions. Our goal is to give readers the same frameworks and tools that we use in our consulting and teaching work to help leaders make sound decisions about their organizations. Each of the referenced tools is included in the Appendix and in electronic form on the accompanying CD-ROM. We encourage you to make use of these tools in your own work. Tools that are included on the CD-ROM are indicated by marginal icons.

We do not want to minimize the complexity inherent in any of the organizational forms examined, although we try to be clear and present the various steps of organization design decisions as distinctly as possible. The rate of change in the business environment continues to increase, and new competitors are constantly entering industries as economies grow around the world and become more interconnected. Today's corporation is more complex than ever before. For example, in 1970, the world's fifty largest companies averaged $29 billion in revenue in 2003 dollars. By 2005, the average was $100 billion. During the same period, the number of consumer products introduced each year increased sixteen-fold. In order to compete successfully, these same companies have to be able to react faster to changes in the business environment. Strategies that depend on developing multiple and fast-changing products, serving demanding customers, and coordinating across organizational unit boundaries complicated by time and cultural distance cannot be achieved with simple organizations. Nor can these strategies be achieved with managers and employees who do not understand why and how their organization is configured as it is and who have not been given the processes, tools, and skills to operate successfully within it. We believe it is worth repeating Harvard Business School professor Chris Bartlett's observation that companies often pursue third-generation strategies using second-generation organizations staffed with first-generation human resources. When first-generation managers attempt to institute third-generation multidimensional organizations, they often fail, and then attribute the failure to the organizational form rather than to their lack of capability (Galbraith, 2000). Our goal with this book is to help you build organizations to successfully execute your third-generation strategies.

Acknowledgments

We thank our many clients who have prompted our thinking on these topics, with particular appreciation to Joe Wong of MeadWestvaco Specialty Chemicals and German Carmona Alvarez of Cemex, who both read sections of the manuscript and contributed valuable feedback. We also thank our colleagues on the board of the Organization Design Forum (ODF), who have furthered the field and our own thinking through the conferences and programs offered by ODF each year. In addition, Paul Erickson and Julie Spriggs provided invaluable research and editing support during the writing process.

Finally, we both thank our families, Sasha Galbraith, and Muhamed, Malik, and Elias Saric, who tolerate all of the travel that makes our work possible.

The Authors

Amy Kates is principal partner with Downey Kates Associates (DKA), an organization design and development consulting firm located in New York City. Amy works globally with leaders and their teams to assess organizational issues, reshape structures and processes, and build depth of management capability. In her work as a diagnostician and designer, she helps her clients to understand organizational options and their implications and to make good decisions.

In addition to her consulting work, she teaches Organization Design in the Executive M.B.A. program at the Center for Technology, Economics, and Management in Denmark and co-teaches, with Jay Galbraith, a seminar on the Design of Customer-Centric Organizations at the University of Southern California. She is also on the board of directors of the Organization Design Forum.

Amy Kates is coauthor, with Jay Galbraith and Diane Downey, of *Designing Dynamic Organizations: A Hands-On Guide for Leaders at All Levels* (2002). She has published numerous articles and book chapters on the topics of organization design and talent management, including "The Challenges of General Manager Transitions" in *Filling the Management Pipeline* (Robert Kaiser, ed.). Her article, "(Re)Designing the HR Organization," was featured in the Summer 2006 issue of the *Human Resource Planning Society Journal* and was awarded the HRPS Walker Prize.

Amy Kates holds a master's degree in City and Regional Planning from Cornell University. Prior to joining DKA, Ms. Kates was a planner and urban designer and was selected to serve as an Urban Fellow by the New York City mayor's office. Amy can be contacted at Downey Kates Associates,

139 Fulton Street, Suite 210, New York, N.Y., 10038, by phone at (212) 349–3522 or by email at AKates@DowneyKates.com.

• • •

Jay R. Galbraith, a senior research scientist at the Center for Effective Organizations at the University of Southern California and professor emeritus at the International Institute for Management Development in Lausanne, Switzerland, is an internationally recognized expert on organization design. He is the president and founder of Galbraith Management Consultants, an international consulting firm that specializes in solving strategy and organizational design challenges in companies of all sizes—from small manufacturing companies to large global firms. His theories on gaining a significant competitive advantage through customer-centricity have been heard and implemented by top-level executives throughout the world.

Dr. Galbraith, creator of the widely used Star Model™, has written numerous publications including *Designing the Global Corporation, Designing Dynamic Organizations,* and *Designing Organizations: An Executive Guide to Strategy, Structure and Process.* His latest book, *Designing the Customer-Centric Organization,* introduces the Strategy Locator™, an innovative tool that helps companies determine the degree of customer-centricity their organizations need in order to offer the types of solutions that their customers demand.

In addition, Dr. Galbraith is regularly sought after for his expert opinion by the media, including *BusinessWeek, The Wall Street Journal, Fortune,* and *The Financial Times.* For more information, please visit www.jaygalbraith.com.

Chapter 1

Fundamentals of Organization Design

THIS BOOK is about five of the most common organization design challenges that business leaders face today. This first chapter reviews some fundamental organization design concepts in order to provide readers a firm foundation for understanding the complex organizational forms we discuss. It also defines key terms, highlighted in italics, that we use throughout the rest of the book. (For an in-depth discussion of organization design concepts and processes, refer to Galbraith, 2002, or Galbraith, Downey, and Kates, 2002.)

The first two questions to address are: What is an organization? and What is organization design? For our purposes, the term *organization* is used broadly to refer to an entire firm, as well as to just one part of it. It can be made up of many thousands of people or only a handful. For a corporate leader, the organization encompasses the entire company, and from the vantage point of a unit manager, the organization may be simply that unit. Most of what we discuss in this book is applicable to the whole organization, as well as to the smaller organizations nested within the larger firm. Although we frequently refer to companies and firms, the concepts apply equally to nonprofit and government entities.

Organization design is the deliberate process of configuring structures, processes, reward systems, and people practices to create an effective organization capable of achieving the business strategy. The organization is not an end in itself; it is simply a vehicle for accomplishing the strategic tasks of the business. It is an invisible construct used to harness and direct the energy of the people who do the work. We believe that the vast majority of people go to their jobs each day wanting to contribute to the mission of the organization they work for. Too often, however, the organization is a

1

barrier to, not an enabler of, individual efforts. We have observed that when left to their own devices, smart people figure out how to work around the barriers they encounter, but they waste time and energy that they could direct instead to improving products and services, creating innovations, or serving customers. One of the main purposes of organizational design is to align individual motivations with the interests of the organization and make it easy for individual employees to make the right decisions every day. Furthermore, a well-designed organization makes the collective work of accomplishing complex tasks easier.

This chapter begins with an overview of the Star Model,™ which provides a decision-making framework for organization design. We highlight the key concepts associated with each point on the star, which we expand on in the other chapters. The chapter concludes with a summary of themes that serve as our design principles.

The Star Model™: A Framework for Decision Making

Organization design is a decision-making process with numerous steps and many choices to make. A decision made early in the process will constrain choices made later, foreclose avenues of exploration, and eliminate alternatives, resulting in far-reaching impacts on the ultimate shape of the organization. Making sound decisions at these early, critical junctures requires a theoretical framework that gives credence to one choice over another. Yet many leaders and their teams still make organization design decisions based largely on their own individual experience and observation. A common framework for decision-making has a number of benefits. It:

- Provides a common language for debating options and articulating why one choice is better than another in objective, impersonal terms
- Forces design decisions to be based on longer-term business strategy rather than the more immediate demands of people and politics
- Provides a clear rationale for the choices considered and an explanation of the implications of those choices as the basis for communication and successful change management
- Allows decision makers to be able to evaluate outcomes, understand root causes, and make the right adjustments during implementation

The Star Model (Figure 1.1), which serves as our framework, has been used and refined over the past thirty years. Its basic premise is simple but powerful: different strategies require different organizations to execute

FIGURE 1.1 **Star Model.**

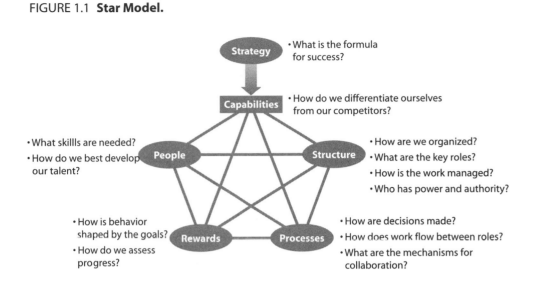

them. A strategy implies a set of capabilities at which an organization must excel in order to achieve the strategic goals. The leader has the responsibility to design and influence the structure, processes, rewards, and people practices of the organization in order to build these needed capabilities.

Although culture is an essential part of an organization, it is not an explicit part of the model because the leader cannot design the culture directly. An organization's culture consists of the common values, mindsets, and norms of behavior that have emerged over time and that most employees share. It is an outcome of the cumulative design decisions that have been made in the past and of the leadership and management behaviors that result from those decisions.

The idea of *alignment* is fundamental to the Star Model. Each component of the organization, represented by a point on the model, should work to support the strategy. The more that the structure, processes, rewards, and people practices reinforce the desired actions and behaviors, the better able the organization should be to achieve its goals. Just as important as initial alignment is having the ability to realign as circumstances change. The configuration of resources, the processes used, and the mental models that contribute to today's success will influence the plans made for the future. In a time of stability, this creates efficiency. In a time of change, such static alignment can become a constraint. The organization must have alignment, but it also needs the flexibility to recognize and respond to opportunities and threats.

It is always easier to change a business strategy than to change an organization, just as it is easier to change a course beforehand than it is to turn a large ship that is already under way. The more rapidly the organization can be realigned, the faster the leaders can "turn the ship" and execute new strategies and opportunities as they arise. This is especially important for large companies that must compete against smaller, nimbler organizations. Therefore, alignment is best thought of as an ongoing process rather than a one-time event.

The ideas of strategy dictating organizational form and of organizational elements aligning with strategy are based on a body of thought called contingency theory (Lawrence and Lorsch, 1967). *Contingency theory* does not prescribe any one best way to organize, but rather suggests that organization design choices are contingent on both the strategy selected and the environment in which the business is operating. Contingency theory has been extended with *complementary systems* theory, which comes to organization design from the field of economics (Milgrom and Roberts, 1995). The notion of complementarity holds that design choices work as coherent systems and that the application of one practice will influence the results of a corresponding practice—whether positive or negative. This underscores the practical application of the Star Model. For example, if a strategy depends on cross-unit coordination, contingency theory suggests it would be wise to formally link those units with processes and create measures and rewards that encourage teamwork. Research into complementary systems goes further, suggesting that in order to derive the full benefit of these choices, they should be employed as a system, and that negative consequences may occur if the practices are employed individually and not together (Whittington and others, 1999). This research confirms what many suspect: piecemeal adoption of management practices has little impact on business performance. It also means that simple benchmarking and copying of another company's structures and processes has little useful application in organization design. For example, using a matrix is neither a good nor a bad practice in itself. But when a matrix is installed without the appropriate and corresponding role clarity, governance processes, reward systems, performance management methods, and training that are needed to make it effective, its introduction can actually have a negative impact on the organization.

Thinking of organization design choices as complementary systems also has implications for the organization design process. While each point on the star in the model represents many choices, they are not as unlimited, and thus not as overwhelming, as they first seem. Once the strategy is set, there are then sets of complementary options available to support that strategy. As we address each major topic in this book, we have structured the discussion around the Star Model and have highlighted the set of complementary choices and considerations that align with each strategy.

Another concept underlying the Star Model is *complexity*. In this context, it refers to the idea that complex business models cannot be executed with simple organizations (Ashby, 1952). The more dimensions a business has—for example, number of products, business units, or customer sets—and the larger its size, the greater the number of interfaces that will need to be managed internally. In addition, when the company is geographically dispersed, new challenges of national culture, time, and distance are introduced. Many strategies today require high levels of cross-organization collaboration at multiple levels. As a result, units tend to have more "surface area" and a greater number of interactions between units required to get work done (Lawler and Worley, 2006). Such organizations will not spontaneously self-organize. Employees in large companies, no matter how good their intentions, are unlikely to be able to gain a broad enough view to make the right decisions about how units should be configured and who should interact with whom. Complex strategies and organizations need firm and clear guidance, and this is an activity for senior leadership.

The design goal should be to keep the organization clear and simple for customers and the majority of employees. It is the job of leaders and managers to manage the complexity that is created by the organization's design. The different elements of a design that will need to be managed—the points on the Star Model—are explained in further detail below.

Strategy

Strategy is a company's formula for success. It sets the organization's direction and encompasses the company's vision and mission, as well as its short- and long-term goals. The strategy derives from the leadership's understanding of the external factors (competitors, suppliers, customers, and emerging technologies) that bear on the firm, combined with their understanding of the strengths of the organization in relationship to those factors. The organization's strategy is the cornerstone of the organization design process. Without knowledge of the goal, no one can make rational choices along the way. In other words, if you do not know where you are going, any road will get you there.

The purpose of a strategy is to gain *competitive advantage*: the ability to offer a customer better value through either lower prices or greater benefits and services than competitors can (Porter, 1998). These advantages can be gained through external factors such as location or favorable government regulation. They can also be secured through superior internal organizational capabilities. We define *organizational capabilities* as the unique combination of skills, processes, technologies, and human abilities that differentiate a company. They are created internally and are thus difficult for others to replicate. Creating superior organizational capabilities in order to gain competitive advantage is the goal of organization design. We will also refer to *transferring capabilities.* To transfer and, when necessary, adapt a company's capabilities or advantages is one of the key jobs of any manager when opening up a new location or unit.

Business model is a broad term used to encompass the internal logic of a company's method of doing business. It encompasses the business's value proposition, target customer segments, distribution channels, cost structure, and revenue model. For example, an Internet music site may operate on a subscription basis (unlimited songs available for a monthly fee) or on a straight fee-per-song basis. Each approach represents a different business model, although both companies are in the same business. Each model is built on a different revenue and cost structure, and therefore each company requires a different set of organizational capabilities to succeed.

A *business portfolio* is the set of product lines or business units that a firm manages. How similar (or different) the business models are for each of the units in the portfolio drives different organization design decisions. A *profit center* (often called a *business unit*) is a unit in an organization that is considered a separate entity for purposes of calculating revenue and cost. How much influence the manager of a profit center has over the variables that generate revenue and costs is also an organization design decision.

Organizational Capabilities: Translating Strategy into Design Criteria

Organization design is a series of choices and decisions. In any decision-making process, clear criteria serve the purpose of allowing alternatives to be evaluated against agreed-on standards. The criteria used for organization design decisions are the organizational capabilities that will differentiate the organization and help it execute its strategy. The organizational capabilities are the link between the strategy and organizational requirements the strategy demands. We use the words *organizational capability* and *design criteria* interchangeably.

Different strategies require different organizational capabilities and therefore different organization designs. The right design choices increase the likelihood of building the right organizational capabilities. Each design decision can be tested against the design criteria to determine if it will be helpful in creating the desired organizational capabilities. We can expand on the definition of organizational capabilities offered above. Organizational capabilities are:

- Unique, integrated combinations of skills, processes, and human abilities. These are not simple programs or technologies that can be copied from other companies.
- Created by and housed within an organization. They are not bought or conferred by regulation or location or monopoly position. Rather, they are developed, refined, and protected internally.
- Factors that differentiate the organization and provide competitive advantage. This is important, as there are many things at which a company has to be as good at as its competitors, but just a few where it truly needs to be better.

How a company chooses to compete determines the most important organizational capabilities. For example, a pharmaceutical company developing novel prescription drugs requires a strong research and development capability and an ability to build relationships with physicians. But a pharmaceutical company that specializes in selling over-the-counter medicines needs efficient manufacturing processes and a strong consumer marketing capability. Some companies build a capability in product innovation. Procter & Gamble has not only a strong research and development capacity but also the capability of bringing ideas to market. Its Crest Whitestrips product comes from blending the company's technological expertise in the unrelated areas of bleaching, dental care, and adhesives. Other companies choose to compete based on marketing or distribution capabilities. The Campbell Soup Company does not necessarily make better soup than its competitors do. Instead, it creates innovative packaging and works effectively with retailers on displays that highlight the convenience of its product. Professional service firms such as Bechtel, which provides engineering and construction services, or Accenture, which provides consulting and outsourcing services, need different capabilities than consumer goods companies do. They compete on their abilities to staff and manage large-scale projects and to create and apply knowledge.

As a company's strategy changes, so do the differentiating organizational capabilities it needs. For example, Thorn Lighting, a U.K.-based firm, had a sixty-year history of innovation in the design and production of light bulbs. In the early 1990s, the company changed its strategy to focus on the more lucrative business of providing lighting solutions. It sold its manufacturing arm and now works with governments and property developers to design and implement lighting projects for stadiums, office complexes, and highways. The company still maintains an expertise in lighting technology. However, the organizational capabilities required by the two business models are quite different. The original business was built on product design, manufacturing, and consumer marketing. The new organization is built on customer relationship management, large-scale project management, and integrated solutions development.

The process of identifying the most important organizational capabilities is the first step in drawing the connection between the strategy and the form of the organization. Once the capabilities have been identified, a set of organizational implications can be generated to form the basis for a discussion of alternatives. Metrics can also be developed as a way to gauge progress. Figure 1.2 illustrates the thought process—from strategy to organizational capabilities to organizational implications—for a Latin American division of a cable television network. This process engaged the network's leadership in collectively understanding and agreeing on the criteria that an acceptable organizational design would have to meet.

The identification of organizational capabilities is carried out by the leader or leadership team that has ultimate responsibility for design decisions. This is not an activity that can be delegated, as it requires the broad strategic perspective of the leadership level. These organization capabilities become the criteria against which all subsequent design decisions are judged, so they must be agreed on at the most senior level of the organization.

Once the design criteria are in place, the question can be asked at each step in the design process: Which option will better help us preserve or build the organizational capabilities we have said are critical to our success? We suggest that the leaders identify no more than five organizational capabilities to serve as design criteria. It is the act of generating possible capabilities and then narrowing them down into those that can truly differentiate the company that creates healthy discussion and debate about what direction is truly most important to the organization. The Developing Design Criteria tool located in the Appendix provides detailed guidance on identifying, selecting, and using organization capabilities in the design process.

Structure

An organization's structure determines where formal power and authority are located. Typically, units are formed around functions, products, geographies, or customers, and are then configured into a hierarchy for

FIGURE 1.2 **Example of Organizational Capabilities.**

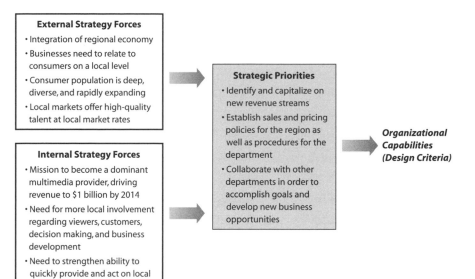

Organizational Capabilities	Organizational Implications	Metrics
Position our networks and products to meet local market interests	• Marketplace expertise/presence in the region • Empowered local business units with decision-making ability related to local matters • Increased level of knowledge and "feeling" of local markets • Improved speed, flexibility, and fluidity in the business • Focus on longer-term strategy and planning	• Relationships, accounts and viewers retained and added • Annual revenue growth • Annual profit growth • Designation of profit/loss responsibilities • Historical profitability by priority markets
Share talent across product lines	• Responsibilities, authority, and resources for identifying and responding to market expansion are clearly assigned • Clear line of accountability and responsibilities between all functions (especially country management and revenue) • Increase innovative capabilities • Talent is broadened, career opportunities are available	• Individual and departmental goals are aligned with business priorities • Goals are met • Talent ready for broader assignments
Execute new ideas efficiently	• Realize economies of scale • Avoid fragmentation • Minimal bureaucracy	• Average cost to produce • Our costs vs. competition • Overhead as a percentage of total costs

management and decision making. The structure is what is shown on a typical organization chart.

Organization design is not limited to structural considerations, and many variations of a structure can be made to work. But if the structure is not approximately right, then it will be harder to align the other design elements with the strategy. The structure sets out the reporting relationships, power distribution, and communication channels. It determines who comes in contact with whom. The structure projects a message about what work is most important. If the structure does not at least nominally support the strategy, then everyone in the organization will find themselves working around a formidable obstacle.

The four primary building blocks of organizational structure are function, product, geography, and customer. We also refer to these as *structural dimensions.* Most companies use a mix of all four and add dimensions as the business grows. Small companies and those with a single product line are typically organized by function. As the firm diversifies, each new major product line becomes a product division, with each division organized by function. We would describe this as a *multidimensional* organization, structured primarily along the lines of product and secondarily by function. When the firm expands into new territories, a geographic dimension may be added. Recently, with the increase in customer buying power, many companies are finding the need to add customer segments and markets as a structural dimension. The complex organizations we discuss in this book generally have multidimensional structures. In order to analyze, understand, and design such organizations, it is useful to briefly review each dimension.

Functional Structure

A functional structure is organized around major activity groups such as finance, human resources, research and development, manufacturing, and marketing. All employees in each function are managed together in order to promote sharing of knowledge and greater specialization. Functional structures promote standardization, reduce duplication, and create economies of scale. The concept of *scale* arises often in organization design. In general, common work done together reduces its cost, providing the larger unit or firm with an advantage. However, grouping work together may also slow it down, and the advantages of scale will be outweighed by a decrease in speed.

The functional structure is suitable for small businesses. It is also good for large companies that are in a single line of business and need to realize the benefits of scale, such as retailers or semiconductor manufacturers. Variations of functional structures can be used successfully for different purposes. A fast food and a pharmaceutical company both use a functional organization. The fast food company is focused on low price and consistency. Its primary functions are therefore supply chain, marketing, training, real estate, and franchisee relations. A pharmaceutical firm's primary functions are focused on research and development, government relations,

FIGURE 1.3 **Functional Structures.**

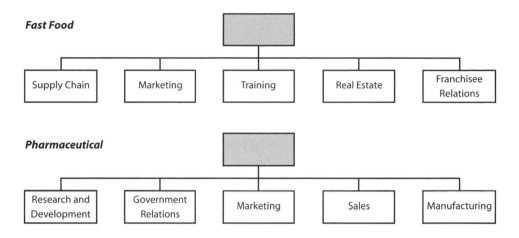

manufacturing, marketing, and sales. Although each company serves a wholly different customer base and relies on a different set of core functions, the functional structure is effective as a primary organizing dimension. Figure 1.3 illustrates a simplified structure for both.

When a company has only one fairly stable product line and long product development cycles are feasible, a functional structure can be used to advantage to create scale, expertise, and efficiency. This structure, however, becomes a barrier once the company diversifies and needs to manage a variety of products, services, channels, or customers, since all the coordination must be done by the senior management team. In a purely functional structure, there is no one with end-to-end responsibility for each product line below the level of the chief executive officer.

The functional dimension is useful under the following conditions:

- Single line of business serving one set of customers (for example, consumers or other businesses)
- Small organization or large, single business
- Need for depth of expertise and specialization
- Common standards are important
- Scale efficiencies
- Long product development and life cycles

Product Structure

Typically a functional structure evolves into a product structure when a company finds itself with multiple product lines that diverge in their underlying business models. For example, the fast food company may want to sell its products in the frozen foods section of supermarkets, or the pharmaceutical firm may want to branch out into medical devices. These new product lines require different organizational capabilities and a different configuration of functional expertise. Therefore, the companies will likely set up a new product division for each business. The launch of a product line that requires its own organizational home will also result in a new profit center as well; therefore, we use the terms *product division* and *business unit* interchangeably.

Separating into product divisions brings three main advantages:

- Product development cycles can be compressed because all the employees focused on the product are housed together.
- Focusing more narrowly on one line of products can promote product improvements and innovations.
- New opportunities can be more easily pursued because of the autonomy afforded by the divisional structure. There is not the constraint of coordinating with other divisions.

Employees and managers generally like working in the product division structure. They develop a strong team identity around the products they produce and the markets they serve. Managers can focus on customer satisfaction and profitability. Measures and rewards are typically closely linked to business unit success, and both managers and employees can see the results from their decisions and actions. The divisions may share some basic functions at a corporate level, such as purchasing or finance, but most of the functions are housed in the discrete business units. The head of a product division is often referred to as a *general manager,* as he or she has control over almost all aspects of the business. As a result, the product division is also an effective way to develop well-rounded executive talent with experience running an end-to-end business. Figure 1.4 illustrates a typical structure for a manufacturer of diverse products with some shared functions at the corporate level.

Caterpillar is an example of a large company that moved from a functional structure to a product division structure (for example, loaders and excavators, tractors, mining equipment) in order to gain more focus and accountability for each of its product lines. As a result, the company has been able to reduce its product development cycle time for heavy machinery from seventy-two to thirty-six months by providing managers with a clearer line of sight and control over the variables important to the dynamics of their business units (Neilson and Pasternack, 2005).

Using the product division as a primary structural dimension does introduce some problems. First, knowledge within functions is not as easily shared; for example, a research and development breakthrough in one

FIGURE 1.4 **Product Structure.**

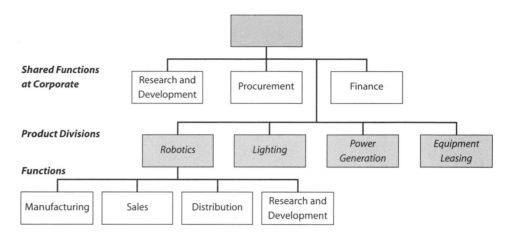

division that could be applied by another division may go unnoticed. Second, as opposed to leveraging scale, which a functional structure does, there may be duplication of effort by the functions housed in each division. This separation also creates policy and system divergence, as opposed to standardization, which may be problematic if there is a desire to build a common culture and operating practices across the divisions. The final disadvantage is that customers who wish to buy more than one product may be frustrated by having to deal with each division independently.

The product division structure is useful under the following conditions:

- Short product life cycles
- An emphasis on quick product development, new product features, and being first to market
- Multiple products that are produced for separate market segments
- Product lines with different underlying business models
- Product divisions large enough to achieve the minimum efficient scale required so that duplication of functions is not costly

Geographic Structure

The geographic dimension is employed as a company saturates its home market and grows by expanding into new territories. It is true that advances in communications and the rise of Internet shopping mean that fewer businesses need to have operations in the same physical locations where they have customers; nevertheless, when culture, language, or political factors influence buying patterns or when consumer behavior differs significantly by region, a geographic structure provides the local focus that can create competitive advantage. The benefit of having local managers focused on these differences is that they can tailor the company's standard products

FIGURE 1.5 **Geographic Structure.**

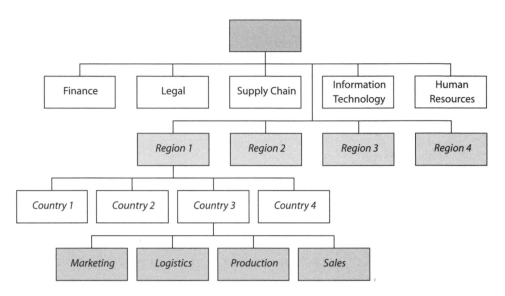

for local tastes and compete successfully against competitors that are more familiar with the local market. A geographic structure is also useful when the cost of transporting products is high or a service must be delivered locally.

Figure 1.5 illustrates the structure of a beverage bottling company that uses geography as its primary organizing dimension. Although the core products are standardized, differences among countries in product packaging, marketing, logistics, and the need to build good relationships with local government officials and retailers all require an organization that allows managers to focus on local conditions.

The disadvantages of the geographic structure are similar to those of the product division. Power and resources are controlled by regional or country managers, who may favor their own unit's needs over shared global or regional needs. As with the product division, the design challenge is to find the elements that can be shared across geographies while providing autonomy for managers to make local adaptations.

The geographic structure is useful under the following conditions:

- Transportation of materials to customers is costly, or the service is delivered on site.
- Buying patterns have strong local differences based on culture and language.
- The host government is active in the economic sector, and strong government and community relationships need to be developed.

Customer Structure

Functional, product, and geographic structures provide benefits for managers, but they do not necessarily provide an easy interface for the customer. Customers, particularly businesses buying from other business, often want a single point of contact, products customized to meet their needs, or an integrated bundle of services and products. The customer structure looks much like the product structure, except that divisions are based on *customer segments,* which are groups of customers who share similar needs, characteristics, or buying patterns.

Such a structure allows a dedicated service relationship and is often found in professional services firms and investment banks. An interesting example of an organization that uses a customer organization is the Internal Revenue Service (Rossotti, 2001). In the late 1990s, this U.S. government agency, which was originally structured by geography, was reorganized into four customer segments that reflect groups of taxpayers with similar characteristics: wage earners, sole proprietors and small businesses, medium and large businesses, and government and nonprofit entities. Each segment has full responsibility for serving its set of taxpayers. Managers therefore can focus on creating programs, services, and communications targeted for each group. Shared information technology services are housed at the corporate level, as are some small units that need to be independent, such as appeals, criminal investigation, and taxpayer advocacy services.

We can also illustrate here how other dimensions can be used at lower levels of the organization to match additional organizational needs. The medium and large-size business category is further segmented by customer into industry groups. Each of these industries has headquarters located in the city where the activity is concentrated, such as financial services in New York City and natural resources in Houston. The wage earner segment, however, is broken into geographic territories one level down in order to create regional offices close to the taxpayers. The high-level structure is shown in Figure 1.6.

The potential disadvantages of the customer structure are similar to those of the product division. Activities may be duplicated, incompatible systems might be developed to serve different sets of customers, and the advantages of scale can be lost. Such a structure also creates barriers when products or services are sold to multiple customer segments. However, when segments are highly differentiated or each segment is large enough to create scale on its own, then this is not an issue. For example, at the IRS, the wage earners segment serves 116 million taxpayers, allowing enough scale to deliver most functional activities cost-effectively.

FIGURE 1.6 **Customer Structure in the IRS.**

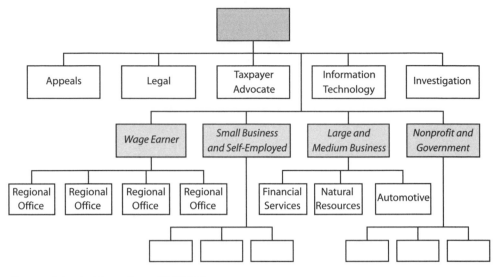

Source: Adapted from Rossotti (2001).

The customer structure is useful under the following conditions:

- Customers are powerful (whether through buying power or depth of relationship with the company) and demand customization and solutions.
- Deep customer knowledge provides an advantage.
- Customer segments can be differentiated in such a way that the products or services offered are unique to each customer group.
- The organization is large enough to achieve minimum efficient scale within each segment.

The *front-back structure* combines the advantages of the customer and product dimensions and is described in Chapter Two. The Structural Options tool located in the Appendix provides a summary of the advantages and disadvantages for each dimension.

Processes

Leaders frequently lament the organizational silos that prevent people from working together. *Silo* evokes an image of an invisible but windowless tower surrounding vertically stacked groups of people. These walls prevent the groups not just from interacting with one another but from even being able to see another group's perspective. "Breaking down the silos" is a common theme in discussions of organizational change.

All structures create silos. Whenever people are grouped according to one logic, boundaries are created that make it difficult for them to interact with groups formed according to a different logic. This is not a problem if the strategy does not require a high level of interaction or collaboration across these boundaries. But if the strategy does require collaboration, then the organization's structure—no matter how well thought out—will create some barriers to collaboration. The organizational challenge becomes how to bridge these internal boundaries and integrate activities. Processes and lateral connections provide the required mechanisms of integration.

We use the term *process* to mean a series of connected activities that move information up and down and across the organization. This includes work processes, such as developing a new product, closing a deal, or filling an order. It also includes management processes, such as planning and forecasting sales, business portfolio management, price setting, standards development, capacity management, and conflict resolution. Processes that cross organizational boundaries force organizational units to work together. Their design has a significant impact on how well units work together vertically or laterally. Clear articulation of roles and responsibilities at the boundary interfaces is essential for the design of good processes. The Responsibility Charting tool located in the Appendix can be used to help provide this clarity.

In addition to processes, *lateral connections* can be used to bridge barriers erected by an organization's structure. Lateral connections are generally less well understood than processes, and so are given more attention here. Lateral connections can be thought of as existing along a continuum, as shown in Figure 1.7. The horizontal axis represents the strength of connection between people or units, with personal networks forming a relatively weak connection and a matrix forcing a strong relationship. The vertical axis represents the cost, management time, and difficulty in using the lateral connection successfully. Costs include such things as reconfiguring information systems to aggregate data in new ways or meetings, which are notoriously time-consuming but are the vehicle for much lateral coordination work. Networks are relatively inexpensive and easy to foster, whereas a matrix is one of the most difficult organizational forms to master. Each type of lateral connection is briefly reviewed below.

Networks are the webs of interpersonal relationships that people form across organizations and serve to coordinate work informally. Healthy networks are the foundation for all other lateral connections. While networks

FIGURE 1.7 **Continuum of Lateral Connections.**

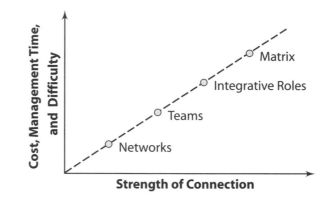

are voluntary and do occur spontaneously, there are a number of ways that management can influence and encourage them:

- Co-locate people who need to work together, and design the physical space to encourage informal interaction.
- Create communities of practice that bring together employees who are in different organizational units but have a shared interest (for example, an emerging technology, a common customer, or research interest), either for face-to-face meetings or virtually, through an intranet.
- Use meetings, retreats, and training programs to build relationships among individuals from different units.
- Rotate work assignments to bring knowledge, relationships, and culture from one unit to another and create understanding and appreciation for different organizational perspectives.
- Use technology and e-coordination to make knowledge sharing easy and help staff find others with complementary skills or interests.

The Relationship Map tool in the Appendix provides more guidance for analyzing and building interpersonal networks.

Teams are cross-business structures that bring people together to work interdependently and share collective responsibility for outcomes. A team can be configured around any dimension. If the primary structure is functional, a team can focus its work on another dimension: product, customer, or geography. Teams are more formal than networks. Participation is required rather than voluntary, and a team's charter will specify accountability and expected outcomes. Teams typically require a leader or project manager, dedicated resources, and senior-level sponsorship and attention and are thus more costly than networks. An example is shown in Figure 1.8. In this illustration of an information technology organization, a customer

FIGURE 1.8 **Cross-Business Team.**

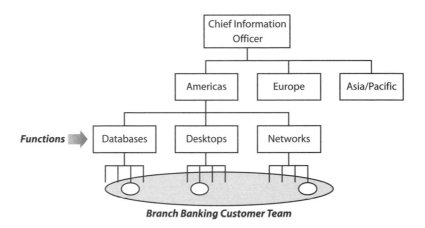

team is used to coordinate across the database, desktop, and network functional units on behalf of the branch banking business customer.

Integrative roles provide a higher level of coordination than teams. Teams are typically staffed by people who remain in their business unit and devote part of their time to the team's mission, or are pulled out of their unit to participate on the team for a limited period of time. An integrative role is a full-time manager charged with orchestrating work across units. A customer relationship manager and a brand manager are examples of integrative roles. They have accountability for results but do not directly manage the resources they need to achieve these results. Successful integrators are people who have high credibility and strong influence skills. An example of an integrative role is shown in Figure 1.9, which builds on the example in Figure 1.8. In addition to the customer team, there is now an account manager for the customer dimension in this illustration to create additional focus and coordination.

A *matrix* is a set of dual reporting relationships used to balance two or more dimensions in an organization. Networks, teams, and integrative roles all serve to integrate a secondary dimension. The matrix allows both dimensions to be equal. Selected roles in the organization report to two managers from different units, representing distinct structural dimensions. Because these managers are required to jointly set objectives, resolve conflicting priorities, and manage performance of the shared resources, they are forced to take a broader view than if they focused solely on one dimension of the business.

In the example shown in Figure 1.10, the organizational dimensions of function and customer are equally important. The matrixed manager has to balance the perspectives and objectives of each organizational

FIGURE 1.9 **Integrative Role.**

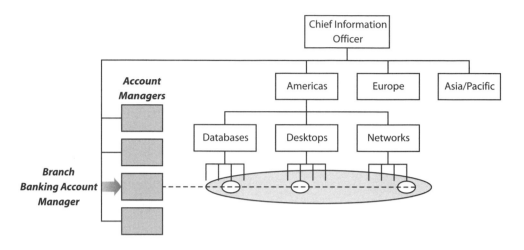

dimension when making decisions. For example, if asked to upgrade the desktop operating system for the branch banking business, he will have to ensure that it meets the global standards set by the desktop functional area and satisfies the needs of the branch banking customer. The matrix forces managers at a lower level in the organization to make decisions from a general management perspective.

The matrix can also promote a much more flexible and efficient use of resources, since teams do not have to be duplicated along every dimension. However, the successful use of a matrix requires a well-functioning management team, above the level of the matrixed manager, that can jointly manage the conflicts that inevitably arise.

Processes and lateral connections are the principal means of coordinating activities. Well-designed processes and lateral connections ensure that the right people are brought together to speed decision making. They allow more decisions to be made closer to customers and the activities affected, and also allow the company to be responsive to multiple constituencies.

FIGURE 1.10 **Matrix.**

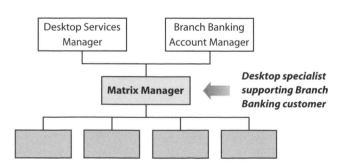

By designing and managing lateral connections, the leader gains increased ability to respond to opportunities and challenges. The carefully considered use of processes and lateral connections can be used to avoid the need to restructure when strategy shifts. The underlying structure can remain a stable home for employees, while processes and lateral connections are quickly reconfigured. A new strategic direction can be implemented with the majority of the organization still focusing on current work. For example, customer teams can be used as an interim step in reorienting a product structure toward customer segments. We refer to an organization's *lateral capability* as its ability to build, manage, and reconfigure its processes and lateral connections in the service of its strategic goals. Strong lateral capability is fundamental to all of the complex organizational forms discussed in this book. The Selecting Lateral Connections tool in the Appendix summarizes the options.

Rewards

Metrics and rewards align individual behaviors and performance with the organization's goals. For employees, a company's scorecard and reward system communicate what the company values more clearly than any written statement can. *Metrics* are the measures used to evaluate individual and collective performance. The *reward system* motivates employees and reinforces the behaviors that add value to the organization through salary, bonuses, stock, recognition, and benefits.

In complex organizations, the overriding challenge in designing metrics and rewards is how to create incentives for collaborative behavior. Rewards based on simple bottom-line measures that work for self-contained units cannot drive business results in organizations that depend heavily on cross-unit coordination. In complex organizations, variable compensation (that is, pay above base salary) typically tends to focus on team, unit, and business performance more than on individual accomplishment. Some questions to consider in designing rewards are these:

- *Level.* At what level should results and behaviors be measured and rewarded: team, department or unit, division, or company? How high up in the organization should results be aggregated before being rewarded? What level will still allow employees to feel they are being measured on the outcomes of their decisions and actions?
- *Locus of measure.* What is the appropriate configuration of profit centers? Should the product, customer, or geographic unit be accountable for business results? How does the organization create accountability

and transparency and minimize overhead cost allocations? How does it apportion credit among the multiple dimensions?

- *Behaviors.* What are the behaviors and actions that are essential to supporting desired strategic outcomes (for example, responsiveness, follow-up and communication, knowledge sharing, leading and participating in teams, cultural acuity, relationship building, influence, developing talent, and other organizational infrastructure contributions)? How do these get acknowledged in the performance management process?

- *Evaluation process.* Who should assess the performance that rewards are based on? What is the role of customers, peers, direct reports, lower-level staff, and colleagues from other departments? How does the organization create rigor around what can become a subjective evaluation of required behaviors?

Throughout this book and in the context of the strategy and organizational form being discussed in a particular chapter, we point out planning, measurement, and reward practices that help to answer these questions.

People

By *people practices*, we mean the human resource policies for selection, staffing, training, and development that are established to help form the capabilities and mind-sets necessary to carry out the organization's strategy. The complex organizations discussed in this book require a sophisticated management team that understands how to use the organization as a lever for competitive advantage. But it is not just managers who need to have strong organizational and interpersonal skills. Complex organizations require employees at all levels to have a fundamental set of competencies to interact across organizational boundaries, participate on teams, and make decisions that take multiple perspectives into account. The competencies that the organization needs to select for and develop include the ability to:

- View issues holistically and from cross-functional and cross-cultural perspectives
- Negotiate and influence without formal authority or positional power
- Build relationships and networks and skillfully work through informal channels
- Advocate and collaborate without bullying or compromising
- Share decision rights and resources and make joint decisions with peers
- Exhibit flexibility and resolve conflicts

- Manage projects with discipline
- Make decisions in situations of ambiguity and change

Management must also model these abilities and behaviors. Transparency and open communication channels between employees and managers create an important foundation for all of these competencies. In our discussions of various organizational forms, we highlight the talent and human resource considerations relevant to each model.

Design Principles

A number of themes run through this book. They are summarized here in the form of design principles. We have chosen these few to emphasize based on our experience consulting with organizations, combined with our understanding of the rich body of research that has been conducted on organizational design.

Requisite Complexity

Ashby's dictum from 1952—that an organization should be as complex as its business requires—still holds true. Today's leaders, while trying to respond to the increased demands of the market and speed of competition yet keep their organizations manageable, have to challenge themselves. Have we simplified too much in a desire to make our leadership task easier? Have we failed to build an organization that can achieve all aspects of our strategy? Conversely, some questions arise about whether an organization is too complex. Have we exceeded human limitations? Have we created too many interactions and interfaces for our people to manage? Can we achieve the same outcomes more simply and introduce complexity only where absolutely needed? Organizations can be designed so that managers have simple roles in a complex structure or, alternatively, work in a simple structure but end up with highly complex jobs. Complexity cannot be avoided, but it can be intelligently designed and managed.

Complementary Sets of Choices

The choices one has among structures, processes, rewards, and people practices are many. However, once a strategic path is set, the number of suitable choices for each point on the Star Model is reduced. The organization designer learns what sets of complementary choices work best together and assists the organization's leaders to build, align, and optimize these alternatives.

Coherence, Not Uniformity

A large, complex organization—particularly one that spans geographic boundaries—rarely has a simple structure. Rather, it can be thought of as a set of differentiated networks, in which each suborganization is designed in accordance with the environment in which it must operate (Nohria and Ghoshal, 1997). Leaders can make their organizations responsive to local conditions and at the same time remain coherent by differentiating where appropriate, and then using integrative mechanisms to link the organization into one system.

Active Leadership

With the interaction of many dimensions in an organization, priorities must be clear, or decision making falters and strategy execution slows. Leaders must clearly and continually communicate strategy and priorities throughout the organization so that employees know where to focus and how to make intelligent trade-offs. Successful complex organizations are guided and led by visible and active leaders who not only communicate strategy but also create the decision frameworks in which employees operate. They do not shy away from conflicts, complexity, or difficult choices.

Reconfigurability

An organization's internal rate of change has to be as fast as the rate of change in its external environment. But the larger the organization is, the harder it is to change. An organization's lateral capability—that is, its ability to bring the right people together quickly around risks or opportunities—is its most powerful means for changing direction. With robust lateral capability, processes and lateral connections can be rerouted and new ones created to shift priorities. They can even be designed in advance in anticipation of changes in strategic direction.

Evolve, Do Not Install

Lateral connections are cumulative. The capabilities developed at a lower level are necessary for the next level to work well. For example, for an organization to be able to use teams effectively, strong, informal networks must have already been developed. Build lateral capabilities by beginning at the low end of the continuum and working upward. As people in the organization gain the necessary skills and behaviors, begin instituting the next type of lateral connection if the strategy calls for it. Installing a matrix, rather than evolving toward it through the use of networks, teams, and integrative roles, is usually a recipe for failure.

Start with the Lightest Coordinating Mechanism

Coordination is expensive in terms of management time and attention. Always use the lightest touch when selecting what lateral form to use, choosing the least costly and least difficult coordination process to meet the required objectives. That is, start with networks and teams, and move to integrative roles and a matrix only if required.

Make Interfaces Clear

To manage complexity, spend time designing and clarifying interfaces. When interfaces between units are numerous and unclear, the amount of communication necessary can become overwhelming, and coordination suffers. Help the people who will be working at the interfaces understand the intentions and implications of the design.

Organize Rather Than Reorganize

Successful companies are continually evaluating and adjusting their organizations. Leaders of these firms form and communicate a picture of the future ideal and move toward it every day. Rather than periodic reorganization events that cause the organization to lurch forward, leaving employees with whiplash, aim for 80 percent initial alignment, with a plan for how to continue organizing toward the ideal.

• • •

In this chapter, we have introduced the fundamental concepts of organization design. The Star Model provides both a decision-making framework and a starting point to help leaders think about the interaction of strategy, structure, processes, rewards, and people. To begin the organization design process requires articulating the organizational capabilities to execute the strategy. These become the criteria for all further design decisions regarding the complementary sets of structures, processes, rewards, and people practices.

We also discussed how the organization needs to be as complex as the surrounding environment demands. The structural dimensions of function, product, geography, and customer should be configured based on the strategy. Different parts of the organization can be configured differently based on the external conditions they face and the challenges that need to be addressed. Decision making and activities are coordinated through processes and lateral connections. Lateral connections—networks, teams, integrative roles, matrices—are key elements of reconfigurability, which provides competitive advantage in a world of constant change.

The following chapters use the concepts introduced here and prepare you to confront five of the critical organizational design decisions that managers face today: designing around the customer, organizing globally, making a matrix work, making decisions about what to centralize and what to decentralize, and how to organize for innovation.

Chapter 2

Designing Around the Customer

IN ORGANIZATION DESIGN, form follows fashion as often as it does function. Probably the most significant development in the field over the past ten years has been a shift toward customer-centric design. As with other management trends, some companies have embraced it for the wrong reasons or have applied it in a clumsy manner, and will likely abandon the effort, cursing it as yet another passing fad. But the underlying factors pushing so many companies toward customer-centric designs are very real and will not be going away soon. Most leaders will find that they need to understand how these factors affect their firm, how their organization needs to respond, and how and where to build at least some customer-centric capability.

Our goal in this chapter is not to sell you on customer-centricity. It is not the right solution for every company or for every part of an organization. For some organizations, the company strategy may be predicated on organizing around markets or customers; this will dictate reconfiguring how all parts of the business relate to one another. In other cases, an underlying organization structure based on products, functions, and geographies provides a sound framework, and these organizations may just need to build some additional customer capability.

This chapter provides an overview of the concept of customer-centricity and gives tools for building customer-centric capability. It is organized into two sections, one focusing on strategy and the other on organization design issues.

The section on customer-centric strategies will help you:

- Define a customer-centric organization
- Identify the factors driving customer-centricity and why they are likely to become stronger in the coming years
- Recognize the components of a solutions-based strategy
- Understand the relationship between customer profitability and customer segments

The second section on customer-centric organizations focuses on design considerations for three levels of customer-centric application.

Light	How to develop a customer-centric capability on top of your existing framework, primarily by using customer teams
Medium	How to build a stronger customer focus by introducing the integrative account manager role
Intensive	How to fully organize around the customer while preserving product and functional capabilities, by employing a "front-back" structure

The section begins with some tools to assess your organization and determine what level of customer-centric organization you require and are ready for. Then a guide is presented to help you think through each level of customer-centric organization (see Galbraith, 2005, for more in-depth examples at each of the levels discussed in this chapter).

Customer-Centric Strategies

The idea of being customer-centric is an appealing one. Therefore, it is all the more important to begin with an understanding of what is meant by *customer-centric* and the strategic factors that make it appropriate for one organization and not another.

What Is Customer-Centric?

Just about all companies, government agencies, and nonprofit organizations say that they care about their customers. Certainly in recent decades there has been no lack of exhortations from the business press to focus on the customer and improve customer service. But this is different from customer-centricity. Since business terminology is often not precise and can lead to confusion, it is important to distinguish between *customer focused* and *customer-centric*.

When looked at carefully, customer-focused strategies and initiatives usually apply to how products are developed and how customer interactions—sales and service—take place. Companies that are customer focused use extensive market research and may even involve customers in the design of their products and services. They create products that customers want rather than trying to build demand for the products they are able to produce. They invest in the training and systems that allow front-line employees to provide smooth and consistent service in transactions. Customer-focused programs, processes, and systems improve an organization, but they do not transform it.

Customer-centric strategies do transform an organization. Put simply, a customer-centric organization brings together and integrates products, services, and experiences from within and beyond the firm to provide solutions to the complex and multifaceted needs of its customers.

In a study of 347 organizations deploying customer-centric strategies, most respondents emphasized that in order to overcome the inertia of the current organizational form, there had to be a powerful strategic reason to reorganize around markets (Day, 2006). Creating a customer-centric organization will have an impact on each point on the Star Model™. Moreover, there will need to be a strong rationale to motivate those within the organization to accomplish such comprehensive change.

Strategy

Most customer-centric companies employ a *solutions* strategy: the company believes that by combining and integrating advice, services, or software with their products, the resulting customized offering will create more value than customers can create for themselves by buying a set of stand-alone products (Galbraith, 2005). Priorities are focused on a portfolio of customers, with an emphasis being given to those that are most profitable. The strategy requires leadership and management commitment to the belief that the internal costs of the integration and collaboration generated by this strategy will be more than offset by increased profitability, customer satisfaction, and share of customer spending.

Structure

The customer-centric organization revolves around customer segments and customer profit and loss centers. New organizational units and roles are often required, including customer teams, relationship managers, account teams, proposal teams, and other integrative roles. The organization may even use fully developed customer-facing front-end units, creating a "front-back" structure. In order to provide solutions that use products and services from outside the company, there will also likely be alliances and joint ventures structured with partner companies.

Process

Within the customer-centric organization, a key process is customer relationship management, often supported by new technology systems that capture customer interactions and make data available to decision makers across the organization. A second important process is that which governs how solutions are developed and priced. Finally, the customer-centric organization must have a strong product portfolio management process in order to determine which products and services are complementary and provide added value when bundled together. And as in the other complex organizational forms discussed in this book, a full and robust set of lateral connections and planning tools must be built and maintained.

Rewards

The performance metrics in the customer-centric organization focus on share of customer spending, customer satisfaction and retention, and the lifetime value of the customer. Power and recognition go to those who have the most in-depth knowledge of customers' businesses, create the highest-value solutions, and retain and develop relationships.

People

With regard to selecting and developing talent, the most distinct difference in a customer-centric company is usually found in the front-end sales organization. The sales perspective moves from the point of view of the seller—"How can I get you to buy more of my products?"—to that of the buyer—"What combination of products is best for you?" The change from transactional selling to solutions and relationship selling often requires a complete reevaluation of the sales and marketing organizations, how they are supported and interact, and the type of people needed. More generally, employees working closely with customers need to be selected and developed to work cross-organizationally at the points of connection with the rest of the organization.

Figure 2.1 summarizes the basic differences between a customer-centric and a product-centric organization, with which it is most often contrasted.

FIGURE 2.1 **Product-Centric Versus Customer-Centric.**

		Product-Centric Company	Customer-Centric Company
STRATEGY	Goal	Best product for customer	Best solution for customer
	Main offering	New products	Personalized packages of products, service, support, education, consulting
	Value creation route	Cutting-edge products, useful features, new applications	Customizing for best total solution
	Most important customer	Most advanced customer	Most profitable, loyal customer
	Priority setting basis	Portfolio of products	Portfolio of customers — customer profitability
	Pricing	Price to market	Price for value, risk
STRUCTURE	Organizational concept	Product profit centers, product reviews, product teams	Customer segments, customer teams, customer profit-and-loss
PROCESSES	Most important process	New product development	Customer relationship management and solutions development
REWARDS	Measures	• Number of new products • Percent of revenue from products less than two years old • Market share	• Customer share of most valuable customers • Customer satisfaction • Lifetime value of a customer • Customer retention
PEOPLE	Approach to personnel	Power to people who develop products • Highest reward is working on next most challenging product • Manage creative people through challenges with a deadline	Power to people with in-depth knowledge of customer's business • Highest rewards to relationship managers who save the customer's business
	Mental process	Divergent thinking: *How many possible uses of this product?*	Convergent thinking: *What combination of products is best for this customer?*
	Sales bias	On the side of the seller in a transaction	On the side of the buyer in a transaction
	Culture	New product culture: open to new ideas, experimentation	Relationship management culture: searching for more customer needs to satisfy

The Drive Toward Customer-Centricity

Companies are increasingly finding that they cannot compete on the basis of commoditized products or simple transactions and cannot wring out more efficiency from their operations in order to lower costs. Rather, new technologies are quickly incorporated by all industry players and provide short-lived advantage. Companies therefore need to compete by adding value. A customer-centric strategy can provide a path to this value by responding to one or more of the dynamics occurring in the business landscape.

Global Coordination

Global customers operating in multiple countries expect the same level of service across geographies from their vendors. They often want one global point of contact and expect the supplier to do the internal coordination to make that happen. Imagine an apparel manufacturer that has operations and customers in dozens of countries. It does not want to negotiate banking services in each country; instead, it would like a global banking partner to coordinate the relationship and ensure that cash management, foreign exchange, and other cross-border banking services are optimized in each location. The manufacturing customer wants the bank to do business the way the manufacturer does business, and it does not care how the bank is organized internally.

Increased Customer Sophistication

In concert with increasing globalization has been an information revolution that has made customers more sophisticated then ever before. Information on public Internet sites makes comparison of product and service features and prices widely available across suppliers and regions. Customers also know that suppliers benefit when customers buy more often or in larger quantities. They expect to be rewarded for this loyalty with discounts or higher service levels. The savvy customer expects merchants and suppliers to have the ability to know how much business they do together and what the last contact or purchase was, regardless of where it was in the world or through what distribution channel the sale was made.

Customization

Buyers are demanding increasing amounts of customization in the products and services they purchase. It may be in the realm of mass customization for consumers, in the way that Levi's has been offering custom-constructed jeans. On the business side, there is a trend toward using a smaller number of suppliers with which the company works more closely in order to create unique solutions that add value to the company's own products. For example, Johnson Controls makes interiors for cars. What it produces for Toyota is quite different from what it creates for Chrysler. As a result, it needs to configure its internal organization in such a way to provide this customization profitably.

Experience-Driven Buying

Customers, particularly individual consumers, are placing almost as much importance on the buying experience as on the utility of the product itself. Some observers have suggested that we are moving from an information age to a conceptual age, where meaning is as important as usefulness. As a result, companies that are fun and easy to do business with, deliver good design, tell a story with their products—perhaps an environmental story or a socially responsible one—and are able to connect with their customers on an emotional level will gain an edge—not just in sales but in customer loyalty (Pink, 2005). For example, Ikea sells simple, inexpensive furniture, but the experience of the store layout, café, product self-assembly, and even the Swedish cultural touches contribute to a unique buying experience. Starbucks is leveraging the customer loyalty that it has built through its coffee-buying experience by expanding into the promotion and production of music, books, and films.

Consulting and Advice

Customers in the developed world have an abundance of choice, but the sheer variety of options can often be overwhelming. Whether it is an over-stretched purchasing manager having to select office equipment or a consumer faced with two dozen possible home theater configurations, advice on how to make good choices becomes something worth paying for. The most trusted advisors will recommend not only their own products but also someone else's when it makes sense. IBM's well-known turnaround story is all about the successful introduction of consulting and advisory services and the fact that IBM will provide a system that includes non-IBM products.

● ● ●

Customer-centricity is not confined to the business sector. Government and nonprofits also feel these pressures. We used as an example in Chapter One the case of the Internal Revenue Service, which has reorganized from a geographic and functional structure into a customer structure aligned around four distinct segments: wage earners, sole proprietors and small businesses, medium and large businesses, and government and nonprofits. Each of these units is an almost wholly self-contained division focused on the particular needs of its customer segment.

It is important to note that not all companies have customers with complex or multifaceted needs, and not all customers want their needs met by a single organization. Some customers may prefer to assemble their own bundle of products and services from a variety of providers. In addition, within a firm's market, there may be a mix of customer types—some who want a relationship and a solution and others who want a simple transaction.

Customer-Centric Strategies

All customer-centric strategies are built on the premise of segmenting the market in some way and then organizing to meet the needs of each segment. The resulting product and service offerings of the company can be thought of as existing along a spectrum from stand-alone and loosely bundled products or services to fully integrated solutions, as shown in

FIGURE 2.2 **Spectrum of Customer-Centric Integration.**

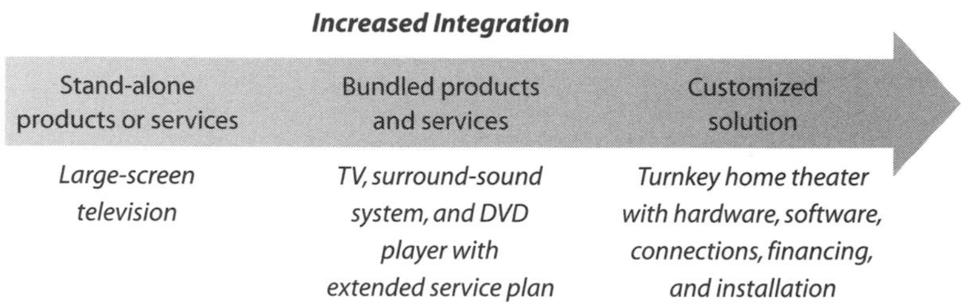

Increased Integration

Stand-alone products or services	Bundled products and services	Customized solution
Large-screen television	*TV, surround-sound system, and DVD player with extended service plan*	*Turnkey home theater with hardware, software, connections, financing, and installation*

Figure 2.2. As the organization moves toward offering integrated solutions, the more that organization needs to be integrated as well.

Bundling Products and Services

Many companies start at one end of the spectrum by adding a fuller range of goods and services and then bundling, discounting, and cross-selling them. They provide value to their customers by serving as a one-stop shop. By diversifying horizontally, they capture a larger share of a customer's spending. For example, a local cable company may offer a package of cable TV, Internet service, and Internet phone. The customer pays less than if she bought the services separately and gains the convenience of a single bill. Another example is the case of a regional bank that buys a small investment bank in order to offer its mid-tier business clients mergers and acquisition services in addition to banking and loans. American Express offers charge cards, concierge, travel agent services, and travel insurance for Platinum members through one telephone number.

In many instances, these efforts provide a thin veneer of customer-centricity. Beneath the surface is still a product organization, with each division operating quite independently. For example, the cultural divide between a commercial bank and an investment bank means that there is more often an internal hand-off of customers between the two parts than any true collaboration.

Bundling and cross-selling nevertheless are a good place to start for many organizations. Doing this builds the capability of bringing together disparate resources from inside and outside the organization around the customer and begins to build a customer-centric mind-set. It also provides a way for the company to learn about customers and test different methods of segmenting customer groups before undertaking any significant reorganization.

Creating Solutions

Further along the spectrum of integration, and what we are concerned with here, are strategies that integrate products and services, including ones not sold by the firm, into a new offering. Often this is done by expanding vertically along the value chain, adding pre- and postsale services. Or it may be through significant customization and even co-creation of new products with customers. These new offerings create a level of value for the customer beyond the one-stop shopping described above and are commonly called "solutions." Rather than just fill a need, as a product or service does, a solution solves a complex problem for the customer. It can be thought of as a miniature form of outsourcing, allowing customers to focus on their core business or interests.

Because of the complexity and abundance of products available, deciding what to buy and how to make it all work together has become increasingly difficult and time-consuming (Iyengar and Lepper, 2000). This is true for both the business purchaser and the consumer. And for many customers, their most precious resource is time. Especially when making large purchases, consumers are willing to pay for advice to help them make well-informed choices, and to make them more quickly. They are also willing to pay for postsale service, because ongoing maintenance tasks (whether for a home computer network or an enterprise resource planning system) can be formidable and beyond generalist technical abilities. Business's strategic response to this customer dilemma is to get in the value chain earlier and stay in longer. The buying process changes from one of a transaction to more of a relationship, as the buyer becomes dependent on the seller not just for individual components but also for expert knowledge on how to make them work together.

Figure 2.3 illustrates the basic steps in buying an information technology system for a company. The points along the triangle represent the steps the customer must take in order to complete the purchase and maintain the system. The more of these needs a company can meet on its own, the more it can avoid competing on price with other vendors, because the intangible value provided by the integration and linkage of each step—although hard to quantify—is both significant and costly for the customer to replicate.

It appears that more and more companies are focusing on postsale "keep it going" services. In 1999, after-sales service accounted for 24 percent of U.S. business revenues. Even better news for companies choosing to provide these services is that they have a high margin; businesses earned 45 percent of their gross profits from them (Cohen, Agrawal, and Agrawal, 2006).

FIGURE 2.3 **Customer Activity Cycle.**

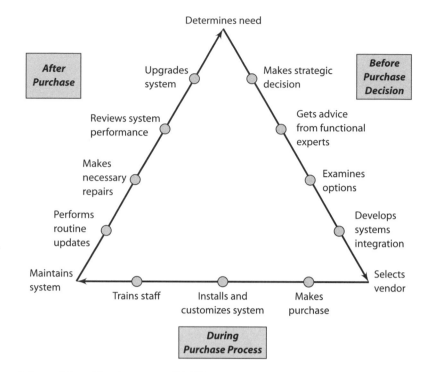

Source: Adapted from Vandermerwe (1999).

Customer Profitability and Segmentation

Conventional wisdom has held that the best customers are repeat customers who refer colleagues, friends, and family members. In fact, this may not be the case; some repeat customers may actually be unprofitable because of the product mix they buy or the level of service they require.

When the Royal Bank of Canada began looking at profitability by customer rather than product, they discovered that 17 percent of their customers provided 93 percent of their profits (Selden and Colvin, 2003). Furthermore, they found that 40 percent of their customers generated no profit at all (Burrows, 2003). Many companies find that their customer profiles look something like Figure 2.4, which shows a company's customers arrayed by profit and then divided into ten equal-sized groups. The profit per customer that the company gains from each decile varies widely.

Understanding customer profitability is important when making decisions regarding which customers to pursue and invest in, and how to configure products and services for them efficiently. An organization may make a deliberate decision to serve currently unprofitable customers. For example, the Royal Bank of Canada found that it was worth investing in some currently unprofitable customers in order to build loyalty for the future.

FIGURE 2.4 **Array of Customer Profitability.**

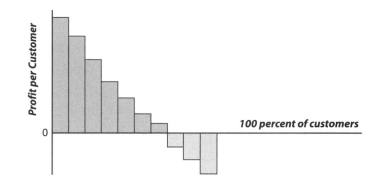

Many banks are stepping up their marketing of credit cards to marginally profitable college students based on studies showing that young adults who open accounts are likely to remain customers for years to come (Kim, 2006). The hope is that they will stay loyal to the bank into their later life stages when they need profit-generating mortgages, car loans, and retirement investments.

Customers can be segmented in any way that creates discrete groups that share similar buying needs and patterns. Some segmentation options are size, life stage, industry, or location. The profitability profile informs the segmentation strategy, but it is not identical to the segmentation strategy. Customers who are highly profitable may have very different needs and interests from one another. Putting them in the same segment will not lead to a strategy that satisfies any of them. Conversely, each segment is likely to have profitable and unprofitable customers, based on buying and use patterns. Each segment needs to be analyzed in order to determine the right mix of products, services, and service level to attract and serve the right customers efficiently.

Understanding the profitability dynamic within a segment is important as a way to differentiate among various offerings. The challenge is figuring out how best to measure customer profitability. Many companies' systems are set up to measure profitability by product and business line, not by customer. As a company starts to contemplate moving to the types of complex sales structures and relationship-oriented approaches required in a customer-centric business, accounting systems that measure customer profitability become critical. Indeed, the first step in Fidelity Investments' customer-centric reorganization was upgrading and consolidating their information systems. Rigorous analysis then allowed them to understand the dynamics of their customers and ultimately focus on those who were most profitable or had the potential to be so. Fidelity segmented customers into four groups: those with high-value, complex portfolios who required significant levels of attention; active traders who generated high transaction volumes; core customers with moderate portfolios who were interested in investing but did not trade actively; and institutions and small businesses. For each segment Fidelity has created a business model, a service offering, and bundles of products that now include even funds from competitors ("Learning How to Profit," 2006). The Customer-Centric Strategy tool in the Appendix can help you think through these factors for your business.

Customer-Centric Organizations

Building a customer-centric organization is not an all-or-nothing proposition. Some organizations need only to assemble an informal cross-unit team to create offerings or services for a customer. Others may create an account manager role, and still others will build a unit that deals directly with the customer. For simplicity, we call these respective organizational choices light, medium, and intensive levels of the customer-centric approach.

You can (and should) choose the level of application that you need in order to meet your strategic needs. The process of creating customer-centric capabilities adds internal complexity to an organization. Integrating across organizational boundaries can slow decision making. In addition, an increased level of management time and attention is needed to bring together products and services from different organizational units with different histories and business models that may not have worked together in the past. Therefore, create only these capabilities to the extent that they are needed.

Strategy Locator: How Customer-Centric Do You Need to Be?

Going too far in realigning the organization around customers when your business model and strategy do not require it will waste management energy. But if your customers and competitors are driving you toward a more customer-centric organization and you fail to create an integrated system that supports this capability, you may end up in the category of companies that failed to execute on their opportunities. The strategy locator shown in Figure 2.5 can help you gauge what level of customer-centricity is most useful for your organization. It has two axes: the horizontal axis measures the level of *integration* of products and services needed to create the offering, and the vertical axis measures the *complexity* of the offering

FIGURE 2.5 **Strategy Locator.**

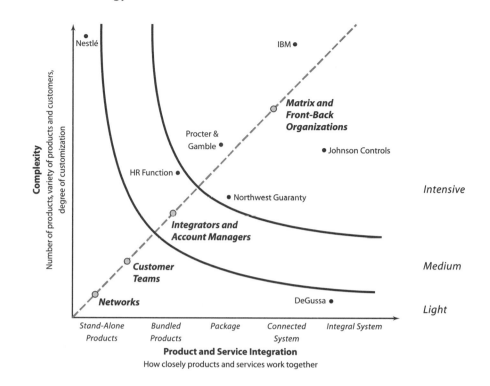

(in terms of number of products, number of customers, and variety of products). How these two dimensions interact will determine whether a light, medium, or intensive customer-centric organization is needed and the type of structures and lateral connections (shown on the diagonal line) that will be needed to build the organization.

The level of integration needed to present an offering to a customer is the most important indicator. The higher the level of integration involved, the more customer-centric the organization needs to be. Integration can be thought of along a scale from low to high:

Very low or none at all	Stand-alone products (perhaps sold under a common invoice)
Low	Bundled products (all retirement products)
Some	Package (investment banking services for an acquisition)
Moderate	Connected system that allows substitutions (computer system)
High	Integral system (car interior)

Complexity is an indirect measure of how difficult it will be for an organization to deliver the offering. One of the factors important to complexity is the *number* of products or services that are likely to be bought from the company by the same customer and therefore must be brought together to create the integrated offering. As a rule of thumb, fewer than four products do not add a lot of complexity, but twelve or more can add significant complexity. When we refer to products in this sense, it is from the internal perspective, with each unique product having a different internal owner or product manager. For example, from the perspective of a small business customer, a line of credit and a checking account from a bank may look fairly similar, and both may come up on the online banking screen together. However, behind the scenes, they may be managed as totally different products, with different objectives and measures.

Another factor that bears on complexity is the *variety* of products or services that must be integrated. *Variety* refers to differences in the business models underlying the products. To extend the example, a credit line and a checking account are similar in that both are largely automated transaction businesses. However, if the bank was also to offer retirement planning advice to the small business customer, this would increase the variety of the offering. Advisory services require a high degree of person-to-person interaction, analytical capabilities, and relationships with external product providers. Some other factors that affect the degree of complexity are the variety of customers who must be served, their geographic distribution, and the level of customization required for each customer.

High numbers of products and a high level of product variety by themselves do not create complexity. It is only when the strategy is to bring them together into an integrated offering that these factors are important. A product-oriented company can sell large numbers of a great variety of products, but it does not need to organize around the customer if it does not plan to integrate those products to create added value. For example, Nestlé offers dozens of products and brands, but it does not seek to present them to customers in an integrated way: no one buys a prepackaged suite of Nestlé products. Nestlé is a highly successful company, but it does not compete through customer-centricity. Nor do all organizations that are customer-centric exhibit the same integration and complexity profile. An organization's profile can help indicate how much customer-centricity it needs. We will use three examples to illustrate. Each is also plotted on Figure 2.5, along with the other examples we use in this chapter.

Johnson Controls, which makes car interiors, is high on integration. In order to create a customer-specific interior, the components delivered must work together seamlessly and cannot be substituted. It is moderate on complexity, however: although there are numerous products to assemble and each interior is customized, the products are closely related.

Procter & Gamble (P&G), unlike its competitor Nestlé, is quite customer-centric. It derives more than half of its revenues from a dozen or so major global and regional retailers (retailers being its primary customers) and provides them with customer insights and marketing advice. The company overall falls at the medium level on the integration continuum. Although there is little product integration for the end consumer, in order for P&G to service its retailers, the right products must be on the right truck and coordinated with the right in-store marketing campaign. A high level of coordination and integration takes place in the supply chain. P&G is moderate on the complexity continuum; although it offers many dozens of products to the same customer, the products do not need to work together (a Gillette razor does not need to be sold with Crest toothpaste, for instance, to make it work), and the variety of products is relatively low: all are in the consumer goods family.

IBM is one of the best examples of a company that has transformed itself from a product-based organization to one that has successfully added a customer-centric component around consulting, integration, and education services. In 1998, Louis Gerstner, then the CEO of IBM, stated, "The greatest competitive advantage in the information technology industry is no longer technology. . . . Technology changes much too quickly now. More and more the winning edge comes from how you help customers use technology" (IBM, 1998, p. 6). IBM is high in internal complexity. The design and installation of the systems for a new call center, for example, require a broad range of products and services, including hardware, software, technical consulting, and training—all of which IBM provides. Integration is also high: a number of internal units need to coordinate to ensure that the components work together.

As these examples show, there are different ways to be a customer-centric organization. The Strategy Locator tool in the Appendix provides additional guidance on determining how customer-centric you need to be.

Customer-Centric Capabilities

In Chapter One, we discussed organizational capabilities and how they form the basis of the criteria for making good design decisions. We stressed that each organization needs a unique set of capabilities that reflects its strategy, history, and context. However, among customer-centric organizations, we see some common capabilities. The capabilities outlined in

FIGURE 2.6 **Customer-Centric Capabilities.**

Level	Typical Organizational Capabilities
Light	• Analyze sales and profit data by customer. • Understand the needs of target market groups and establishing strong relationships based on fulfilling those needs. • Convert customer information and knowledge into market-leading products and services. • Develop core products which are flexible enough to be customized to specific market segments. • Deliver end-to-end (pre- and post-sale) customer service that enhances the value of products. • Build a sales support infrastructure that enables relationship selling. • Manage matrixed customer teams. • Collaborate at all levels across organizational boundaries to make profitable decisions. • Offer and integrate outside products or services when asked. • Create a cross-organizational planning system.
Medium	• Use information and accounting systems that allow for customer relationship management at all touch points. • Manage complexity. • Assemble and disassemble multiple teams against opportunities. • Select and develop account managers who can both collaborate internally and advocate for their customers.
Intensive	• Create decision-making and conflict resolution processes/governance structures to manage complexity and conflict. • Deliver project management support throughout the organization to support team projects. • Create pricing rules and market mechanisms for front-back interaction.

Figure 2.6 are additive—that is, what is needed for the light level of application is also needed for the medium and intensive levels.

Most organizations should start with a light level of application and focus on a few customers who are asking for (and willing to pay for) integrated solutions. This experience will help the company build its capabilities, test assumptions, and learn from the experience without totally disrupting the organization. After confirming the customer-centric business model, it can take additional steps to build further capability and move toward a medium or intensive level of application, if that is required by the strategy. The Customer-Centric Capabilities tool in the Appendix will allow you assess these capabilities.

Customer-Centric Light

Customer-centric "light" is a way to introduce capability without changing the underlying framework of the organization and is achieved primarily by using customer teams. For some organizations, this level of application may be enough. For others, it is a good place to start and gain experience

FIGURE 2.7 **Star Model for Light Customer-Centric Application.**

before moving toward more intensive applications. Figure 2.7 shows the Star Model for light customer-centric organizations.

Strategy

The first tenet of customer-centric organizations is to do business the way the customer wants to do business. As we have noted, not all customers value or are willing to pay for bundled products, complex solutions, or customization. Creating such offerings for these customers and building the organizational architecture to support such offerings will be a waste of resources. But at some point, these originally uninterested customers may evolve, or your company may decide to move out of the market that serves them. Alternatively, you may be able to meet their simple needs at the same time as you serve the complex needs of other customers.

It is those complex customers whom we focus on here. The first step is to create customer teams for customers who want them. How do you know a customer is ready? Some indicators are when your customer:

- Buys multiple products from you
- Requests a complex, customized product
- Complains about having to deal with multiple salespeople or points of contact for service
- Asks for presale advice or postsale service support
- Has complex needs that require in-depth understanding and dedicated resources to uncover and respond to them
- Is willing to pay a premium for advice, service, integration, or some combination of all three

Example of Light Customer-Centric Application: Degussa Catalytic Converter Business

As an example of the light customer-centric approach, we look at Degussa, a specialty chemistry company based in Germany with a business unit that supplies catalytic converters to automobile manufacturers. Catalytic converters are the elements of exhaust systems that reduce emissions and pollution. Although the basic components of the converters are similar across vehicles, the converter itself must be designed to work with each specific engine and platform that a given car manufacturer uses. Therefore, Degussa's customers require dedicated teams within Degussa that understand both the engineering requirements of their vehicles and local regulatory requirements. Degussa's customers do not want to buy the converter parts and build the component themselves, as this is not their core business. They are willing to pay some premium in price to have Degussa develop a solution for them.

The Degussa catalytic converter business is low on the Strategy Locator in terms of internal complexity because it provides essentially one product to its customers. However, it is quite high in terms of integration: its product is complex and must be customized for each customer, requiring a high level of internal cross-functional and geographic coordination. Degussa achieves this level of integration through cross-functional customer teams.

Structure

A customer team is essentially a lateral integration mechanism placed on top of an existing structure. The team brings together functional expertise across product lines or regions on behalf of a customer. Degussa's customer team for Volkswagen is shown in Figure 2.8. The core members of Degussa's Volkswagen customer team are marketing and sales representatives from each country in which Volkswagen is located and makes buying decisions. Also included on the team are functional representatives from Germany, where both Volkswagen and Degussa are based.

The Degussa example illustrates some important considerations when structuring a customer team.

Team Charter and Goals All teams need a clear mandate and set of objectives in order to focus their energy. Customer teams are no different and should be chartered with a set of defined outcomes—for example:

- Anticipate customer needs by staying in close contact with the customer and relaying information to research and development. This may also involve educating the customer and influencing his or her preferences.

FIGURE 2.8 **Degussa's Volkswagen Customer Team.**

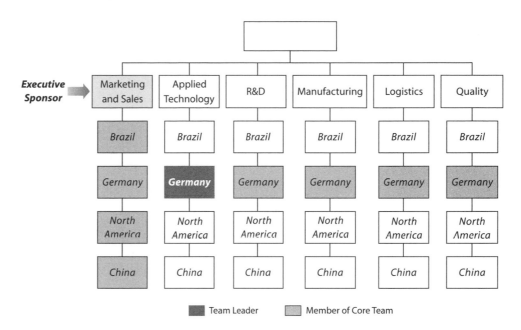

- Coordinate the design of new products, and advocate for the customer's requirements.
- Establish pricing for the customer when costs vary across regions, or determine when discounts are necessary to stay competitive.
- Determine sourcing of products, and decide when outside products need to be brought in on behalf of the customer.

Executive Sponsorship A customer team cuts across the existing power structure of the organization and may be seen as a threat, particularly to the sales organization, which has historically "owned" customer relationships. Therefore, the team needs resources and authority to get its work done. Although an initial foray into customer teams may be undertaken as an experiment, the team is likely to fail if it is underresourced in terms of talent, visibility, and clout. Rather than deliver an integrated solution to the customer, the customer will be exposed to all the internal dysfunctions of the organization.

One way to support the success of customer teams is to provide them with an executive sponsor who can speed decision making and resolve conflicts. This executive team member can be from any part of the organization, and different leaders can have responsibility for different customer teams. This link will help to ensure that the nascent customer teams are not overpowered by the concerns of the existing functional and product groups.

Location of the Team The team can be a virtual one, as in the Degussa example, where team members working to serve Volkswagen are located on four continents. If the customer is located in multiple geographies, then it is best for the team leader to be located in the same region (or country, if possible) of the customer's headquarters in order to build the deep level of insight and the close relationships required by this model.

Processes

The creation of a customer team states to others in the organization—and to the customer as well—that the company will be making new and different decisions on behalf of the customer. Structuring the customer team is a fairly straightforward proposition. Creating the linkages back to the organization is more difficult but just as important. We look at some key considerations.

Customer Information In order to make decisions on behalf of a customer, the customer team needs the company's accounting and information systems to provide it with new and different data. The team will need data on customer profitability across all products and services. From this, the team will need to analyze and predict what aspects of their offering the customer values the most, as well as the lifetime value of the customer. Then the team will need to assess how vulnerable the company is to losing the customer and what the cost of that loss would be. This data-driven analysis feeds into making decisions about how solutions are put together and how they are priced.

You may ask which comes first: building the supporting systems or forming the customer teams. The practical answer—and to a large degree the ideal course to follow as well—is that it is an iterative process. The team needs enough information to build a profile and hypotheses about the customer. It may need to start with off-line spreadsheets because the accounting systems do not aggregate the information in a useable way. As the team works with the customer, it will develop a set of specific information needs that can start to drive changes in underlying systems and form the starting point for an integrated customer relationship management (CRM) system. The need to invest in enabling systems is another reason that the customer team needs to have an executive-level sponsor, since these investments will likely not be initially supported by other functional units within the firm.

Matrix Management This customer team is a form of a matrix. Each member has to have strong accountability to the customer team as well as to the functional, geographic, or product group that he or she is drawn from. The seemingly simple addition of a customer team can work well only when a firm has the strong underlying networks and lateral enablers that any set of matrix relationships needs to succeed. For example, all matrixed teams require strong working relationships and agreed-on processes that make clear the involvement and responsibility for potentially contentious decisions. Specifically, for a matrixed customer team, there needs to be clarity around these topics:

- Who will make product portfolio decisions
- To what extent products will be customized
- How pricing and discount decisions will be made
- The process for the development of new products
- Performance expectations for order fulfillment

Without this clarity, the conflicts that arise will be blamed on the customer strategy, the customer team, or the matrix, and the attempts to organize around the customer will fail. (For more on how to make matrixed relationships succeed, see Chapter Four.)

Rewards

One of the ways in which a customer-centric team such as we have been describing is different from a team that is merely customer focused is in the way in which performance is measured. Many companies configure teams around customer issues or even particular customers. These teams may have deliverables for which they are held accountable—for example, resolving an issue, redesigning a process, or making a recommendation—and may even receive rewards for their efforts and results. But a truly customer-centric team is measured in terms of business outcomes.

The basis for these measures is the planning process. Goals and milestones are put in place based on the relevant customer metrics for the business. These might include share of a customer's total business, customer satisfaction, customer retention, or number of new customers. Depending on the underlying organizational structure, these results can be accounted for in various ways.

At Degussa, results are measured at the level of the regional business unit. Since customer teams by definition span organizational boundaries, including geography, the dilemma is how to account for customer results without double-counting. Degussa's customer team results are included in the region in which the customer is headquartered, regardless of where the revenues and costs are accrued for that customer: GM and Ford are rolled into the North America business unit's results, Volkswagen and Daimler-Chrysler into Europe, and Toyota and Nissan into the Asia region. In this way, each customer team can be treated as a profit center and can be compared to other customer teams or to goals established in the planning process.

While it is imprecise to attribute some global results or costs to one region over another, this approach permits the introduction of fully accountable customer teams without disrupting the company's underlying accounting systems. This approach is also a useful halfway step that can be employed during the time that a firm's underlying systems are being redesigned. The challenge of refashioning a company's measurement and rewards systems is not to be underestimated. As noted earlier, in most cases, the teams will need visibility and direct connections to the executive level in order to overcome the organizational inertia that has governed how decisions around giving credit for results have been made up to this point.

People

At the light level of customer-centric application, the team leader and members need to be A-level players; this is not a place to put people who are merely available. The selection of the customer team members can be used as a form of recognition to reward high performers. Team members should be senior enough to command respect from their internal counterparts and deal with the customer organization as equals. Those selected need strong technical abilities as well as the collaboration skills that will enable them to work across boundaries. At the same time, they have to be comfortable advocating on behalf of the customer, which may mean occasionally challenging more senior functional managers. Human resource systems have to be realigned to select, develop, and reward people for both collaboration and successful advocacy in the customer's interest when required.

Strong senior leadership is required. The introduction of customer teams can create conflicts over pricing, customization, cost allocations, and standardization. The leaders will have to continually educate the broader organization about the purpose, role, and expectations of the customer teams and how they fit into the strategy and operations of the underlying organization. This, of course, requires that senior leaders support the customer-centric strategy, understand the organizational capabilities required to deliver it, and see addressing and resolving disputes quickly as a key part of their role.

Customer-Centric Medium

The addition of customer teams begins to build customer-centricity around key customers who will benefit from and value it. However, if your organization is fairly high on the integration spectrum on the Strategy Locator and you have the added complexity of offering a greater number or wider variety of products and services to your customers (see Figure 2.5), more internal units will have to coordinate in order to deliver to the customer.

Many organizations meet this challenge by using an integrative role, often called an account manager or customer relationship manager. The account manager is a new role introduced into the organization, with focused and clear accountability for coordinating and integrating products and services on behalf of a customer. This person is a facilitator of the organization-customer relationship. This is a dedicated role, with more authority than the team leader in the customer team. It is an addition to, not just a part of, the existing organization.

Making the role of account manager work is not simple. The account manager can become a bottleneck rather than an integrator. Others in the organization may perceive the new role as an interloper and jealously guard their preexisting relationships with the customer. Or those selected to be account managers may define the role as a gatekeeper, and slow access and decision making. The role of single contact point for the customer can breed frustration from others in the organization, who often rightly believe that they need to be in direct contact with the customer themselves in order to do their job properly.

Our discussion of the medium level of customer-centric application focuses on how to design the account manager role so that it operates successfully. Figure 2.9 shows the Star Model for medium customer-centric organizations.

Strategy

In the light application example, Degussa's customer team brought together people from different functional or geographic areas, but they were all working on the same product for the customer. If your business has a variety of related products that you want to bring together on behalf of a customer, the task of internal integration becomes more complex, and one team for a customer may not be enough. With increased complexity, you will need different team configurations for different solutions. The products may come from parts of the organization with different business models and may be

FIGURE 2.9 **Star Model for Medium Customer-Centric Application.**

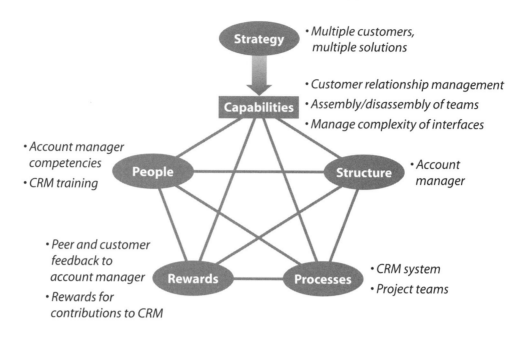

located in units with different histories and organizational cultures. Now you are trying to integrate people representing a multitude of products and facing the challenge of weaving together the work that they do in a way that does not leave your employees hopelessly confused.

Example of a Medium-Level Customer-Centric Application: Human Resource Function

For our example of the medium level of customer-centric application, we will look at a typical human resource function in a large company. Many companies are implementing customer-centric organizations for their internal staff functions, particularly when business lines are diverse and each has a different set of needs from the others (Kates, 2006). As the work of the business units becomes more complex, the units are demanding true solutions—instead of just services—from their internal support functions.

Where does the HR function fall on the Strategy Locator? It provides products that are fairly diverse, including payroll and benefits administration, training, staffing, compensation, employee relations, and organization development. On the Strategy Locator, HR is moderate in terms of internal complexity. Until the past fifteen years, it was also low on the integration scale, as each of these products and services was provided relatively independently to its internal customers.

However, the typical HR customer (a business unit manager) has started to ask for more holistic responses to issues. Sometimes the business unit just wants a new employee, or a training program, or a compensation package. But more often the unit wants a talent management solution that includes integrated selection, development, and compensation systems to support a start-up business unit, for example. Or perhaps a change in strategy requires the use of a matrix, and the business unit turns to HR to conduct an organization assessment, identify organization development interventions, and provide the best practices, training, and facilitation to support the transition. The customer does not want to have to assemble the team to do this. At the same time, the HR leader—who is typically under tremendous pressure to lower costs while providing more sophisticated services—does not want to have to provide a dedicated team of specialists for each business unit. Rather, she wants to be able to configure teams around solutions on an as-needed basis in order to use and develop resources efficiently.

Structure

These strategic pressures on the HR function to deliver integrated solutions and become more customer-centric have pushed many to the account manager model (which in HR is sometimes called the *business partner model*). The same trends have been seen in other staff functions, such as finance and information technology. The account manager role may be performed by one person or by a small team, dedicated to a line of business if internal, or to one customer or customer segment if it is facing externally. A typical structure for the account manager in a staff function is illustrated in Figure 2.10.

The role of the account manager is to uncover the customer's (business unit) needs, pull together a team to develop options from the product areas, and present the customer with a recommendation. The account manager may or may not also be involved in the delivery of the recommended

FIGURE 2.10 **HR Account Manager Structure.**

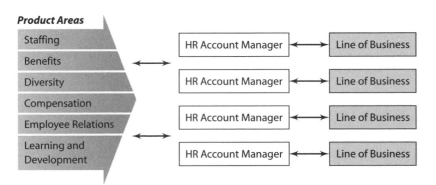

solution. The product areas (in staff functions often known as "practice areas" or "centers of excellence") are staffed by specialists. For HR or other staff functions, the product areas typically develop responses to regulatory requirements and create enterprise policies, systems, and programs. As in any true customer-centric organization, the account manager can offer products and services drawn from outside the organization—that is, use vendors or consultants—if these external resources are more capable or less expensive than internal ones.

The account managers are usually members of the organization's leadership team. Rather than an executive-level sponsor, as is used with the customer team, in this model the customer's voice is now directly represented—through the account manager—at the executive committee level.

Although this is a powerful idea, the account manager role often runs into four predictable problems in the reality of organizational life:

- *Specialists need more contact with the customer than the account manager role allows.* In many organizations, in order to keep the interface with the customer simple, the account manager is set up as the "relationship owner" and becomes a kind of go-between for the customer and the specialist groups. However, configuring solutions that use the expert knowledge of specialists requires that the specialists conduct their own assessments, since the account manager may not have the depth of knowledge to do an adequate diagnosis. In addition, many in the specialist groups gain job satisfaction through direct client interaction and come to resent always having to go through an intermediary.

- *The account manager role is hard to staff.* It is difficult to find people with relationship building, interpersonal, and selling skills who also have the requisite technical expertise to staff the account manager role. Account managers need to be able to manage a client relationship as well as influence and guide their internal functional colleagues. It is a highly visible and stressful position.

- *The account manager lacks credibility, and the customer and specialists go around him.* When the account manager role is introduced into a situation where the customer and the specialist or product staff already have existing relationships, the new role is often met with skepticism, particularly by those from the account manager's own organization. While coworkers will often admit that they see the value of the role in certain situations, the role is often viewed, at least initially, as unnecessary overhead. If the account manager fails to quickly prove his or her value, the specialist and product staff will continue their direct relationships with customers, further undermining the role.

- *The same model is applied to all customers.* In a desire to create internal consistency, the role is often designed the same way across customers. However, customers, both internal and external, need to be segmented by profitability and how they prefer to do business. In our human resource example, not all business units have the same complexity of human resource needs or make the same strategic contribution to the overall enterprise. Thus, not all customers merit the same level of investment above the basic level of service that is provided to all. The mistake is to create a model that provides internal consistency and is easy to manage but does not meet the needs of different customers.

Given these potential pitfalls, the design of the account manager role needs to be well thought out before it is staffed or implemented. The following are some considerations:

- *Discourage the notion of client ownership.* Groups using an account manager model can get caught up in competition over who "owns" the client. It is helpful to make clear that providing a single point of contact for the customer (if that is what the customer wants) and simplifying the interface does not imply ownership or exclusivity in the relationship. The emphasis has to be on coordinating and communicating internally, so that the customer can deal with the organization in the way that it prefers. If the customer continually resists using the account manager, the design or implementation of the role is flawed; it is not that the customer needs to be more thoroughly "trained."

- *Define the role as collaboration, not control.* The role is not a gatekeeper but rather a coordinator of interactions. The account manager makes introductions to internal colleagues who can better solve problems, or educate the customer, or sell customized solutions when opportunities are identified. To gain credibility with peers, the role has to be designed as one that facilitates rather than controls. To develop complex solutions, specialists need to talk to colleagues at multiple levels between the customer and supplier organizations. The account manager does not need to be the expert in every area and cannot be threatened by colleagues who are true experts. Their role is to connect the right internal staff with the person at the right level in the client's organization.

Figure 2.11 shows the common "bow-tie" problem, where the account manager becomes a constraint on communication. An alternative way of conceptualizing the relationship and role of the account manager is shown

FIGURE 2.11 **Common "Bowtie" Relationship.**

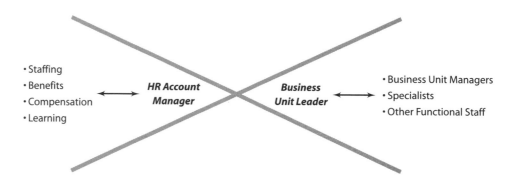

in Figure 2.12. In this model, each level has direct contact with its counterpart, and the whole relationship is facilitated by the account manager and the customer relationship management system.

Processes

As with the light level of application, developing appropriate customer information systems and good matrix relationships is critical. In addition, two new capabilities are needed: (1) the ability to quickly form and re-form project teams to build customer solutions and (2) more robust customer relationship management systems to manage customer touch points.

Project Teams In addition to the account manager role, teams are used extensively at the medium level of application. The account managers will likely work with a fairly stable core group of individuals or teams within the product and specialist areas because of the customer-specific or sector

FIGURE 2.12 **Account Manager Facilitating Interaction.**

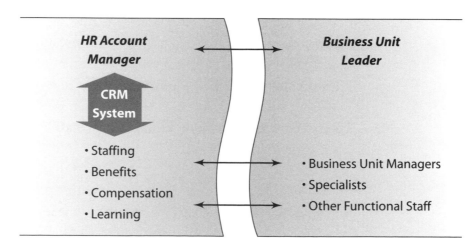

knowledge that is required. However, because medium-level solutions are more varied than those in the light level of application and often draw from differing sets of products and services, the organization will need to become more project based. The ability to assemble teams and staff them appropriately is a key capability at this level of customer-centricity. Project teams should be staffed not just based on an evaluation of who will get the work done, but also with an eye toward developing and motivating staff and transferring solutions across business lines.

Customer Relationship Management Systems The customer relationship management and contact systems require added capability to support a medium level of customer-centric application. At this level, rather than having one team looking at one customer or customer segment, there are multiple views into the customer. In our simple HR example, a client business unit may interact with the account manager to identify needs and solutions. In addition, the product areas may need to interact with the client to gather information or roll out an enterprisewide human resource initiative. The CRM system needs to be able to capture all of the customer activity, reflect the status of issue resolution, and track the progress of projects for that client across the organization. The account manager needs this information in order to identify opportunities and solutions or uncover needs that the client may not even be aware of. At the same time, robust CRM information allows the client to access the HR organization through a variety of channels and get an answer to a query without having to go through the account manager. The internal coordination required should be invisible to the customer.

Rather than limit customer interactions, the goal is to manage and register them at all touch points. This requires systems that provide a view of interactions by product (the status of a new training program, for example), customer portfolio (all projects underway by business unit), and project view (status of cross-organizational projects). It also requires qualitative information to be fed into the system. Often the biggest barrier to making CRM systems work is not the technology itself. Rather, it is the fact that it is difficult to get everyone who interacts with the customer to see the value of documenting their interactions in the CRM system.

Rewards

The account manager role requires the design of new measures and rewards. It is a difficult position that requires a mature, highly skilled person with credibility both internally and with the client. One account manager at a global bank reflected on the role this way: "I know I'm doing my job when I'm pushing in both directions and everyone is a little displeased. I need to educate the clients so that they accept solutions they may not have even considered. And I need to push internally to get from my colleagues what is best for my client." Therefore, the performance management system needs to incorporate both client and peer feedback, measuring not just results but also the desired behaviors with both groups.

The account plan is a key tool for supporting the account manager model. The planning process brings together all the players with an interest in the customer to develop the project plan (for an internal customer) or revenue plan (for an external customer or segment). Ideally, planning is done face-to-face, as this is a good way to build networks among those who will have to deliver on the plan. A face-to-face meeting also helps to avoid the assumptions and misunderstandings that can occur when planning is conducted by conference calls or e-mail. The plan is then transferred into the CRM system to help guide decision making and track progress.

Finally, this level of customer-centricity is made possible by a robust information system, which will most likely need active contributions regarding customer needs, inquiries, and contacts. You may need to create rewards and incentives to encourage people to contribute to the CRM system and to proactively share customer information.

People

The account manager is an integrative role. As we noted, it is a role that is notoriously difficult to fill because it requires a wide range of competencies. These are people who need to have a high level of technical competence in order to build credibility with their functional organization, but they also need excellent influence skills because they have to deliver for the client without direct control over resources. Many times they have to choose between getting things done and getting credit, as they will not be able to do both. If the organization has evolved to the account manager from the customer team level, you may look to select the account manager from among those on the customer team who have shown promise in being able to span both the internal and customer worlds. Some organizations have also found success by hiring people from their customer organizations.

Client relationship management is not the sole province of the account manager. Training and education in how to manage customers is beneficial for those sitting in the product areas, as well as for those with more direct client contact. Along with training in using the contact database,

FIGURE 2.13 **A Front-Back Organization.**

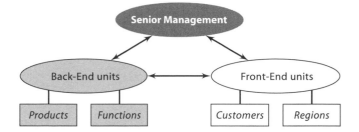

CRM training builds an understanding of the business model, clarifies why various decisions are made, and shows how each role in the organization contributes to meeting both the customer and enterprise needs.

Customer-Centric Intensive

What we call the intensive level of customer-centric application reflects a strategy that requires fully organizing around the customer while simultaneously preserving product and functional capabilities. This usually results in what is called a front-back structure, where the front is a set of customer units and the back is made up of product units. Figure 2.13 shows a simplified diagram of a front-back organization.

Procter & Gamble uses a front-back structure. At the front end are regional units and global customer teams. Global teams are housed within the regional units where the customer predominates. For example, the team that serves Tesco, a large British grocery chain, is in the Western Europe region. However, Wal-Mart, a global customer for P&G that spans multiple regions, is provided its own customer unit. At the back end are the global business units organized into two product divisions: Beauty and Health (grooming, oral care, pharmaceuticals, and skin care) and Household (home and fabric care). In the back end are also functional units including technology, supply chain, finance, and operations.

Front-back configurations can be found at any level of the organization. The smaller the organization, the simpler it is to make the connections between the front (customer units) and the back (product units). However, when divisions or whole companies are organized this way, the complexity increases substantially.

The intensive level of customer-centric strategy application, resulting in a front-back structure, is an attempt to gain the benefits of both a product and a customer organization. Rather than focusing on optimizing one or the other, you are attempting to create an organization with multiple

FIGURE 2.14 **Star Model for Intensive Customer-Centric Application.**

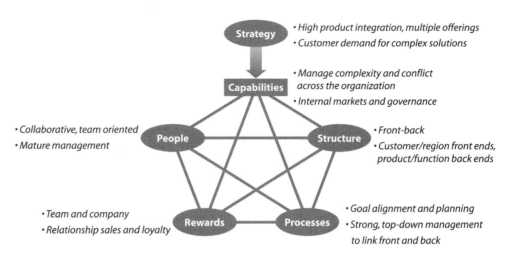

capabilities that can do both things well. Figure 2.14 shows the Star Model for intensive customer-centric organizations.

Strategy

At the level of the firm, a number of well-studied companies have employed variations on the front-back structure as their organizing framework. In addition to Procter & Gamble, these include IBM and Nokia, and much has been learned from their experience (see Galbraith, 2005). For our discussion here, we use a small company, which we will call Northwest Guaranty, to illustrate the key points that must be taken into consideration when designing a front-back organization.

Example of the Intensive Level of Customer-Centric Application: Northwest Guaranty

Northwest Guaranty is a small bank of 750 employees serving agricultural producers, farm-related businesses, fishermen, part-time farmers, and country home owners in the northwestern United States. Its primary products are life and crop insurance and home and business loans.

Over the past fifteen years, the farm industry has gone through significant changes. At one extreme, diversified medium-size farms have given way to much larger single-crop agribusinesses. At the same time, riding a wave of new money, part-time farmers and ranchers have bought up properties in the Northwest. Each group represents a set of sophisticated financial customers with very different needs.

As a small player in this new climate, Northwest Guaranty found it was under pressure from the large insurers, as well as from community and regional banks. It could not continue to compete in generic lending and insurance products, so it developed a strategy to capitalize on its ninety-year history of working in farm communities and its deep understanding of the needs of its customers. The strategy had two components.

First, Northwest Guaranty broadened its offerings to include leasing and appraisal services, business management programs, real estate advisory services, and legal advocacy and assistance. In the language of the Strategy Locator, it increased the number and variety of products. To match the increased specialization and sophistication of its customer base, Northwest Guaranty also invested in hiring more product and service specialists. For example, it hired and developed specialists who could help a farm family through business succession planning.

Second, Northwest Guaranty segmented its customers. It first did this according to the size of typical loans, but it found that loan size did not adequately capture the different profiles of customers. It then created three customer categories:

- *Agribusiness*, which has complex business credit and insurance needs but also requires bankers knowledgeable about the business dynamics of the products that a farm specializes in, whether it is a potato farm, a cattle ranch, or a vineyard.
- *Young Producer*, aimed at young farmers, small farmers, and minority farmers. Northwest Guaranty has identified this segment as a niche that is growing and represents an opportunity to build early customer loyalty.
- *Country Home-Owner*, offering loans, advice, and services aimed at the new ranch or farm owners who have moved into the area and have limited or no experience in rural life.

By creating customer segments, Northwest Guaranty increased the level of internal organizational integration necessary to service these customers. Each customer segment required a variety of products that needed to be delivered as an integrated solution. For example, an agribusiness customer might need property and equipment refinancing, along with a specialized insurance product to protect its investment. Northwest Guaranty went from very low on the integration continuum of the Strategy Locator to medium. Although the bank's products can still serve as stand-alone products, they require a much deeper level of customer knowledge and information sharing in order to configure and deliver them as integrated solutions than existed previously. Even a modest rise in integration, however, increases complexity and the attendant coordination requirements.

As it built a more robust solutions capability, Northwest Guaranty also focused on creating a cost-effective, efficient operational system to deliver its commodity products. For example, it decided to continue to offer straightforward loans on a transactional basis for customers who did not fit into a market segment or did not want additional services.

Northwest Guaranty illustrates the three main components underlying an intensive customer-centric strategy: do business the way the customer wants to do business, expand along the value chain to provide integrated solutions that the customer cannot easily assemble themselves, and explicitly segment the market. Northwest Guaranty's experience also serves to highlight that the move to this level of customer-centricity does not happen spontaneously or emerge out of a mere aggregation of business unit strategies. It requires a deliberate decision by senior management and an ongoing, centralized strategy-making process to ensure that one coherent enterprise view on how the company will move forward is implemented and articulated.

Structure

Historically Northwest Guaranty was organized into three main business units: Insurance, Corporate Credit, and Homeowner Credit. Products were sold primarily through branch offices, with staff from the three business units located in the branches but working largely independently from each other with their own portfolios of customers. As part of the reorganization to support the new strategy, this structure was changed to reflect the emphasis on solutions and segments, as shown in Figure 2.15.

The bank's IT and operations functions were upgraded, streamlined, and centralized. The intent was to remove processing and administrative burdens from branch staff so that they could focus more on building relationships with customers, uncovering needs, and developing new products or services to meet those needs. The IT upgrade also allowed Northwest Guaranty to enhance its competitiveness in order to serve customers who wanted an Internet-based interface and simple, transactional services. Product development staff remained in the corporate offices aligned by product categories. Together, the operations and product areas constituted the new back end of Northwest Guaranty.

The major change for Northwest Guaranty occurred in the forty-three branches, which became the new front-end sales units. As the distribution of customers differed across the geographies that Northwest Guaranty served, not all branches were designed similarly or catered to all segments in the same way. Branch staff now worked in teams. A loan officer would take the

FIGURE 2.15 **Northwest Guaranty Structure.**

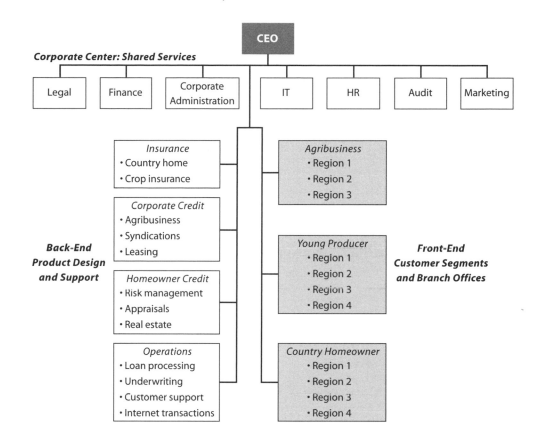

lead on a client account, supported by a team of specialists from the branch, corporate product areas, and even other branches when necessary.

To build this front-end, reconfigurable-team capability, the company first progressed through an account manager model (as previously described in the discussion of the medium level of customer-centric application). Before the reorganization, customers had different contact points for different products. Moving to the account manager model, in which one loan officer coordinated an account, was useful but failed to build enough deep expertise beyond the account manager around the specific needs of the three segments: Agribusiness, Young Producer, and Country Homeowner. Northwest Guaranty's next step was to reorganize the branches fully by segment teams in order to put more expertise and specialization closer to the customer. Branch staff still have product expertise, but they now sit primarily on a segment team and participate in setting strategy for the segment and planning how to execute the segment strategy.

The front-back structure is one of the most complex organizational forms to manage. Therefore, differentiation should occur where it adds value for the customer—that is, in different front-end configurations—and not at the back end where it adds cost. Northwest Guaranty centralized its support functions and kept a simple product structure that allowed product development staff to focus on their areas of specialized expertise. On the front end, they allowed variation in the branches to reflect geographic and segment differences. We can highlight some considerations in the design of the front end:

• *Front ends are now profit centers.* They are not simply about account management. Instead, the front-end unit replicates the product organization—often by selectively matrixing some staff—to create a condensed business team for the customer. While at the light and medium levels of customer-centric application, customer profit is measured and tracked, at the intensive level the customer segments become strong profit centers in their own right.

• *Front ends can be configured in multiple ways:*

• Customer segment (for example, by demographics or buying behavior)
• Geography (physical or national boundaries, stage of market development)
• Industry segment (defense, hospitality, financial services)
• Channel (such as distributors, original equipment manufacturers, retailers, direct marketing)

Frequently a front-end unit is a combination of more than one of these possibilities. For example, at Northwest Guaranty, the front-end units are structured around a mixture of geography and customer segment. Where possible, segments should be configured to avoid overlap; the front-end units are thus discrete entities, and staff can focus on and identify with their segment. The front ends should be designed to reflect how the segment is organized and do not have to be parallel with one another.

Figure 2.16 uses an example drawn from an industrial firm to show how the front end of a global company can be organized around these multiple dimensions. Although the sales front end now has a customer structure, it is likely to retain some geographic focus as well if face-to-face selling is taking place, regardless of the size of the customer. There is almost always an advantage to locals calling on locals, and geographic sales territories are easier to manage.

• *The size of the front-end units will vary.* Units need to be small enough to allow focus on a market, and the managers of those markets need to feel a sense of direct ownership. However, front-end units must be large enough to gain the attention of back-end units and warrant dedicated resources. Just as their structures will differ, so too will the size of the front ends,

FIGURE 2.16 **Organizing a Front-End Unit Around Multiple Dimensions.**

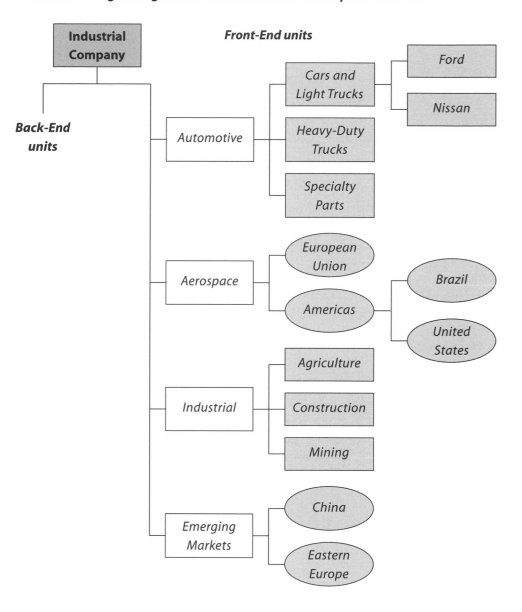

with start-up segments being supported by smaller teams and established markets with larger teams. The bias in the design process will likely be to aggregate the units, but we suggest starting by designing small units that are truly differentiated and have minimal overlap. Then you can reaggregate them to achieve scale around shared customers, channels, growth profiles, or the potential for sharing back-end functions (for example, by grouping plants, distribution, or technology).

- *Sales and marketing are brought closer together.* In a fully product-centric organization, marketing is the strategic function that focuses on brand and product positioning. The sales function is the execution arm, and typically there is a hand-off between the two functions. As a firm reorients to service large, complex accounts, however, marketing and sales need to make joint decisions about product, price, and brand. Large customers may have buying teams representing multiple interests and dimensions of the buyer's organization, and they may want to negotiate customization and pricing. Account managers, product managers, and advertising managers will find they need to work more closely together (Shapiro, 2002). In addition, the marketing function becomes more complex. The back-end product marketing units are focused on next-generation products and features, while the marketing units at the front end are concentrating on building brand loyalty around advice and trust. The front-back structure requires central, senior-level marketing leadership to ensure that these messages are aligned.

- *Project management units appear.* The preparation of proposals for large accounts and the creation of complex integrated solutions require a robust project management capability. Many organizations find they need to add these roles to help support the sales and product teams.

- *Service moves closer to the front end.* For the organization pursuing an intensive customer-centric strategy, postsale service becomes as important as the presale consulting and the product itself. Therefore, managing the service function and capturing customer information from it becomes of critical interest to the front-end segments. For example, a call center may be run operationally as part of the back-end functions in order to optimize site selection decisions, gain scale, and use best-in-class systems and technology. However, the performance of the staff in that call center who handle inbound queries, outbound telemarketing, and problem resolution is managed by the front-end segment managers. In this way, goals and rewards are closely linked to the strategies of the segments.

Processes

After shifting to a front-back structure, in essence you ship your organization to your customer when you make a sale. As a result, the products you sell will work together only as well as the organizational units that produced them work together. And as we have seen, a front-back structure creates more organizational units. Not only have you introduced teams, but these teams will likely reconfigure themselves frequently around new customers, new opportunities, and new solutions. These teams create more points of interface, resulting in a need for more coordination and communication among the units.

The front-back structure is set up both to create and manage conflict. The product units function like a product organization. They ask the question typical of such organizations: How much product can we push out to customers? The front-end customer units are accountable for meeting the needs of the customer. These units can be thought of as buying products from the back end on behalf of their customers. And they may find that a third party's products can meet the customer's need better than their internal partners can.

When these internal conflicts are managed successfully, the organization provides its customers with excellent products and truly integrated solutions, and builds a trusted relationship. For example, Wal-Mart provides Procter & Gamble with otherwise proprietary sales information about how P&G's products are selling, because their incentives are the same: keeping the shelves stocked. It is unlikely that an organization can build this kind of trust with a customer if a high level of trust does not exist internally between the units that must coordinate and collaborate ("Avoiding the Cost of Inefficiency," 2006).

Robust processes and lateral connections, led by strong top-down management, are the essential ingredients in building the trust required in a front-back structure. In addition to the lateral capabilities discussed for light- and medium-level application, the intensive customer-centric company needs a mix of alignment and governance mechanisms that aid decision making, as well as market mechanisms that spell out the rules for how the front-end units "buy" from the back.

Goal Alignment As soon as you create segment strategies and treat the segments as profit centers in order to create customer focus, you create conflicts with the product centers. A product general manager may feel that a customer unit is not featuring her product line as prominently as it should. To manage these disputes, a leader at a level above both the product and customer units needs to get everyone around the table and agree on plans by segment and product line. This can be done using a simple spreadsheet, as shown in Figure 2.17.

The tool is simple. What is difficult is reconciling the natural conflict that will likely arise from having to manage two different strategies. For example, when an agribusiness account manager at Northwest Guaranty is working with a vintner to refine the vineyard's business plan and put together a package of crop insurance and a credit line for expansion of the winery, the account manager may find that an external provider has a product that can complement or even substitute for one provided by Northwest Guaranty. This is the proper approach to give the customer the best solution and should result in customer loyalty in the long run. In the

FIGURE 2.17 **Segment and Product Line Spreadsheet.**

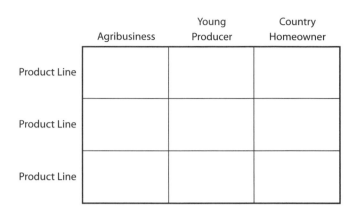

short term, however, it may cause internal tensions from a product manager who does not feel his product was pushed hard enough.

Product Portfolio Strong senior management is also needed to guide the portfolio planning process. The more that products and services have to work together seamlessly, the more that research and development decisions have to be aligned across the product lines and customer segments. Something that may be a good stand-alone product may not advance the development of solutions. For a business like Northwest Guaranty, which ranks at the medium level in terms of integration on the Strategy Locator, this is not as big an issue as it would be for a company such as Nokia, which is delivering smart-phone technology. Nokia's switches, transmission products, software, and handset hardware must all work together seamlessly, which requires an extremely high level of alignment among research and development and engineering groups.

Solutions Development The solutions development process is a corollary to the product development process. Decisions need to be made regarding the limits of customization and about which solutions can be replicated and sold to other customers. If every solution is a one-time customization that cannot be reused, the organization will be customer-centric but unprofitable.

Pricing and Market Rules Providing integrated solutions, which draw on a wide range of products and services from different parts of a company—each with their own cost structures and pricing guidelines—creates the risk either of selling products that are loss leaders or selling solutions with such complicated pricing schemes that they alienate more customers than they attract. The pricing for a solution may be more or less than the sum of the costs of each component part if bought separately. This will cause conflicts over which product or service area takes the discount or where credit is given for value-added intangibles. One option is to use a standing committee that includes representatives from both marketing and sales to resolve pricing and discount issues. The finance function may also become involved to create pricing models and templates that lay out standard transfer prices. Other rules will be needed to specify what can be bought on the open market for solutions and what must be bought internally.

Rewards

Rewards in a front-back organization tend to emphasize contributions to team, unit, and division or company success rather than individual results. The most significant changes have to be made in the compensation structures for sales and other front-end units. Solutions sales tend to be larger and less frequent, requiring redesign of sales compensation packages and providing more rewards for the up-front investment in sales prospecting efforts. Customer satisfaction and customer relationship measures should be factored in as well.

At Northwest Guaranty, for example, branch personnel had been rewarded primarily for product sales. The new emphasis on building relationships and selling solutions requires the branch teams to engage in marketing, customer analysis, and customer relationship management. With this shift, the difference in segment dynamics became more important than the difference in the products, with an agribusiness sale being much larger and more complex than a sale in the young producer segment. New incentives were created to reward these complex sales, encourage people to willingly bring in colleagues with expertise, and compensate the team for making the best decision on behalf of the customer regardless of the size of the sale.

People

As part of our discussion of the light and medium levels of customer-centric application, we have covered many of the talent challenges raised by the transition to a customer-centric strategy. In the front-back organization, in addition to having the multiskilled account managers who were present in the medium level, whole teams must now be both technically adept and astute in customer management.

Having some of the product specialists sit on both product and segment teams in matrixed positions can help to create links between the front and the back. In addition, co-location, where possible, brings product managers closer to customer needs and information. Rotational assignments help to build understanding of the differing objectives of the front and the back and between the sales and marketing functions.

The more complex the solution, the higher up in the customer organization the purchase decision will be made. Selling these solutions requires a more sophisticated senior salesperson or account manager. In addition, there is a greater need for team selling and for account managers to also be team managers. The talent profile for the sales organization can change significantly.

●　●　●

The customer-centric organization is an appealing organizational form with its promise to put customers at the center of attention. In this chapter, we have reviewed the drivers in the business environment that are leading more companies toward organizing around the customer and defined what a truly customer-centric strategy is. But we have also cautioned that a customer-centric organization is not necessary or right for everyone.

Leaders who believe that a customer-centric strategy is warranted can use the Strategy Locator we have described to determine to what level they need to change their organization. The light form uses customer teams to coordinate for those few advanced customers that want solutions, not just stand-alone products. For many organizations, the light form is all that is needed. Even for those that need more customer-centricity, it is also a good place to start as a way to learn and build capability. The medium form adds account managers to the customer teams in order to coordinate across multiple product lines to create multiple solutions for customers. We have reviewed how to design this difficult role for success. Finally, the intensive application of customer-centric strategy results in a front-back structure, with fully developed customer front-end units organized by segments that draw on the product and functional capabilities of the back-end units. This most advanced and complex customer-centric form requires strong, top-down leadership and a mature management cadre to manage the multitude of interactions and conflicts that trying to implement such a structure entails.

Chapter 3

Organizing Across Borders

WITH THE OPENING OF THE FORMER SOVIET UNION, the growth of China, the easing of global trade through international bodies such as the World Trade Organization, deregulation, and increased disposable income in many places in the world during the past fifteen years, corporations have expanded rapidly to reach across international borders. Companies from North America and Europe have long sought new markets in which to leverage their brands, capital, and other strengths. The signal change in the past decade is that multinational firms from developing countries—such as China's Lenovo; India's Infosys, Tata, and Wipro; Israel's Teva Pharmaceuticals; Mexico's Cemex; and South Africa's SABMiller—have enjoyed similar success in expanding globally.

International expansion has always been an attractive option for growth. When domestic markets become saturated and mature, the options for a firm are to diversify into new products and services or seek new locations in which to grow. Even the United States, with its enormous buying power, represents just 5 percent of the world's population; growing middle classes on other continents present attractive market opportunities. In addition, international expansion allows a company to spread risk across different economic cycles, lessening its dependence on the health of a local or regional market.

A successful multinational firm brings many strengths to bear as it expands outside its home country. These include admired and desired brands, research and development expertise, global scale and efficiency for purchasing and manufacturing, financial power, and advanced management and human resource practices. But even the most successful domestic company faces a new array of complex challenges as it moves into the international arena:

- How to manage power relationships and decision rights among country managers, global product managers, customer segments, and corporate functions
- How to bridge differences of time and culture when adapting home-grown success formulas to new environments
- How to manage the balance between local nationals and expatriate staff and build a global talent pool
- How to create new channels for learning and overcome the dangers of both arrogance (from being successful at home) and ignorance (not knowing what to keep the same and where to differentiate)
- How to move innovations, regardless of where they are generated, across the global network

Traditionally organizations have grown internationally by creating geographic divisions and using strong country managers to run and expand local operations. However, beginning in the 1980s, the promise of free trade and a more common global culture led many to envision markets without borders. The corporate response was to create business units to manage global product lines, diminishing the role of the country manager and the importance of national boundaries. Recent experience, however, has shown that local cultures and buying patterns are still strong and that local competitors can be formidable. As John H. Bryan, former CEO of Sara Lee Corporation, the parent company of Hanes, has noted, "Even underwear has national characteristics" (Forteza and Neilson, 1999, p. 2). Although the growth of the European Union (EU) has brought European countries closer together from a trade perspective, the largest opportunities for many firms are in emerging and developing nations that have active host governments and specific ways of doing business. Many companies find that they still need strong country management to deal with national regulations and manage the local brand and reputation issues that allow a newcomer to compete against established local providers. Geographic and cultural differences have not diminished as quickly as expected.

Today's aspiring global company can choose to organize geographically, around global products, or around global customers, or it can pursue a combination of these three strategies. In addition, it must decide what the role of the home country will be and how functional capabilities and centers of expertise can best be distributed around the world.

This chapter provides an overview of global strategies and the options for organizing internationally (for a more comprehensive examination of the topic, see Galbraith, 2000). The chapter has two sections, the first focusing on strategy and the second on organization design issues. The first section, "Levels of International Strategy," will help you understand the different types of international strategy and the capabilities needed for each and choose a form for your international organization that matches your strategy. The second section, "Design Considerations," makes up the bulk of the chapter and is focused on three international strategies and the organizational form for each:

Geographic	Expanding by setting up operations outside the home country, using geographies and regions as the primary organizational units
Multidimensional network	Adding a global product or customer dimension to the geographic form
Transnational	Changing the role of the geographic units to become global centers of expertise

Levels of International Strategy

The international strategy you pursue will determine the capabilities and organizational structure that you need. In general, there are five types of international strategy that a company can pursue. They can be thought of as five levels. As an organization moves from level 1 to level 5, more value is added to the firm by the assets and employees outside the home country, and a more complex set of capabilities and a greater level of organizational coordination are needed. The five levels are summarized in Figure 3.1 and described below.

Level 1: Export

The export mode is the simplest level of international strategy: the international unit is simply a sales organization. For a product company, the sales subsidiary is the primary link to distributors. For service companies, once the service—such as consulting, advertising, or banking—is sold, the home office does the work. Before entering the foreign market, the home office must develop a product and branding strategy that aligns with the demands of the new market. This is the beginning of the development of capabilities in international product development and brand management.

FIGURE 3.1 **Levels of International Strategy.**

Strategy	Description	Organizational Characteristics	New Capabilities Required
Level 1: Export	• Sell products and services abroad that are manufactured in home country	Sales units	International product development International brand management
Level 2: Partner	• Create partnerships or joint ventures with local firms • Increased level of assets outside home country • Partnering is used as a means to gain market access in foreign country—may be required by government • Usually a stepping stone or learning platform	Varies depending upon the partnering model used	All level 1 capabilities plus International partnering
Level 3: Geographic	• Expand business by setting up complete operations • Fully fledged business in one or more geographies • Competitive advantages transferred from home country • Integration achieved through home country functional units	Geographic division appended to home country structure	All level 2 capabilities plus Transfer and modification of advantages from home country
Level 4: Multi-dimensional network	• Higher level of integration across geographies through global product lines or global customers • Significant portion of assets outside home country, but home country still dominates and transfers advantage	Organized along multiple dimensions: geography, business, function, and/or customer	All level 3 capabilities plus Cross-unit integration Balancing power among multiple dimensions
Level 5: Transnational	• Significant portion of assets outside home country • International units play leading and contributing role in generating advantages • Home country is no longer the center or most important location	Peer model with a distributed power structure Multiple centers of capability based on where activity can be done best	All level 4 capabilities plus Management of a distributed organization

Beyond making sales, the subsidiary can provide input to the home office to build these capabilities and improve the company's offerings.

Level 2: Partner

A firm often chooses partnering when it has limited international experience or if the market it is entering is very different from those with which it is familiar. By entering into a joint venture, a company can minimize risk as well as learn about a new business environment, and determine whether and how its advantages can be transferred. In addition to the international product and marketing capabilities necessary for the level 1 export model, a level 2 partnering strategy requires skills in selecting partners, negotiating deals, maintaining contacts at multiple levels, and managing alliances and relationships.

Level 3: Geographic

The next level of international strategy is the addition of geographic units to the existing corporate structure, which means that the company expands operationally. Now, in addition to international product development, marketing, and partnering capabilities, the home office must learn how to transfer its resource advantages to its new international operating subsidiaries. These advantages may include supply chain or innovation capabilities, technology, financial expertise, or acquisition and integration experience. A geographic strategy can result in a separate international division appended to the home country division, or it can evolve into a set of regions and countries roughly equal in power and importance to one another.

Level 4: Multidimensional Network

As the company increases its foreign direct investments and begins to operate in more and more countries, the simplicity of a separate geographic division that reports to headquarters may no longer be adequate. In addition, based on the firm's strategy, the home country may be organized along more than one dimension—by function, geography, product, or customer—and the firm may find that it is ready to extend this structure to the geographies. At this point, a multidimensional network can be used. In a level 4 firm, the home country remains the dominant force, transferring competitive advantages to the subsidiaries. The geographic dimension is still important, but now it shares power with global product lines or global customer units as well as global functions. The new organizational challenge that has to be met is the integration of these various dimensions. The company must develop appropriate lateral processes and multidimensional networks to integrate the company's work around the globe.

Level 5: Transnational

In contrast to the other levels, in which subsidiaries implement advantages and strategies generated in the home country, in a transnational company all of the firm's units around the world play both leading and contributing roles in creating capabilities. This strategy is implemented less through structural decisions than through process and behavioral supports (see Bartlett and Ghoshal, 1998). The original home country may no longer be the largest, most important, or most expert geography. Another way to think of the level 5 firm is as a peer model. Capabilities are located where the work can be done best, and the geographic units are mutually interdependent. An important difference to keep in mind is that these are not just functional support units that are located where labor is cheapest; these are the core business units. The key capability to be developed here is the ability to manage a distributed organization with multiple "headquarters."

For most companies, there is some progression from one level to another. However, these five levels are not necessarily developmental stages. One can design a start-up organization at level 5. For example, Logitech, the computer peripherals maker, began with its product development, finance, and hardware research and development functions located in Switzerland; software and marketing housed in the United States; and manufacturing in Taiwan and China. But starting up at level 5 will still require all of the level 5 capabilities, in addition to those required in levels 1 through 4. Note that in using the term *level*, we are not implying that a higher level is better. Depending on the business strategy, an export strategy (level 1) can be more profitable than a transnational approach (level 5). Finally, many companies will be at different levels in different parts of the world, operating in the way that makes sense locally. The International Strategy tool in the Appendix can help you clarify where your company is in its level of international development, its aspirations, and the capabilities needed to realize its strategy.

In this discussion of designing an organization to operate across borders, we focus on the configurations that correspond to the geographic organization, the multidimensional network, and the transnational strategies. The other two strategies—export and partnering—have less impact on organizational form and therefore are not addressed here.

Design Considerations: Geographic

International expansion is usually driven by success in the home country coupled with limited growth potential in the home market. Figure 3.2 shows the Star Model™ for the geographic international organization.

A company can choose to expand organically or by acquisition to build a local presence in a selected additional country. The decision criteria for establishing which country to expand into first often include a country's physical or cultural proximity to the home country or the presence of a similar development and customer profile. Companies that choose to grow organically do so because the market does not exist in the target country (for example, Amazon expanding from the United States into the United Kingdom by building a business there) or because they believe that existing firms do not meet their standards (such as Toyota choosing to build,

FIGURE 3.2 **Star Model for Geographic International Organization.**

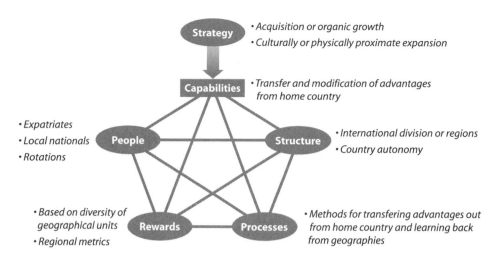

rather than buy, manufacturing plants in the United States). Alternatively, a company can choose to grow through acquisition. This is typically done when there is already enough local capacity in the sector and the acquiring company believes it can improve operations or achieve synergies with its current products or processes. For example, there are already enough cement plants in most parts of the world. When the large global players in the cement field, such as LaFarge or Cemex, move into a new geography, they do it by acquiring local facilities and upgrading them.

After progressing through export or partnering or local acquisition, when the firm's nondomestic activities are robust enough, they are often put into a geographic division appended to the home country's structure. The work of the geographic division is to localize the company's success formula and transfer its advantages, making whatever adaptations and modifications to local conditions are necessary. When we talk about transferring advantages, we are essentially referring to organizational capabilities. For example, when Wal-Mart expanded internationally, it brought with it the company's tremendous buying power, efficient store management practices, supplier management technology, and logistics expertise. Whether exporting to Japan to sell through local retailers there, forming a joint venture partnership in Mexico, or acquiring and transforming an underperforming chain in Canada, Wal-Mart's international success has been largely based on its ability to transfer the capabilities it has honed in its home market and adapt them to local conditions (Govindarajan and Gupta, 1999). Nevertheless, the company has stumbled in some regions and pulled out of Germany and South Korea after finding that local shopping habits and strong competitors did not give the Wal-Mart success formula an advantage and that the company could not adapt enough to compete successfully.

Geographic Example: Cemex

To illustrate some of the considerations to be made in designing a geographically based international division, we use as an example Cemex, the third-largest cement company and the leading supplier of ready-mix concrete in the world. As of 2006, it was a $15 billion company, with over fifty thousand employees in fifty countries. Cemex was founded in Mexico in 1906 and remained a small regional player in the cement industry until the liberalization of the Mexican economy in the 1980s. Cemex then consolidated the Mexican cement market and from this position of strength began to expand internationally in order to keep pace with the other leaders in the industry.

Through the 1990s, Cemex built a geographically based international business by first exporting and trading cement—without making any direct investment in other countries—in order to learn about conducting business outside Mexico (an example of a level 1 strategy). It then moved to a level 3 strategy, expanding first to its neighbors: south Texas and Central and South America. Its first foray into Europe was to Spain, which offered cultural similarities to Mexico. Expansions into Asia were first through the Philippines and Indonesia, emerging markets with similar levels of economic development as Mexico.

Structure

The geographically based international division usually has a fairly simple structure. If there are just a few countries in the international division, they can all be managed by a single executive. As the number of countries grows, however, they may be grouped into regions, either still managed by one executive or, if the regional groupings are large enough, each region may have a leader who is a member of the company's executive team. At the corporate level, the functional groups—finance, human resources, IT, product development, supply chain management—are usually fairly strong in order to gain scale, manage standards, and leverage the organization's capabilities across the regions. Often functional managers in the countries are matrixed to the country manager and to a regional or corporate-level functional manager to ensure a focus on both local and enterprise interests. Figure 3.3 illustrates a typical geographic division with functions matrixed at the country level.

FIGURE 3.3 **Geographic Division with Matrixed Functions.**

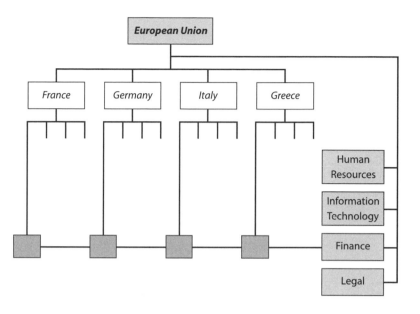

Cemex began with Mexican and International divisions. As the international business grew, it was divided into regional groups for North America; Europe; Asia, Africa, and Southern Europe; and South America and the Caribbean. A simplified structure for Cemex is shown in Figure 3.4.

Benefits of Structuring an International Business by Geography

Regardless of how the home country is organized, the most common way to move across borders is to add on geographic units, usually aggregated into what is called the "international division" reporting to the CEO. The geographic groups are based on country boundaries, and each unit is led by a country manager, who serves as a business manager for all the activities in that country. This structure has a number of benefits. First, organizing by geography minimizes travel and transportation for local marketing,

FIGURE 3.4 **Simplified Cemex Structure.**

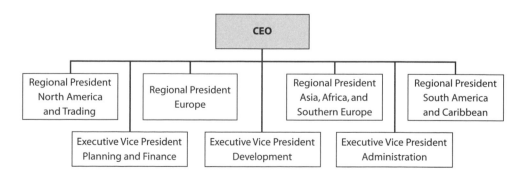

sales, distribution, and service. Second, although market boundaries may not match perfectly with national boundaries, there are usually enough differences between countries in terms of regulation that having an organizational structure that matches the political boundaries between countries makes sense from a management standpoint.

Perhaps the most important argument for separating the geographies from the existing business into an international division is that it offers greater focus. Geographic expansion is usually limited when it starts, and if these fledgling businesses are not separated out into their own groups, they frequently do not receive the level of attention that they need. For example, if international sales represent 10 percent of total sales and the international sales unit is left in the larger business unit, the unique concerns of the international business are likely to be overlooked or downplayed. In many ways, geographic expansion can be seen as a start-up within an existing company, with the same needs as we discuss for new businesses in Chapter Six. The international units may need different product designs or business processes and may not fit with the standard and established ways of the home country. At the beginning, units in new geographies may produce little profit given the management time and attention required to get them up and running. A dedicated division provides separation, emphasis, and focus.

Standardization of Structures Across Geographies

Once a firm has established itself in more than one new region, a question may arise as to whether to standardize the structure of the country units. The benefits of using a similar structure within each country (having the same roles reporting to a country manager, for example) are twofold. First, the job of regional or international division management becomes easier. These managers can assess and compare performance across geographic units. Second, having similar jobs and structures makes it easier to move people between different units. For example, a supply chain manager may be moved from a smaller to a larger country for career development purposes. The manager will find that the scale of the job has increased, but if the units are similarly structured, he should also be able to quickly assimilate and fit into a familiarly configured leadership team.

The push from the corporate perspective to standardize, in order to ease oversight and talent development, should be tempered with an analysis of what is best from a local perspective. The size of a country, the size and complexity of the business, the diversity of a country's internal markets, and local growth strategies should all be taken into account. Each country structure should be designed from the ground up to reflect the local context and business and then assessed for fit against an overall template that will facilitate linkages back to the corporate center. For example, at Cemex, local functions that are run from corporate (such as IT, purchasing, and human resources) are structured consistently across country units. The way in which the business operations are configured, however, is left up to the country manager.

Determining the Rationale for Clusters

When the number of countries in an international division becomes so large or diverse that it is not practical for one executive to oversee them all, they are typically grouped into regions or clusters, with the new role of regional director added. In such cases, the home country—regardless of its size—often remains on its own, because it is still the firm's primary source of expertise, talent, and other competitive advantages. The value of regional groupings, beyond concerns around span of control, is that member countries can leverage assets and knowledge based on some shared market characteristics. When this occurs, it is useful to have an intermediate level of coordination at a regional level. There are a number of options for configuring regions:

- *Proximity.* This is the most obvious option, as it reduces travel time for the regional manager, and countries that are adjacent often share some market commonalities. In addition, if the countries can share manufacturing or distribution capabilities, clustering by proximity reduces transportation time and cost.

- *Common market.* The European Union and Mercosur in South America serve to diminish the importance of country boundaries for purposes of trade, and make for natural clusters.

- *Development level.* Grouping by economic development level may offer more synergies than does grouping by geographic proximity. For example, in the Balkans, Slovenia and Croatia are more developed markets in terms of gross domestic product than Bosnia or Serbia, although they are neighboring countries with some cultural similarities. The former may be better clustered with Hungary and Austria than their southern neighbors.

- *Customer profile.* If customer buying patterns differ significantly across countries, it may make sense to group countries by market characteristics. For example, the Polish grocery sector is dominated by large retail chains, much as in Western Europe. For Coca-Cola, Poland has more in common with Italy from a customer perspective than it does with its Eastern European neighbors, which tend to still have a large number of small independent retailers.

• *Business life cycle stage.* Another grouping scheme might be based on how developed the business is in the country. Units that are starting up operations may have more in common with other start-up units and thus can share learning. Or the regions may be purposefully mixed, so that start-ups can gain from the experience of countries with more established businesses. British Petroleum used to group its oil fields based on proximity, but leaders noticed that the lack of common experience meant there was little sharing or exchange when the field managers got together. They reconfigured the fields into four peer groups based on life stage (exploration, start-up, production, and decline), as members of these groups were likely to face similar technical and commercial concerns (Roberts, 2004).

In sum, based on the overall business strategy and the nature of the countries in question, arguments can be made for grouping along a number of dimensions. In addition, arguments can be made for grouping similar profiles together in order to leverage commonalities, or purposefully grouping units into diverse clusters to promote a different type of learning. Which route is chosen is a design decision that should be based on an explicitly articulated rationale and a set of clear criteria, and it should be revisited periodically as the international businesses develop and the political and market context changes. The Region Configuration tool in the Appendix can help guide this discussion.

Role of Division and Regional Management

The geographic division has two levels of management. On the ground are local or expatriate managers, running the local operations and led by the country manager. The second level is the regional or division leadership, which is usually staffed with managers from headquarters who have had extensive tenure with the company. The role of the division management is to:

• Set overall international strategy
• Make acquisition, investment, and divestiture decisions
• Translate corporate policy and standards for application at the local level
• Provide functional expertise and oversight

- Serve as a liaison between the geographic units and the home country and represent the international units to important home country constituencies
- Select and manage the careers of country managers and key functional managers in the countries

A major organization design decision is the role that regional management will have. At one extreme, the region can consist of a single regional director with no supporting staff. In this case, the regional executive plays primarily a coordinating and coaching role, reducing the span of direct reports up to the company's senior management level.

At the other end of the spectrum—and when there is enough volume to justify the cost of regional overhead—the regional structure can replicate the corporate functions. This makes sense when the countries are grouped together on some basis that allows leverage of regional capability. In this case, the regional management will create a regional strategy and may measure results on a regional basis. Cemex has traditionally had a fairly light regional structure, but as the business has grown, it has begun to coordinate more formally within regions. For example, in the Caribbean basin, all customer calls are routed to call centers in Colombia. Call center representatives are trained to speak Spanish in local accents so that customers are not even aware that calls are not being handled in country.

Country Autonomy

Another key organization design question to ask when launching a geographic subsidiary is, How autonomous should the division be? The geographic units will argue for maximum freedom and autonomy in order to learn how to do business in the unfamiliar geography, but the home country will want to keep a fairly high degree of control in order to transfer advantages and integrate the subsidiary into its network. Consideration of three factors can help guide this decision.

- *Amount of cross-border coordination.* If the business strategy is to progress to the level 4 multidimensional network (for example, a global product line delivered through the geographies), the country units will eventually have to be closely integrated into the home country business. A bank serving multinational customers who want access to consistent products and services regardless of location will need to achieve a high level of product line coordination across geographies. In this scenario, the countries would be given less autonomy. More decision-making power would be given to the central staff in order to make consistent enterprise decisions that will prepare the company for the goal of an integrated, global business. In addition, if the supply chain crosses borders, there is a potential for transfer of technology, or if trade is conducted between country units within the company, more coordination and guidance from a higher level is needed. But if there is not an eventual objective of creating global business lines, the geographic units are very different from one another, they function largely as stand-alone businesses, and they have active host governments with specific requirements for doing business, then they need to be given more autonomy.

• *Cultural distance.* Cultural distance is a measure of how different the international units are from the home country in terms of language, national culture, history, customer buying patterns, and business practices. If the cultural distance is great—for example, a German company expanding into China—then it is less likely that the advantages that exist in the home market, such as management systems and practices, will readily transfer intact. More local customization will need to be done, and it will be more important to have some local nationals who have experience with the corporate vision but can adapt the corporate success formula to suit local conditions. These managers need to be given autonomy to make these decisions. In addition to management practices, if the firm has to recreate local supply chain, workforce, customer relationship, or other resource advantages, the geographic subsidiary will require greater autonomy. Successful execution may require quick decisions. If the units' decisions always have to go through headquarters for approval, ground may be lost to nimbler local competitors.

• *Portfolio diversity.* Most companies tend to have a more diverse business and product set in the home country than abroad. As a company expands, it leads with its winning products. If the strategy is to develop a diverse portfolio internationally, then it will be difficult for one country manager to understand the complete business, and it is more likely that business line managers at a regional or corporate level will need to manage the product lines across the regions. This speaks to less autonomy for the country unit (see the discussion of multidimensional networks later in this chapter).

On balance, during the start-up phase of the geographic division, most companies do well to err on the side of giving the units greater autonomy when the issues at hand are not central to firm strategy. In this way, the units are not dominated by the home country in such a way that they lose the ability to respond rapidly to local conditions and opportunities. The Country Autonomy tool in the Appendix can provide more guidance on this topic.

Processes

The processes that are designed first in a company that is expanding geographically are those that link the home country to the geographic units. Often overlooked, but also important, are the processes that enable the transfer of new information back to headquarters and thus foster sharing among countries.

Transferring Advantages to the Geographies

The first process to be implemented is a method to transfer the firm's capabilities to the new geography. This is usually accomplished by expatriates familiar with the business formula who transfer it to local nationals. If the strategy is to expand through acquisition, the due diligence and integration phases present the opportunity to transfer and embed the home country's practices.

Cemex considers its postmerger integration (PMI) process a competitive advantage. In the cement industry, there is already enough worldwide capacity. Therefore, major global players achieve growth largely through acquisition and consolidation. Cemex chooses its targets carefully and eventually pursues only 15 percent of those candidates that it has considered. The due diligence team is made up of a dozen people, with at least half having prior due diligence experience. After a deal is completed, the PMI process takes anywhere from a few months to a year—half the time most of Cemex's competitors take. It is a rigorous, systematic process focused on building and integrating IT systems and training local staff on their use, improving operational efficiencies, and inculcating Cemex standards and management culture. The PMI team is carefully selected to be multinational in makeup, and up to half of the members stay on as expatriates to help run the acquired plant. Talented managers from the acquired company are sent back to Mexico to learn about Cemex's culture and practices. Through this process, the Cemex way of doing business is rapidly transferred to acquisitions and new geographies.

Listening and Learning by the Home Country

The country managers and geographic division leaders must be continually communicating with and educating managers in the home country. Clearly the headquarters will be interested in business results, but there also must be a mechanism to keep senior executives informed during periods of adaptation so that they can decide where standards need to be rigorously maintained and where they can be relaxed to foster innovation. Communication is difficult between different regions under the best of circumstances, and start-ups in new countries rarely offer the best of circumstances. Cultural distance, along with inexperience in the home country managing remotely and across cultural boundaries, can make communication anxious and tense, particularly if the issues are unexpected or challenge the management competencies of the home country managers.

One of the ways that Cemex formalizes this communication is by having the functional managers in the countries make presentations each month to the country manager and regional director, covering all aspects of operations. Then, also on a monthly schedule, the country managers, regional directors, and corporate functional leaders all meet with the CEO. These frequent and structured meetings ensure that information flows upward, downward, and laterally without becoming distorted (Ghemawat and Matthews, 2004).

Gaining the Benefits of Size: Leveraging the Home Country

In a geographic division structure, each country is essentially a field unit. All of the issues of centralization and decentralization described in Chapter Five apply but are compounded by issues of physical and cultural distance. As we discuss in that chapter, determining where decisions are best made is not a simple choice between corporate and local. For each element of the business, choices need to be made regarding who will make which decisions and at what level.

Cemex has given a lot of thought to decision processes and has divided them into *integrated*, *coordinated*, and *local* levels, as shown in Figure 3.5. Activities and decisions that fall into the "integrated" level must be done the "Cemex Way," with little (if any) local discretion allowed. Integrated processes and activities are those that the company believes are best managed centrally and are carried out in a similar fashion across geographies. These include finance, audit, procurement, IT, and human resources. For example, the finance function is one that Cemex leadership believes should be controlled strongly from the center. Centralization of this function—or integration, as they call it—leverages scale, allows consistent control, and enables corporate managers to develop deep expertise. The finance directors in the countries report directly to the regional and corporate finance functions, with no reporting link to the country manager. This allows them to remain independent and make even the most local of decisions with

FIGURE 3.5 **Cemex Coordination Model.**

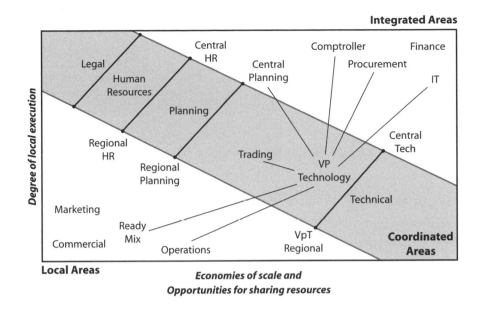

an enterprise perspective. In addition, the position is usually staffed with an expatriate or a person who has spent time in the regional or corporate finance function.

At the other end of the spectrum are local processes and activities, deemed to be best handled completely at the local level. If a regional or corporate function exists in these areas, its role is merely to loosely coordinate, lend support when requested, or focus on corporate activities that have little direct bearing on local operations. For example, Cemex sells Ready Mix, premixed concrete delivered from a local depot to construction sites in the familiar cement truck with the rotating drum. Once mixed, the concrete is good for only a certain amount of time and must be kept in motion to prevent it from hardening prematurely. Therefore, the Ready Mix business is an exceptionally local business. At Cemex it is managed on a country basis, with no linkage to any corporate function at all.

To bring clarity to global coordination, Cemex determines what will be managed at the corporate level and what is left to local decision makers. More difficult is determining how decisions are made for activities that fall into the middle segment, which at Cemex are called "coordinated" activities. An example that illustrates the tensions of autonomy is the cement technology function. It is a small unit housed at the corporate level whose primary role is to monitor operations, identify and transfer improvements and innovations, acquire and develop new plant technology, and gather market intelligence. For each of these roles, the leader of the technology function has to decide when his group should dictate from the center (for instance, when a plant is failing and centralized expertise has to be sent in), when it should "sell" ideas out to the geographies (perhaps to spread the use of new technologies and practices), and when it should wait to be invited to participate (a plant is experiencing a decrease in yield and cannot diagnose the cause, for example).

The key questions that must be debated and agreed on are common to all functions that do not fall neatly into being either centralized or decentralized. Well-developed management processes—those that are intentionally designed, frequently assessed, and adapted as the environment dictates—are the differentiators between companies that struggle with managing their geographic units and companies that strike the right balance between central control and local autonomy.

In general, in order to foster innovation and local responsiveness and develop the judgment of managers close to the customers, our recommendation is to provide freedom to make decisions at the local level and establish clear boundaries governing when decisions should be escalated to a higher level. Key questions to ask when determining these boundaries include:

- Is this a high-risk decision? If it is made incorrectly at the local level, what is the risk?
- Is this a high-cost decision? Do the savings and other benefits of standardization outweigh the trade-offs in reducing local autonomy?
- Is corporate or regional involvement in this decision important for control purposes or for informational purposes? If it is for informational purposes, is there a way to gather the information without being part of the decision-making process?
- Is there a way to set the boundaries and criteria for decisions and then let the local managers determine their own course within those parameters?

The Centralization—Decentralization tool in the Appendix provides more guidance on structuring these decision boundaries.

Leveraging Regional Groups

In our discussion of structure, we noted that the country units can be clustered in more ways than just according to physical proximity. To gain the benefits of clustering—whether by size, development, customer profile, life stage, or something else—formalized connections need to be made among units. This can be facilitated by the regional director, or it can be self-managed by the country managers. Since giving assistance to a peer will take attention and resources away from the country manager's primary focus, there need to be some reciprocity, self-interest, and rewards designed to encourage this behavior. British Petroleum organized its oil fields into clusters based on life stage and then encouraged what they called "peer assists." Any member of a cluster (usually comprising about ten oil fields) could call for a peer assist. A peer elsewhere in the cluster who could help with the issue would be expected to send expertise. Asking for help became an accepted and encouraged norm, and responding was rewarded through recognition and reciprocity. This notion evolved into peer challenges, whereby members of the cluster reviewed others' performance targets, made capital allocation decisions for the cluster, and then took collective responsibility for meeting the group's targets (Roberts, 2004).

Rewards

Metrics and rewards for the geographic units tend to vary based on the diversity of the local markets. If the local conditions are quite different and there is little or no support that one country can provide another, then the rewards for the country manager and his or her team are based largely on performance against their local goals. Once regions or clusters are formed, however, if the region also functions as a profit center, then the country units also have to be assessed against their contribution to the overall regional performance and their support of other units in the cluster.

Adding regional goals raises the complexity in measuring and rewarding performance. For example, one country may take the lead on product development, or another may provide manufacturing capacity for the other countries in the cluster. Regional management then has to develop scorecards to measure not only quantifiable outputs but also responsiveness, knowledge sharing and transfer, and collaboration.

People

The key talent consideration in the geographic model is the strategic deployment and management of expatriates and local nationals.

Expatriates

An expatriate is a staff member from the home country or other area who is brought into a country unit for a specific and limited amount of time. Expatriates are paid differently from local employees, and they have a particular role to play. They know the firm's capabilities, have expertise that is not available locally, and carry the corporate culture to the geography. Expatriates are often used as country managers in the early phases of a geographic expansion. They may also be used in key roles. For example, at

Cemex, the country-level finance officer is almost always an expatriate. This brings greater independence to the role and ensures that conflicts of interest from past local ties are avoided. Expatriates may also be used where local talent is thin or the company's capabilities are closely linked to a particular role, such as marketing for a consumer goods company. When there is a regional management level, expatriates are often used in these roles as well. Typically regional headquarters are located in cities with a good expatriate infrastructure (transportation, schools, clubs, global arts, and culture) and are therefore attractive locations for managers and their families to live for a defined period.

Cemex uses the idea of "centurions" to underscore the importance of bringing a core group of experienced people into any expansion. The centurions were respected professional officers of the Roman army who led and inspired small groups of soldiers (usually around one hundred—thus, their name) by example, fighting from the front of the formation. They were loyal to Rome, and regardless of their time away from the capital, they never became part of the local community. At Cemex, they tell the story of a local manager who was having some problems with his business. Sitting with a manager who had come from the regional office to help understand the issue and lend assistance, the local manager became frustrated: "If you were on this side, you would see it a different way." The Cemex centurion responded, "I'm on the Cemex side. What side are you on?"

Local Nationals

The other key talent decision to be made is in regard to the use of local nationals. These are people who are hired into the company from the geographic unit. If they are talented, they can eventually become part of the expatriate cadre after gaining experience in the company, moving to the regional or corporate level and other geographic units. The primary value of local national managers is that they know the local business environment. They are often hired from local competitors and have ties to the community.

In the past, multinational companies were attractive options for well-educated local residents, and the multinational had an advantage when hiring in the local talent market. Unfortunately, many companies do not have strong mechanisms to identify high-potential local nationals, and they fail to put the same effort into local development as they do for managers from the home country. As local competitors have become more sophisticated in their management of talent and business practices, many companies have found that top local nationals may not be as interested in working for a multinational if the leaders of the country or regional unit are always expatriates. One option to overcome this is to challenge the assumption that an expatriate must be in the leadership role. Ninety percent of Unilever's foreign operations are headed by local nationals, with expatriates filling roles at the next level down (Quelch and Bloom, 1999). However, the local nationals are required to have worked outside their home country in order to have exposure to the broader Unilever culture and way of operating.

Rotational Assignments and Development

The geographic division provides an excellent way to develop talent. The country manager has broad responsibility for all aspects of the business in his or her country and thus develops the general management skills needed at the executive levels of a company. Many companies rotate staff through these roles as a way to develop their general managers. For example, Wal-Mart's approach to general manager development places heavy emphasis on learning from experience, perhaps the single greatest source of leadership development. New general managers may start by overseeing twenty stores, then move to another country to manage the same number of outlets, and next to a position with more stores in a third country. Wal-Mart talent managers have learned to pace development so that individual capacity and capability grow with the complexity of the job. Moves for managers identified as having high potential for success are carefully planned and sequenced (to the extent that market changes, family situations, and individual interests allow) in order to expose the manager to the right set of developmental experiences (Kates and Downey, 2005).

A key question is how long to leave a manager in an assignment. The general rule of thumb has been three years, but many companies are now considering longer stretches. Given how much there is to learn in a new environment, the value of customer knowledge and relationships, and the importance of seeing the operational results of strategic decisions, the trend is toward lengthening the time in assignment to three to five years. Jeffrey Immelt, in his nineteen-year career as a GE manager, spent between just eighteen months and three years in most of his positions. Now, as CEO, he is keeping managers in place for at least three years to provide more stability and improve accountability for decisions made and actions taken (Kranhold, 2006).

Design Considerations: Multidimensional Network

The geographic structure works best for a single business—that is, a business with one set of closely related products, as is the case with Cemex. The

FIGURE 3.6 **Star Model for the Multidimensional Network.**

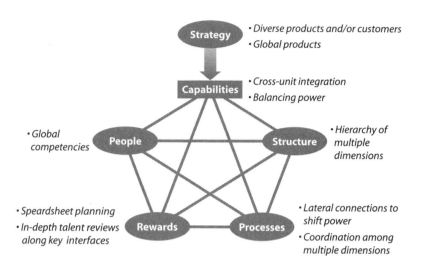

multidimensional network emerges as the firm increases the percentage of its operations outside the home country and introduces additional product lines to its international business. Figure 3.6 shows the Star Model for the multidimensional network.

Strategy

While the geographic division can be two-dimensional—countries and regions as the primary organizing unit, with functions playing a strong role—a level 4 strategy adds another strong organizational dimension—either product or customer—that cuts across geographic borders. Although there is still a geographic element, it is no longer dominant. For coordination, subsidiaries are connected to each other and to appropriate units in the home country through a variety of lateral mechanisms, giving the company a network-like quality. Figure 3.7 shows the Black & Decker regional structure with business teams. The company makes a variety of tools and household products. It is organized geographically, but uses cross-border business teams to coordinate new product development and global brand management. In Chapter Two, we also used an example of a multidimensional network structure: the Degussa global customer team (see Figure 2.8).

The primary challenge for level 4 companies is developing appropriate cross-unit coordination capabilities—linkages and networks—across borders, functions, businesses, and customers that will help drive the firm strategy. The multidimensional network model attempts to achieve multiple objectives: manage multiple product lines for global scale and efficiency, maintain responsiveness and flexibility at the geographic unit level,

FIGURE 3.7 **Black & Decker Regional Structure.**

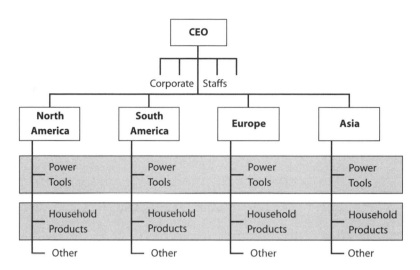

coordinate for global customers, and deploy functional expertise to foster cross-border learning.

Structure

A mixture of geographic and product orientations is a common form of multidimensional organization. We use the terms *product* and *business* interchangeably here, as the multiple business units result from an expansion of product lines. One of the design decisions for a leader to make is how to distribute power between the geographic units and the global business units. Figure 3.8 provides the range of options, some examples, and the factors that go into the decision.

Portfolio Diversity

The first factor to consider when making decisions about the structure of a multidimensional global organization is the diversity of the portfolio. This means not only how many different products and services are offered, but how different the business models underlying them are. When a company adds to its international portfolio a new business that requires different manufacturing, distribution, or sales processes, it may be too difficult to coordinate through the country manager alone, and global business management will become more important.

For example, as long as the Coca-Cola bottling business in Europe is selling various carbonated soft drinks (CSD), a geographic structure works well for local manufacturing and distribution. Product management can be coordinated at the corporate level, but the country managers are the experts at running a local CSD business. The launch of a water, cold tea, and juice

FIGURE 3.8 **Distributing Power Between Geographic and Business Units.**

Structure / Factors	Geographic Units (Cemex)	Geography Dominant (Black & Decker)	Geography and Business Matrix (IBM)	Business Units Dominant (Hewlett-Packard)	Global Businesses (DuPont)
Portfolio diversity	Low	Low	Moderate to high	Moderate to high	High
Consistency of markets (amount of adaptation needed)	Local adaptation	Local adaptation	Local adaptation	More standardization of products	More standardization of products
Customers (buying patterns)	Local	Local	Global and local	Global and local	Mostly global
Product transportability (opportunity to make in one place and sell in another)	Very low	Moderate	High	High	High
Host government role (as buyer and regulator)	High	Moderate	Moderate to low	Low	Low

These are opportunities for border coordination (bracket spanning Consistency of markets, Customers, and Product transportability rows)

business, however, will mean a new set of manufacturing, sales, and distribution practices. Although this business will draw on the capabilities of the CSD business, it is different enough that now there may need to be another executive at the corporate level looking at how to build and manage this business. With the introduction of multiple product lines, the company has introduced a new dimension and a new level of complexity. Country managers will need to coordinate activities with two product executives, and new discussions of priorities and investments will emerge. In Figure 3.8, the expansion of the business portfolio would move it from *geographic unit only* to *geographic dominant in structure*. It would no longer be a level 3 organization, organized by geographic dimension alone; now it would become a *multidimensional network*, in which the geographic dimension remains dominant but must be coordinated with a product dimension.

DuPont, in contrast, is structured without full-time geographic managers. Rather, it is structured around worldwide business units, each with different product lines and business models, in pharmaceuticals, agricultural chemicals, packaging material, coal, and fibers. The customers and competitors for these business units are mostly global. If geographic coordination is required on a regional basis, an executive manages it as a secondary responsibility.

The next three factors listed in Figure 3.8 all relate to the levels of cross-border coordination that are possible. If there is little cross-border synergy possible—because the product must be highly customized for local tastes, or it is both produced and sold locally, or it is expensive to transport—then more power is given to the geographic manager, and results will be measured at a country level. If there is benefit to coordinating at a regional or global level, the business unit becomes the profit center.

Consistency of Markets

The greater the extent to which products can be sold as is, with little customization for local tastes, the more sense it makes to manage products globally. In luxury goods, brand consistency and image is primarily what is being sold. Customers of Gucci or Louis Vuitton would not want either company to alter its product designs because they are buying the status that a global brand and product bring. McDonald's, however, has different menus to cater to local tastes: in Italy, customers can buy an espresso; in India, the restaurants use lamb instead of beef; and in Athens, McDonald's sells spanakopita as a snack food. These adaptations reinforce the need for strong country-level management.

Even where local adaptation is required, the strategy is usually to standardize as much as possible on global production platforms and customize where there is the greatest impact closest to the customer. Nestlé cereals are largely the same around the world, but packaging and promotion are modified for local markets. The more that products can be standardized, the more they can be managed on a global level, increasing the importance of the business or product dimension over the geographic.

Customer Buying Patterns

The existence of global and regional customers, as well as local customers, is also a factor in companies choosing to organize multidimensionally. It may be in a company's interest to negotiate separately with customers on a country level to maintain price differentials. But at some point, when the customer becomes organized on a regional or global level for buying, they will not want to negotiate separately with managers in each country. If strong industry opponents also force competition on price across borders, then the company will have to respond with coordination of pricing that will take place at a level above the country manager. It will be in no single country manager's interest to bear the cost of discounting.

Transportability

The more a product or service must be consumed near to where it is produced or the more costly it is to move a product from its site of production, the more power is given to the geographic dimension. Cemex Ready Mix concrete illustrates this well. Since the product must be consumed locally and is expensive to transport (it has a low value-to-transport cost ratio), Cemex has over fifteen hundred concrete plants around the world to serve local customers.

Other industries, however, are not as constrained by challenges associated with the production and transportation of their products. Advances in telecommunications have made services such as retailing, banking, and education more transportable. Not long ago, these businesses had to be located and managed near their customers. With the advent of the Internet, they can be managed more as business units, with less importance given to the geographic dimension.

Role of Host Government

Another factor to consider—one that operates independent of those already discussed—is the role of the host government. An active government may have specific business regulations, or it may require that foreign firms do business with a local partner, as is currently the case in China. The government may also be a significant customer of the company's products. In these situations, more power needs to be given to the geographic unit, so that this unique country-level relationship can be properly managed. Companies that do business in both developed and emerging economies may end up with different approaches in different regions. For example, Royal Dutch Shell is largely run as a global business, but it uses a strong country manager in places such as Malaysia where oil is a strategic industry managed by a state-owned company that serves as regulator, partner, and competitor. Few companies will be organized completely as geographic units or completely as global business units. Thus, they will simultaneously need sufficient capabilities to manage both dimensions and the ability to manage different models in different parts of the world.

Moving Along the Spectrum from Geographic to Business

As business strategies and external factors change, companies often move along the spectrum, shifting the balance of power between the geographic and business dimensions. One example is ABB, the Swedish-Swiss electrical equipment manufacturer. Until 1998, it was structured as a product-geographic matrix and was widely hailed for its ability to manage the complexity of running a global organization that included functional, customer, and other dimensions. But with deregulation and privatization of utilities, railroads, and other infrastructure, the role of local governments as customers for ABB's products diminished. At the same time, regional customers—who were more interested in speed, standardization, and cross-border supply agreements—were increasing. ABB shifted toward a strong business unit structure, reducing the role of the geographic units. Although the shift was made in response to changes in the external environment and customer needs, it also served to simplify the internal demands on management. A matrix, especially when used to organize an entire company, is extremely difficult to manage well. (See Chapter Four for more on designing and managing a matrix.)

The Citibank corporate banking strategy in the 1990s is another classic example of a company that shifted power among its structural dimensions in response to a change in strategy. As Citibank expanded its presence around the world, it used a geographic unit form. It had some global businesses (such as cash management and foreign exchange) and global customers, but power clearly rested with the country managers. Bank leaders realized that this model gave Citibank little advantage over local competitors when it came to serving local clients. Citibank was rarely the largest local bank in any market, and with its geographic structure, it was unable to bring its global capabilities to bear in the local market. In addition, the geographic structure became a barrier to mobilizing resources on behalf of global clients that did not want to deal with the bank on a country-by-country basis. Over time, the bank shifted its power structure and organized primarily around global customers, even going as far as dropping local customers in some markets. Product lines were secondary, and geography was relegated to the third organizing dimension.

The Multidimensional Structure tool in the Appendix can provide more guidance on analyzing the various factors for determining which dimension should be dominant.

Processes

Cross-unit coordination is the capability central to the success of level 4 multidimensional network companies. We described the four basic modes of lateral organization in Chapter One (see Figure 3.9).

Lateral connections are used both to link units together and shift power among the dimensions as strategy changes, as illustrated in Figure 3.10. When one dimension is dominant, then informal networks, teams, or integrative roles can be used to coordinate along the other dimension. For example, in a primarily geographic structure, product teams can be used to give some power to the business unit dimension. When a balance between two dimensions is required, a matrix is an option.

The use of lateral organizing mechanisms is a cumulative process. As more complicated forms are added, simpler forms are not abandoned; for

FIGURE 3.9 **Continuum of Lateral Connections.**

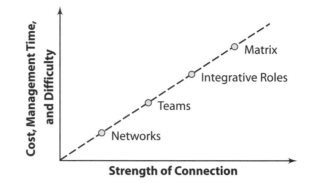

instance, strong informal interpersonal networks are essential in a company that is also using formal teams to coordinate work. One adds more complex forms until the desired level of coordination is reached. The caution is not to push coordination attempts ahead of the organization's capacity; internal conflicts will consume an organization when it tries to execute a coordination approach that exceeds its current capability. We can revisit the use of each of these in the context of creating a multidimensional network.

Interpersonal Networks

Work-based relationships and networks are the basis of all coordinating mechanisms. When the company is small and people work in the same location, these can develop naturally. For the global company, management must take more deliberate action to create communication networks among

FIGURE 3.10 **Shifting Power Between Dimensions.**

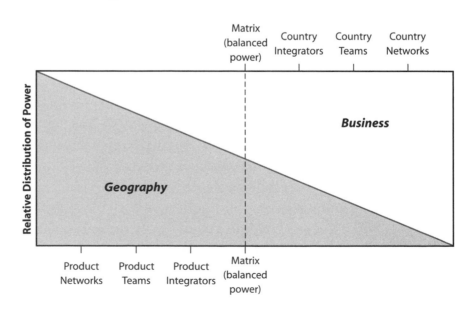

people who share a common interest but do not have contact as part of a reporting structure. For instance, we used the example of the Coca-Cola bottling company in Europe as a predominantly geographically based business. With the addition of juice, tea, and water product lines, the leaders may decide that it will be enough to bring together the commercial managers from the countries selling these products to discuss the unique issues facing them in sales and distribution. Typically such a group would meet face-to-face once a year to cover a common agenda, reinforce the network, and improve communication processes. Throughout the year, communication would be maintained through newsletters, e-mail, telephone and video conferences, intranets, and other avenues.

In such communities of interest, coordination is informal, and participants choose whether to act on the information they receive through these networks. If such networks are adequate, then nothing more complex is needed. If a more structured form of coordination is required, however, there are steps that a company can take to more closely connect geographically dispersed staff.

Formal Teams

In order to guarantee coordination and increase accountability, management may create a formal group, such as a cross-border product team, and give it power and legitimacy within the organization. In order to function effectively, such a team requires more effort and resources than an informal network does. In addition to the design and management work required to create a successful domestic team, building a global team introduces the need for cross-cultural training and remote communication support.

The defining difference between a formal team and an informal community of interest is that a team has a charter and is accountable for defined results. These results may be to coordinate services for a cross-border customer, coordinate the launch of a product simultaneously in multiple locations, or negotiate a cross-border contract with a supplier. Teams can be used to bring together and coordinate any dimension of the organization. If the predominant structure is geographic, then teams can be used to coordinate the work of staff dispersed across the geographic units that are focused on common functional activities, product development, supplier management, or customer needs.

Integrators

When an even higher level of cross-border integration is needed, management may choose to create a role whose specific task is coordinating activities across geographic units. These integrators (also called coordinators, project managers, global account managers, process owners, or brand managers) are responsible for driving decisions for products or customers on a regional or global basis. In contrast to the team, whose members carry out their team tasks in addition to other responsibilities, now there is someone in the company who is thinking full time about business or customer issues on a cross-border basis. To extend the Coca-Cola example further, a community of interest or team may be adequate to coordinate the new juice, tea, and water business because these products are similar to the carbonated soft drink business. However, if Coca-Cola bottling should decide that it can leverage its extensive distribution system and launch or acquire a food business, it would need a stronger level of coordination to identify priority conflicts, create standards, and ensure that the new business line gets the right level of attention at the country level. The same would be true if it wanted to negotiate with large retail chain stores on a regional basis, removing pricing decisions from the local level. A senior-level role would be needed to manage these dimensions of the business.

Since integrators do not run businesses but instead coordinate business activities across geographies, the people chosen for these roles must have strong influence skills, credibility, and networks. They also need their own budgets and resources, as well as clarity around the scope of their decision responsibility. Information systems that aggregate information can provide the data for decision making and influence. For example, a business unit coordinator's position is strengthened when business revenues and profits can be measured across countries. Without this information, if countries are the profit centers, a struggling business within the country may be ignored by a country manager if the overall profit picture is positive. The view into the product line across geographies can empower the integrator, who can use these statistics to initiate action within the countries.

Matrix

The most complex level of lateral organization is the matrix, in which a power balance is created between two or more dimensions. For example, if there is a need for strong cross-border coordination, as well as coordination within borders, the business manager and geographic manager need to be equals.

In a successful matrix, many decisions are made by one manager or another, but a few decisions are made jointly. These joint decisions focus on hiring, setting goals, and evaluating the performance of the people who report to both managers. Matrixed reporting is frequently used for select positions to ensure that decisions are made with a dual focus. For example, country-level human resource directors may be matrixed to the country manager as well as to a regional head of HR to ensure that talent decisions are made with both a local and global perspective.

A true matrix is difficult to manage. Most companies now avoid it for organizing at the global level, finding that having one dimension dominant reduces the conflicts caused by the organization's inability to make joint decisions, resolve conflicts, and communicate that often emerge in a matrix. However, as illustrated in Figure 3.10, the matrix can be an effective transitional form to shift power between dimensions.

Using Lateral Connections for Flexibility

The skillful design and use of these lateral forms are essential to a firm's ability to manage the complexity of a multidimensional global business. The deliberate development of a lateral capability can also build experience toward the ultimate in organizational advantage: reconfigurability. When a company has become reconfigurable, it can maintain a relatively stable underlying structure based on geographic units or business units and then extensively use networks, teams, integrators, and matrixed reporting relationships to bring together the right staff around opportunities and problems as they arise.

For example, we have discussed different ways in which to group countries into clusters. A company can choose one characteristic—perhaps proximity—as the primary basis for grouping. But if it would also be useful to bring together all the country managers in emerging markets at a certain stage of development, this can be achieved through an informal network or team. If there is strategic benefit, why not have multiple simultaneous groupings? Figure 3.11 illustrates a four-dimensional network of this kind. The profit centers are configured by geography into a region, but the company can deploy lateral connections with varying levels of power, such as networks, teams, integrators, and matrix, to address a range of other business concerns. These might include:

- Using networks to link business units that purchase a particular commodity
- Assigning teams to combine products from different businesses into solutions for a particular customer segment
- Hiring integrators to link research and development units that are working on a common technology

FIGURE 3.11 **A Four-Dimensional Network.**

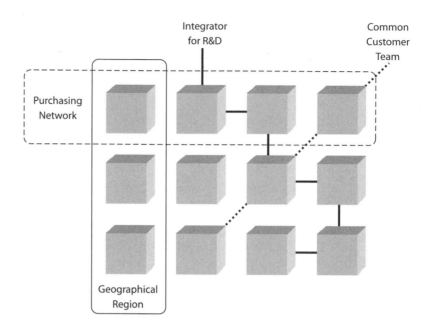

The advantage of a reconfigurable mind-set and a leadership team that thinks in terms of using lateral forms as strategic tools is that opportunities can be tested and pursued without the disruption brought by the major reorganizations that usually accompany a change in direction. Building the capability to reconfigure using lateral forms needs to be a deliberate act by a leadership team that believes the investment in time will address otherwise overlooked opportunities or problems. It also requires a leadership team that is not afraid to make clear which dimension of the business takes priority at any given time and to articulate when that needs to change.

Rewards

In a multidimensional network, the number of interfaces increases geometrically from the geographic division form. At each interface—such as customer team with country team or research and development with business teams—the interests of each party have to be clarified and aligned.

The Spreadsheet Planning tool, shown in Figure 3.12 and included in the Appendix, is a simple yet powerful way to achieve goal alignment wherever two dimensions interface.

In a multidimensional network, the assessment of staff at the key points of interface also becomes more subjective, since a wide variety of metrics can be used. Managers need to be comfortable with the relative power of

FIGURE 3.12 **Spreadsheet Planning Tool for a Multidimensional Organization.**

	North America	Europe	Asia
Product 1			
Product 2			
Product 3			

the dimension they represent and should strive to demonstrate values and behaviors that are aligned to the overall goals of the business. One model of evaluation that can be used is that of the professional service firm or investment bank. These organizations are typically multidimensional, with partners specializing in subject areas, industry sectors, and geographies but working in teams that span these boundaries. Because individual contributions are not easy to quantify, these organizations invest a lot of time in rigorous (yet admittedly subjective) evaluations of managers. These assessments focus on elements such as contribution to relationships and knowledge networks, effectiveness in leading and participating on teams, internal and external influence, and contributions to talent development. Reviews are done by managers and peers and frequently include feedback from subordinate staff as well.

In a multidimensional network organization, these types of reviews are conducted for the highly visible roles that must work across organizational boundaries. For example, they may be used to assess product managers working across geographies or customer account managers working across product lines. In this way, a fuller picture of success is measured. An additional benefit is that the values and behaviors necessary to make such a complex organization work are communicated and reinforced through the process.

People

The primary consideration for talent in the multidimensional network is to develop a cadre of managers who have the competencies to work cross-organizationally and cross-culturally. The best situation is to hire people who have these qualities, but they can also be developed through assignments, feedback, training, and mentoring.

General Competencies

The increase in global business in the past decade has spurred research into the competencies required by the managers working outside their home country (see Thorne, 2002; Rifkin, 2006; and Kanter, 1995)—for example:

- An understanding of and sensitivity to cultural differences and the ability to build relationships with people from other cultures
- A cosmopolitan view that can see similarities across environments and bridge differences among local nationals in order to promote the acceptance of standardization where it makes sense
- The ability to let go of the headquarters mind-set and be able to assess where situations are truly the same and established techniques will work, and where situations vary, calling for different approaches
- An openness to new ideas and a willingness to incorporate local innovations into corporate practice
- Drive, energy, and stamina to manage the added complexity and stress of operating in an unfamiliar culture and with the additional burden, in some circumstances, of communicating in a second language

Role-Specific Competencies

In addition to these general competencies, different profiles are needed for people working along the various dimensions of the multidimensional network—the global business manager, the country manager, and the corporate functional manager—whether as members of teams or as integrators (Bartlett and Ghoshal, 2003).

Global Business Manager   The manager who has responsibility for a product line or business unit at a regional or global level focuses on developing brand strategies, configuring assets and resources against a business plan, recognizing new opportunities, and coordinating transactions across national boundaries. This manager seeks out similarities in product characteristics and customer needs but must be able to recognize when local brands and features truly make a difference and to decide if how a product is sold (channel, packaging, branding) or the underlying product features need to be localized. This type of coordination takes up a lot of time and requires a person with robust technical, administrative, and interpersonal skills, as well as a personality that values coordination and integration rather than depending on control. When staffing business unit teams or integrator roles, it may be worthwhile to select people from outside the home country product division. If these roles are staffed by product managers from headquarters, there can be an assumption that the roles serve more of an enforcement function, attempting to impose dictates from headquarters, rather than the function they should be serving: to coordinate units across borders.

Country Manager The country manager is counted on to be sensitive and responsive to the local market and defend the company's market position against local and other competitors. At the same time, she has to be innovative, entrepreneurial, and good at gathering information, predicting its importance, and then translating local knowledge, trends, and responses in a way that regional and corporate managers can apply elsewhere.

Functional Manager Functional managers at a regional or corporate level who participate on cross-border teams and councils have a unique view into the organization, whether they are in marketing, finance, legal, human resources, IT, or research and development. The nature of their work is to look across business and geographic lines and spot opportunities and trends, connect people to build networks, and identify potential innovations or problems as they emerge. The best-run organizations are using the people in these roles not just for their deep, specialized technical knowledge but also as facilitators of worldwide learning.

Design Considerations: Transnational

The transnational form is a variation on the multidimensional network. The major difference between the transnational form and the two forms that we have just discussed—the geographic and the multidimensional network—is the role of the non-home-country components. In the transnational model, there is truly equal power given to locations where the competency is located, not where history dictates that power should reside; in some cases, the geographic units are given even more power than the home country. For example, Citigroup has its foreign exchange operations headquartered in London, private banking in Switzerland, and derivatives in New York, as those locations are where the talent, markets, and the most hospitable venues for those activities can be found. So although Citigroup is headquartered in New York, a private banker in New York would see Switzerland as the power center for his particular business.

Strategy

In the transnational model, the original home country organization may contribute a small portion of total company revenue. Innovation, centers of expertise, and traditional headquarters functions are placed in locations that can best do the work. The home country functions more as a relic of history, albeit often with continuing significance to the organization's identity, than a traditional center or headquarters, although it may continue to manage regulatory affairs.

While location-specific advantages have been used for centuries, the focus on lead markets is newer. The trend is for many companies to place the leadership for a business where that unit's most advanced customers are located. For example, many of Procter & Gamble's beauty product innovations come out of Japan. Japanese women spend more time and money proportionately on hair and skin care than women in other parts of the world, so it makes sense for Japan to be a skin and hair care product development center for P&G.

Transitioning to the transnational form requires a true belief among home country managers, even if they were instrumental in building the original firm, that they can now learn from others. The model also requires that units around the world take both leading and contributing roles in generating capabilities and that there are mechanisms to recognize and transfer these capabilities to other units. The transnational model rests on a distributed power structure that shifts power to the units that exercise a leadership role.

The transnational approach is an appealing form, with its flattened, less hierarchical, networked quality. But it is still an emerging model and is more easily embraced by new companies that do not have to overcome the strong, historical pull of the home country. Although many of the organizational considerations for the transnational model will be the same as for the multidimensional model, we will highlight some of the design considerations that are unique to the transnational form.

Structure

The transnational strategy can be achieved through a variety of underlying structures. The defining difference between this approach and the models we have already discussed in this chapter is that the various geographic units also take on a role of developing capabilities on behalf of the rest of the organization. This development aspect is crucial. Companies have long housed low-value support activities in one region or another for cost purposes. A firm may decide to locate all accounts payable processing in Costa Rica because there is an educated population that speaks English well and is available at a low cost. The management, policy, and technology still come from the home country. The firm has not selected Costa Rica because

FIGURE 3.13 **A Transnational Organization (Medical Device Company).**

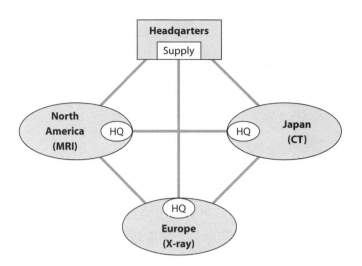

it is a hotbed of innovation and expertise in accounts payable, and it is not looking to local talent to move the field forward.

The transnational model is different from the previous examples because core capabilities are now distributed. New products, processes, and ideas are expected to come out of the distributed centers. Figure 3.13 shows a medical supply company operating in three regions. Rather than produce its three major products—MRI, CT, and X-ray machines—in all three locations, each region takes the lead in development and manufacturing for one product on behalf of the others. Assembly, sales, and service still take place in each region for all the different products in order to meet local customer and government requirements. What had been an American-led company, with subsidiaries in Japan and Europe, has become a company of peers, with each region equally dependent on each other for success.

Processes

Although seemingly simpler than some other forms in that it reduces the tension between headquarters and the operating units that is inherent in so many companies, the transnational form increases the number of interfaces that need to be managed, requiring capabilities in addition to all those needed in managing a geographic division and a multidimensional network: norms and values of reciprocity and redesigned business processes.

Reciprocity

The multidimensional network organization facilitates coordination across regions through the use of processes that may be weak (interpersonal networks) or quite strong (matrixed reporting relationships). The transnational model requires strong cooperation among regions. If the lead responsibility for customer management is delegated to one region, then there need to be explicit norms of reciprocity: "I will take care of your customers; I trust that you will take care of my customers." In this organizational form, everyone's goals and success are closely linked because achievements are so interdependent.

Redesigned Business Processes

Setting up mutually interdependent centers requires the redesign of underlying work processes, such as new product development or global order fulfillment. Often when such projects are undertaken in traditional organizations, there is strong representation from the relevant functional groups in the headquarters but just token outreach to the regions. The effort to redesign these processes creates an opportunity to build transnational capability. The design teams should be cross-functional and cross-regional, and their own process for making decisions should begin to model how the parts of the organization will work together.

The design of the centers as well as the governance bodies also presents potential for building the relationships, trust, and mutual understanding that have to underlie a model where power is so dispersed. Companies experimenting with the transnational form have found that rotational job assignments (where people move physically) as well as rotational team and leadership assignments not only build international experience for individuals, but also help to create the informal networks that reduce conflict and speed decision making.

Rewards

The transnational model requires a different set of measures from the geographic and multidimensional forms. In this model, regional leaders wear two hats: managing sales, profits, and market share for their region as well as the product line for which they are responsible. In addition, if functional centers are also headquartered in the region, the regional manager is responsible for their success as well.

The high level of interdependence among units reduces the ability to create simple bottom-line measures for a self-contained unit, such as a region or product line. Rewards for leaders in the transnational organization tend to be based on global measures. Many managers are uncomfortable being rewarded for results over which they have no significant control. They are more motivated by clear line-of-sight accountability. Therefore, the leaders in a transnational organization have to be experienced and comfortable working in such a team-based environment.

People

A major design differentiator between the multidimensional network and the transnational form is the role of the management team. The regional leaders must now truly make decisions collectively rather than interacting with executives in the home country on an individual basis, as is the norm in a traditional headquarters model. The profile for success includes the requisite levels of technical experience and credibility, cross-regional knowledge, and cross-cultural teamwork skills, as well as a global mind-set, excellent relationship and interface management capabilities, and comfort with dependence on peers for success. The transnational model is dependent on the success of the top management team working together, often virtually. It is likely to take several years of deliberate internal development to build such a team.

The transnational form also highlights the need for a global leadership team. In older companies, the executive suite tends to reflect the company's recruiting strategy of thirty years ago rather than the profile of the company in its current state. Some companies are deliberately changing their leadership profile as their global business becomes more dominant. For example, General Electric, while increasing revenue from global sources from 40 to 50 percent during the period from 2001 to 2006, tripled the number of non-U.S. citizens among the company's top five hundred managers in same time period (Kranhold, 2006). Procter & Gamble has also increased the number of foreign-born executives on its leadership team to 50 percent to match the fact that over half of the firm's revenues come from outside the United States (Colvin, 2006).

• • •

This chapter has presented a review of the basic strategies for international expansion and the organizational forms that support them, with particular attention to the geographic and multidimensional models, which remain the most common forms. The transnational model, an appealing but challenging ideal, is presented as a model that many organizations are trying to move toward in the new climate of globalization. We have focused mainly on the coordination of geographies with business and product units. However, the increasing need to coordinate not just around countries, product lines, and functions but also around global customers adds another significant dimension to the multidimensional, multinational organization, and it creates additional complexity for the global manager.

An important task for global managers is choosing the right form for different regions, to reflect the reality that most companies operating internationally are not at the same level of development in all parts of the world. For example, a European business may employ a multidimensional network in North America, exporting and partnering in Asia, and establishing a few geographic units in South America. Matching organization to strategy and then managing the heterogeneity that results is the true challenge of the global organization.

Chapter 4

Making a Matrix Work

IN AN EFFORT TO ACHIEVE MULTIPLE strategic objectives with the smallest number of resources, many organizations are using matrix reporting relationships as a way to link disparate parts of the organization and encourage collaboration. Using a matrix presents a dilemma, however. Three decades of study of the matrix have shown that it is one of the most powerful ways to force interaction among business units and integrate the diverse parts of an organization. At the same time, experience has demonstrated that it is most successful in organizations that already have a strong foundation of teamwork, joint accountability, and the management processes that support collaboration. Therefore, leaders who jump to a matrix structure in order to get the promised benefits without first putting in place the required enabling support mechanism quickly find that they have introduced complexity, confusion, and frustration without achieving the expected gains. Predictably, they soon revert back to a simpler configuration, feeling wiser for the experience and not inclined to attempt the matrix again soon. They join the many others who have abandoned matrix structures as too hard to do.

The reality, however, is that most businesses today are complex. They need to serve multiple products, markets, and geographies, and if they are to reap the rewards of growth and scale, they need to integrate laterally and find synergies among all the dimensions of the business. Complex business models result in complex organizations, including matrix relationships. And the organizations that can best manage this complexity without making it burdensome to either customers or frontline employees gain competitive advantage.

The complexity created by the matrix is usually borne by the mid- to senior-level manager who provides the connections among all of the elements of the business involved in pursuing multiple strategic dimensions. Attention to organization design does not remove complexity for these managers; rather, it ensures that the organization is an enabler, not a barrier, to these managers as they try to achieve the required business results.

Implementing a matrix is a significant leadership decision and not one to be made lightly. This chapter summarizes what we have learned about designing and implementing a matrix so that it promotes efficiency as well as intraorganizational linkages. We begin by defining the matrix and summarizing the strategic benefits it can provide and the common pitfalls. We then use the Star Model™ as a guide to designing a successful matrix. We hope to demystify this much-maligned and underappreciated organizational form and offer tools to maximize the chance of success.

What Is a Matrix?

Strictly speaking, a matrix is an organization in which some employees have two or more bosses, representing different organizational objectives. It was pioneered in the aerospace and defense sectors in the 1960s and 1970s in response to expansions of scope and complexity represented by initiatives such as the development of large airliners and the space program. For example, an engineer at Boeing working on the development of the 747 airliner might have reported to manufacturing and also to a manager in the commercial aviation products division. In making the engineer fully accountable to both supervisors, the goal was to maintain robust functional expertise while creating a project team with enough dedicated resources and leadership to get a complicated, multifunctional job done.

Soon firms in other sectors experimented with using the matrix. Many of these businesses did not have the robust underlying processes and discipline that were present throughout much of the aerospace industry. Rather, they introduced a complicated organizational form into companies that lacked the mature management structures or rigorous processes that the matrix requires. The results were mixed at best. In the early 1980s, Tom Peters and Robert Waterman claimed in their best-selling book, *In Search of Excellence*, that no companies they identified as excellent used a matrix design (Peters and Waterman, 1982). Companies that have failed while using a matrix have tended to blame it for all manner of ills. For example, in 1994, as Digital Equipment was in the process of cutting twenty thousand jobs and taking a $1.2 billion charge, its chairman was quoted in the *Wall*

Street Journal as saying that Digital would eliminate its "matrix management" structure, as it represented a cost that the company could no longer afford (Wilke, 1994). Many other firms have abandoned their own attempts at shifting to a matrix, citing it as overly complex, rigid, and cumbersome.

The mid-1990s saw the matrix return to some level of favor. One driver was the need to hold down costs. For example, having a systems analyst located in New York report to a local functional manager as well as a product manager in Chicago meant that the Chicago office did not have to hire a systems analyst of its own. Having the same person simultaneously working on projects for the New York and Chicago offices also meant a greater degree of standardization, which might also provide additional cost savings.

A second main driver has been globalization. Outsourcing and offshoring to low-cost manufacturing and processing centers have left North America and Europe with companies that do mostly knowledge-based, project-centered work—precisely the conditions that rely on high levels of collaboration and lateral integration, and the kinds of work that the matrix promises to facilitate.

Today a matrix in some form can be found in most large companies. Sometimes it is used extensively. For example, Nike is organized along product lines (footwear, clothing, equipment), by sport (golf, soccer, basketball), by brand (ACG, Jordan, Presto), and by regions to account for all the dimensions of its business. But rarely is a matrix used as the overall framework of a company. More often, it is used to tie together key roles and ensure that decision makers take multiple business perspectives into consideration. For example, the research and development function is often configured as a matrix. Researchers have a home in their specialized groups but take part in projects that bring them together in cross-functional teams. Another example can be found in the sales function. Sales departments are usually structured on a regional basis in order to minimize travel time and exploit local knowledge. However, national accounts, global product lines, and different distribution channels (for example, resellers and retailers) frequently cut across these regions. In order to coordinate along customer, product, and channel dimensions, as well as along geographic lines, sales managers may be matrixed, reporting to both head of sales for a region and head of sales for a product line.

The matrix is also commonly and successfully used to organize professional service firms. For example, a global accounting firm might have a managing director focused on the financial services industry who will oversee the work of consultants working with financial services clients around the world. However, the dozens of partners and hundreds of consultants who report to her from twenty or more countries will also report to regional directors who help to manage their assignments and career paths. Some of those consultants may also report to a managing director for audit or tax who is charged with building the firm's functional expertise in those areas.

Strategic Reasons to Use a Matrix

There are a number of strategic reasons why a leader may turn to a matrix.

Balanced Perspective

Whenever a choice is made about primary organizational structure—whether by function, product, geography, or customer—a decision has been made about power. The way the organization is structured at the top exerts a strong influence on the agenda of the leadership team and the decisions that they make. No matter how broad an enterprise view the team tries to have, a team of functional managers will have a very different discussion on a given topic than would a group of product division managers. In many organizations, there are two or more dimensions that need to be given equal representation at the table and equal power in making decisions. The matrix formalizes this strategic need.

Flexibility

A matrix is also used to better allocate scarce or expensive talent and flexibly configure and deploy teams around projects, opportunities, customers, problems, and products. It allows the organization to shift resources in response to changing business needs or conditions while preserving a stable framework underneath.

When employees are "locked up" in a unit—whether a product team or a functional group—they often become invisible and inaccessible to the broader organization. The unit is always able to generate enough work to keep them busy, but it is hard to determine if they are working on the tasks that will have the greatest impact for the overall business. The matrix creates a mechanism to share these resources and assign them where their talents and skills can be best used.

Integration

The matrix builds linkages across organizational boundaries and can help promote integrated solutions and consistent service delivery. For example, a marketing team that is matrixed by function and line of business will consider the need for a new campaign from two perspectives: what the state-of-the-art solution for the business is *and* how it can build or buy a program that fits with existing systems (or can potentially be leveraged by another business line). The resulting campaign should be one that meets the needs of the individual line of business and serves the broader needs of the enterprise.

Learning

Another benefit of the matrix is the potential for learning and sharing best practices across groups and locations. In a matrix, there is opportunity for the transfer of knowledge across lines of business as employees participate in multiple teams and projects that cut across the structure horizontally and diagonally. Variations on the matrix are often found in staff functions (for instance, IT, legal, human resources, or finance), since it provides these groups with a unique window onto the enterprise. These staff functions can serve as a vehicle for sharing not only functional information but also business information across the units. This potential is beginning to be leveraged in companies that have routinized low-level transactional work and are starting to use their staff groups more strategically. For example, a human resource group that has matrixed its staff by business and function can use occasions when the group comes together as a function as an opportunity to identify issues occurring in several businesses and address them systematically.

Employees may also have increased learning opportunities as individuals. Working in a matrix is hard, but it does often result in employees' having the chance to do a greater variety of work, build a broader range of contacts within the firm, and develop valuable management skills. In addition, the matrix avoids the need to completely remove employees from their functional home base in order to work on customer or project concerns. One of the benefits of a functional structure is the deep technical learning and sharing that occur when, for example, engineers work closely together. The matrix provides the possibility of continuing those engineers' functional development while deploying them to business-focused teams.

Challenges of a Matrix

The potential benefits of a successful matrix are numerous. An effectively deployed matrix should result in cost savings. Units do not need to duplicate expensive resources, scarce talent can be shared and deployed where they are most needed, and solutions are developed that are both effective and efficient.

But when it is not effectively deployed, the matrix introduces a significant cost: the diversion of management time from products and customers to internal negotiations. Rather than strengthen collaboration, it consumes valuable management attention that must be spent sorting out disagreements. Matrix is still a code word among many observers of organizational life for "cumbersome" and "overengineered." *The Economist*, in a major feature, "The New Organisation," in 2006, derided it as "the corset from which many companies are still trying to struggle free" ("The New Organisation," 2006).

The pitfalls of the matrix are well documented. In their 1978 *Harvard Business Review* article, "Problems of Matrix Organizations," Davis and Lawrence clearly laid out many predictable challenges of a matrix. Nearly thirty years later, we see organizations making exactly the same mistakes they cautioned against. That these pitfalls have persisted does not make the case that the fundamental idea of the matrix is flawed. Rather, it speaks to the need for each new generation of management to study and learn from the lessons of the past. The majority of these risks and costs of a matrix result from confusion and friction about priorities and accountability. We review some of the most common pitfalls.

Power Struggles

Most managers dislike sharing resources or being told that the results they are accountable for are less important than someone else's. All the power struggles that are inherent in any organization are magnified in a matrix. In every organization, there is a tension between the leader—who needs all the pieces of his organization to collaborate—and the managers at the next level—who, despite politically correct talk about teamwork, would prefer to have full control over the resources required to deliver the results for which they are held accountable.

The matrix increases the number of interdependencies and the level of reciprocal need among these managers. If managers perceive themselves to be in competition or involved in a zero-sum game with colleagues and allow negotiations over priorities or resources to become personal, the close interactions the matrix forces can become destructive.

Determining "Best Practices"

If the matrix is being used to drive integration and the sale of core products and services across regions or lines of business, then someone needs to determine what will be standardized and under what circumstances differences are legitimate and allowable. This is not easily done and can be a significant source of conflict.

Many global companies struggle to come up with a truly global product. For example, in the early 1990s, Ford set the goal of producing a "world car"—a single car that is sold in essentially the same form in all markets—which would benefit the company by standardizing parts, engineering, and production and by capitalizing on Ford's international production and R&D expertise. The design team for the car was divided between Ford's North American and European operations. After a development effort that cost over $6 billion, the car was introduced in Europe as the Mondeo, but by the time regional differences were negotiated, the U.S. version was barely recognizable as the same car. Although the cars shared features under the skin, the only external items the Mondeo had in common with the Contour, as it was called in the United States, were the windshield, front windows, front mirrors, and door handles.

On even mundane levels, the conflict over whose process is best can consume valuable management time. Whether at the level of product design or setting the performance management calendar, wrangling over regional and line-of-business variations can quickly exhaust management patience. Strong leadership is needed to set clear criteria for decisions at lower levels and quickly arbitrate disputes when they are escalated.

Decision Strangulation

The matrix gives equal weight to two or more business dimensions. Ideally, as portrayed in the discussion of benefits above, this tension results in better and more creative solutions to problems and opportunities. It certainly means that more people will be involved in making decisions and that they will have to go to more meetings. If the organization does not have good meeting practices, clear decision rights, and strong conflict resolution processes, the result can be slow decision making or no decisions at all. Managers will put off issues that are too hard to deal with, make compromises that benefit no one, or continually elevate disputes up the chain to senior management that should rightfully be settled at their own level.

Personal Stress

Most people prefer a work environment in which they can clearly state what their objectives are, what they are responsible for, and, most important, whom they are accountable to. A matrix requires a certain amount of personal flexibility and a level of comfort with ambiguity and change. It also requires an ability to understand and adapt to the styles and expectations of two or more supervisors and the fortitude to confront and sort out conflicting directives that may come from above.

The organizational flexibility that the matrix promotes also weakens the sense of team identity that is important for many employees. Staff may find themselves sitting on a number of teams, each with differing subcultures and operating procedures. This is the nature of a project-based environment, but for employees used to a more traditional hierarchy, it can be a major change. The greater dependence on influence and negotiation rather than on clear-cut rules and procedures can create stress and job dissatisfaction.

Matrix Design

The Star Model shown in Figure 4.1 summarizes the design considerations for creating and implementing a successful matrix.

Structure

To illustrate how a matrix is typically structured, Figure 4.2 shows an example based on a large U.S. bank's information technology (IT) group. Many companies organize their IT groups and other staff functions by both line of business and function, with the goal of gaining scale and consistency while remaining responsive to specific business needs.

This bank has five lines of business, all with very different information processing needs. Three are outward facing: Wholesale, Lending, and Retail. Corporate refers to centralized and other staff functions, and Operations refers to all the processing units of the bank. Although these two are

FIGURE 4.1 **The Star Model for a Matrix.**

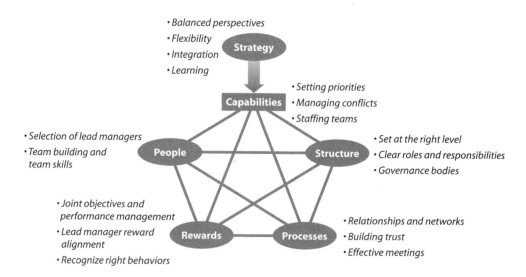

FIGURE 4.2 **A Typical Matrix Structure: IT Group Example.**

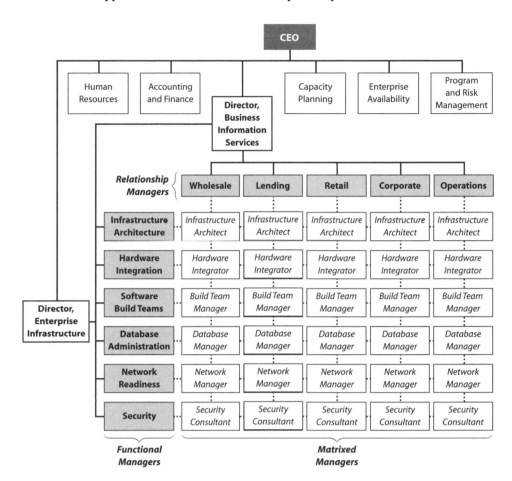

internal functions, they are considered lines of business, or clients, by the IT department because of their size.

The business managers want dedicated points of contact who know the business and can lead teams to develop and implement IT solutions that will drive customer service and revenue growth. The IT relationship managers across the top of the diagram fill this role and provide the link between the lines of business and the IT function. Each has a dedicated team for a given business unit. These relationship managers are measured and rewarded for how well they meet the needs of the line of business that they support.

The bank as an enterprise, however, has objectives that are different from those of its individual lines of business. The bank wants to hold down IT costs by using common platforms, systems, and applications wherever possible. Commonality and standardization mean easier transfer of customer and product data across business lines, allowing customers, the sales force, and service center staff to access information centrally. Commonality also means economies of scale in purchasing from vendors and servicing and securing the IT systems themselves. The six functional managers along the side of the diagram lead dedicated groups focused on building the long-term, efficient infrastructure for the bank in terms of core applications, hardware, data centers, networks, and security. The functional managers are measured and rewarded for meeting these goals.

In the illustration, there are thirty "matrixed" managers (we call them managers, because they typically manage projects or processes, even if all do not directly manage teams of people). Each of these managers has a relationship manager and a functional manager as supervisors. The matrixed manager is measured and rewarded against both dimensions. At any time, he may be working on business-specific projects and infrastructure projects. As in almost all other organizations, there are never enough resources to meet everyone's needs. Every day trade-offs are made and priorities are reset. By setting up a matrix, the organization's leader ensures that these thirty managers make decisions about how they and their teams spend their time based on a balanced calculation of the priorities of the lines of business and the functions. The matrix forces to the surface the underlying tensions in the organization about how to allocate scarce resources. It is intended to compel the relationship and functional managers—whom we will call the lead managers—to discuss trade-offs openly.

Although the thirty matrixed managers in Figure 4.2 are dedicated to both lines of business and functional areas, they are visible to and "owned" by the entire IT function. If a major project arises—such as an acquisition in the retail sector—the IT leadership can reallocate managers and their teams to retail business projects. The intention is for the senior managers to discuss as a team how to get the portfolio of work accomplished (and what work to delay or drop) rather than to force a negotiation for resources among individual managers.

From this very typical example, it is clear that introducing the matrix changes the fundamental dynamics of an organization. The centers of power are purposefully aligned against one another. Before using a matrix, this IT group had been organized completely functionally. The businesses had to put their requests into a long queue and hope for the best. The line-of-business dimension was added to bring more attention to the needs of different customers. Adding this dimension was so dramatic that, six months into the transition to the matrix, one functional manager described the change this way: "I feel like we've been acquired." The impact of introducing a matrix on the status quo of an organization should not be underestimated, and the change management aspects of the implementation should never be given short shrift.

It is important to note that a matrix itself is not an organizational structure but, rather, a set of reporting relationships that tie the organization together laterally. Organizational structures define the hierarchical alignment of people. In the example, the underlying structural framework is *customer* and *function*. It could as easily be along the dimensions of *geography* and *product*, such as in the example of the sales force referred to above. Technically we consider a matrix a form of lateral connection. However, it still needs to be consciously structured in the common sense of the word.

The matrix sits atop the structure as a way to formally link each business dimension together so that the underlying structure remains stable. In a matrix configuration, not everyone is in a formally matrixed position, but the goal is to instill in all employees a simultaneous focus on multiple organizational priorities—what we call a matrix mind-set. The IT function in the example has over two thousand employees. The vast majority formally report to just one manager. However, many of these employees also work on cross-functional project teams and have accountability to other managers. The formalized matrixed reporting relationships help to force the desired mind-set and behaviors.

We have found a number of structural elements that are important to consider when designing a matrix. All address the need to develop efficient ways to resolve the disputes that inevitably arise. Each element is discussed below.

Set the Matrix at the Right Level

A matrix works best when the matrixed positions are placed at a fairly high level in the organization. This means that when the matrixed manager has to raise an issue with her two managers, they are in a sufficiently high position of authority and knowledge to resolve the issue. If the matrixed manager is placed so low in the organization that her managers do not have a broad enough view to make decisions and are forced to raise them up another level or two, then the matrix will become a barrier rather than an enabler of decision making. Figures 4.3 and 4.4 illustrate the same organization. In Figure 4.3, the matrixed position is so low in the hierarchy that almost all conflicts will have to be escalated up two or more levels. There are four levels between the matrixed manager and the top executive on the functional side and three levels on the business relationship side. In this case, the matrixed manager is too low in the organization to have a broad enough view to resolve complex issues. Issues must rise two or three levels before they can be addressed by sufficiently senior management. In Figure 4.4, the matrixed

FIGURE 4.3 **Matrixed Position Too Low in the Hierarchy.**

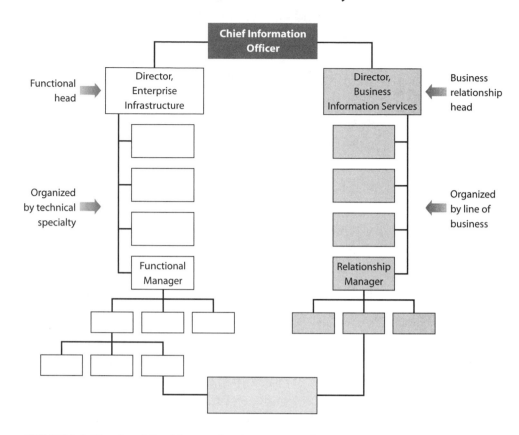

FIGURE 4.4 **Matrixed Position at the Correct Level.**

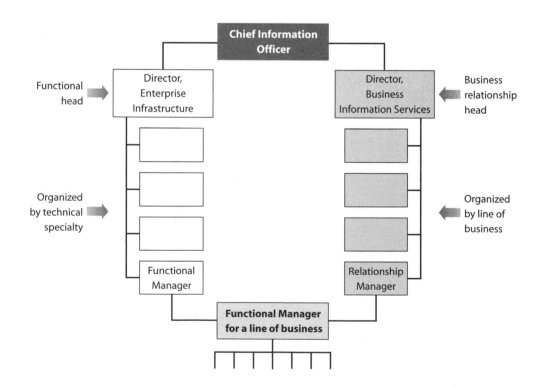

position is placed right below two senior managers with the authority to resolve issues. There are only two reporting levels from the most matrixed manager to the executive that has jurisdiction over both dimensions of the matrix. This puts the matrixed manager in a senior enough position to either resolve issues or to escalate to a level that can resolve them.

Those who are designing a matrix should try to minimize the number of management levels between the matrixed manager and the leader who ultimately has control over both dimensions of the matrix. We recommend no more than two reporting levels between the head of the unit and the matrixed managers.

Avoid Dotted- and Solid-Line Discussions

In a matrix, the issue of who has a dotted-line relationship and who has a solid-line relationship frequently arises. A solid line is a direct reporting relationship implying the usual objective setting, supervisory, and performance management relationship that a manager has with a direct report. A dotted line is taken to mean something weaker. The manager has input in such activities and influence over consequences but not in the same way as a traditional supervisor. The practical implication is that if requests come from both managers, the person reporting to them both will respond to the solid-line manager first.

In order to avoid such situations and game playing, it is best if all managers sharing resources act as if they have dotted lines downward. In other words, they should assume that the staff member in the matrixed position has been given other priorities from other managers that need to be identified and perhaps reset before more work is given out. All matrixed managers, however, should assume that all their reporting lines upward are solid. All managers' requests should be given equal importance, and when they are at odds or time is limited, the matrixed manager needs to highlight the conflict and be sure that priorities are reset in the interests of the organization rather than based on assumed relative importance of the managers.

Clarify Roles and Responsibilities

In a matrix, many interactions are structured around a series of requests and promises rather than by a set of sharply defined tasks and responsibilities. Whereas job descriptions are important in many companies for setting compensation, they are less useful as a way to describe where one role ends and another begins. They may speak to the activities or outcomes that are expected, but they are a poor tool for communicating how

FIGURE 4.5 **Process Map.**

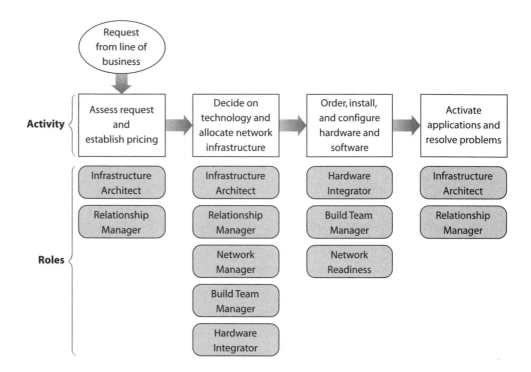

people are expected to interact with one another (Lawler and Worley, 2006). In addition, the effort to keep them up-to-date is Herculean and rarely achieved.

For job design, it is important to focus on the activities within a role. For organization design, we find it more useful to focus on the boundaries and interfaces between roles. The matrix will change the way work moves through the organization. The goal is to anticipate gray areas of understanding and preemptively address situations where clashes may occur. Simple process mapping will help test assumptions about who touches the work and what roles are involved at each step. It is not necessary to map every process, just the key ones that cut across the organization and are likely to cause the most confusion. An example is shown in Figure 4.5 for the process of building a new server for an internal line of business client.

Once the simplified process map is complete and agreed on, a responsibility chart can be used to clarify who makes decisions. This is a simple yet powerful tool that has been in use across a broad range of organizations for at least thirty years. You will encounter many variations on it. It is sometimes known by the acronym RAVCI, which distinguishes between the following five roles in a decision:

Responsible	The individual who actually makes the decision. This person is responsible for action. Responsibility can be shared.
Accountable	The individual who will be held ultimately accountable for the quality of the decision. This person may not make the decision but sets the criteria, time frame, involvement expectations, parameters, and process for the decision. The person accountable determines who is the "R." Ideally, there is only one "A" assigned to a given decision, but in a matrix, accountability may be jointly shared.
Veto	This veto is not the normal oversight that a superior often has in a decision. This "V" represents what is often a hidden veto from a role that can thwart a decision based on compliance to a standard. Vetoes of this kind are often found in places such as legal, compliance, and information security functions. Anticipating who might have a "V" can avoid surprises.
Consult	These are the individuals to be conferred with prior to a final decision. Their ideas, concerns, and suggestions may or may not be incorporated into the decision but will have been fully considered.
Inform	The individuals who need to be informed after a decision is made.

An example is shown in Figure 4.6. The full Responsibility Charting tool is provided in the Appendix.

Use Governance Bodies

A look at any matrixed organization quickly reveals that it does not have a traditionally recognizable leadership structure. The typical group of five to seven direct reports that an organizational leader usually brings together to set strategy and make decisions that require cross-functional agreement does not exist. In the example of the IT function that we have been following, who is on the leadership team? Is it the seven direct reports to the CIO? Is it the two group executives? What about the eleven lead managers? How is this important level engaged in leadership decisions?

FIGURE 4.6 **Responsibility Chart.**

Roles / Decisions	Relationship Manager	Hardware Integrator	Infrastructure Architect	Security Consultant	Build Team Manager	Director, Business Information Services	Director, Enterprise Infrastructure	
1. Staff a server installation team	I	C	C		R		A	
2. Determine standards for new system build	C	R	A	V	C	I	I	
3. Create pricing for a line of business project	C	C	R		I	C	A	

R = Responsible
A = Accountability
V = Veto
C = Consult
I = Inform

Rather than focus on the hierarchy of an organization, we suggest identifying the range of issues that need to be addressed and then creating councils and operating committees with the right mix of people based on the specific topic. These topics might include setting standards, pricing, exception processing, resource allocation and staffing, and customer engagement, to name just a few.

Bad experiences with committees and the unproductive meetings they spawn often discourage leaders from setting up such governance bodies. It is true that they must be carefully monitored lest they become gatekeepers that slow decision making or power bases with agendas of their own. Perhaps worse is the tendency for them to lose focus and tie up precious management time with regularly scheduled assemblies without tangible outcomes. To make these bodies effective, each needs a charter setting out its mandate and scope of authority. And like any team, each needs to have a set of objectives and deliverables against which to measure their success. These councils need to be held accountable for output and results just like any other organizational component.

The IT organization that we have been following uses a number of such bodies. One is the systems architecture council. The charter for this group is to ensure that:

• The firm's systems architecture effectively supports the business strategies

- Architectural standards are clearly stated and accessible, and development groups understand what other groups are doing
- Development tools, organization, and procedures can efficiently support the technical architecture
- Components of the architecture are deployed effectively and at reasonable cost

The council meets regularly with an agenda to continually update and communicate the standards as technology and business needs change, as well as review and approve requests for major exceptions to the standards.

Consider a Matrix Guardian Role

Implementing a matrix is a major undertaking. It is difficult for the leader, along with all of his or her other responsibilities, to fully manage the myriad aspects of change that have to be attended to during the transition to a matrix and beyond. We find that organizations run into trouble in sustaining their focus and energy through the planning and transition phases to create the supporting capabilities that are required to give the matrix a chance of success. One way to help ensure that the change is managed as a project, rather than merely installed and left to sink or swim, is to put in place a new role to oversee the transition. In one study of matrixed organizations, 92 percent of senior managers surveyed identified the lack of such a role, which the survey called a "matrix guardian," as the top obstacle to achieving the desired results (Sy and D'Annunzio, 2005).

The matrix guardian works to ensure that each of the teams is established, roles and boundaries are clarified, and lateral connections are fostered and supported. The role requires someone who can effectively communicate with those who are affected by the implementation, overcome reluctance, and keep a focus on all the work required to make the change a success. Ideally, the role reports to the top leader of the organization and is given enough power to function as a peer to the top managers in the organization. It can be a good role for a well-respected executive nearing retirement or an up-and-coming manager ready for a high-visibility assignment. Some organizations find that the role can be phased out after twelve to eighteen months, when the new organizational routines are well established. Others find, especially in larger organizations, that it is essential to continue to have someone completely focused on building and maintaining the necessary organizational infrastructure as long as the matrix is in place.

Processes

For a matrix to be successful, it must be introduced into an organization that already has a firm foundation of lateral capability. In other words, there must be in place a strong organizational infrastructure and a high level of management maturity onto which this last, most sophisticated of organizational linkages is built. No organization starts with a matrix; it builds toward a matrix.

At the very base of this foundation is social capital: the set of values, norms, and relationships shared among members of a group that permit cooperation among them. The inclusion of the word *capital* also implies investment in these relationships, with some expected returns (Lin, 2001). If human capital is the "know-how" in an organization, social capital is the "know-who." A robust base of relationships, trust, and problem resolution mechanisms helps managers solve problems together and candidly raise and resolve conflicts.

In this section, we walk through a list of characteristics of lateral capability. None of these notions is unique to a matrix. Any one of them will add capability to almost any organization and would be worth investing in, but they are absolutely critical for a matrix. We would go so far as to say that an organization that does not attend to all of them is more likely to experience the pitfalls rather than the benefits of the matrix.

Foster Strong Individual Relationships and Networks

A successful matrix is heavily dependent on good working relationships at every level. We define a good working relationship as two people who assume good intent on the part of the other, have had enough positive interactions to establish mutual trust, and are willing to make a personal contribution to the other's success. A matrixed manager may have two or more formal bosses and even other project managers to whom he is accountable. He has to work with peers on at least two formal teams and perhaps on other projects as well. He may also manage an ongoing team or a set of project teams. In addition, there are clients, vendors, and partners in other parts of the company with whom he needs to establish relationships.

Everyone builds some relationships at work. However, relationships that are not built deliberately have a tendency to fall narrowly into two categories. The first category of relationships is based on day-to-day transactions: Whom do I need to interact with to get my work done? The second category consists of people who share some common interest: Whom do I like to spend time with? While both of these kinds of relationships are important, they are not sufficient to support a matrix environment.

In addition to their formal reporting relationships, managers working in a matrix need a robust set of relationships with people they can call on for advice, resources, political support, and expertise. The flexibility of a matrix depends on the ability to form and re-form teams. The more people on a newly formed team who have a prior positive relationship, the more quickly the team can become productive. These connections in what is sometimes called the informal organization often do not fall into the two categories we have noted; rather, they must be sought out and cultivated.

A network is a set of relationships that link together. The power of networks is often underused. People fail to see the value of investing in relationships that have no immediate payoff, feel uncomfortable with the whole idea of networking, lack the skills to do it effectively, or focus only on networks that involve people with whom they have face-to-face interaction. But someone who invests in only current interactions or in people he or she personally likes misses out on developing relationships that will pay off down the road. For example, in the IT example we have been using, imagine an infrastructure architect who worked on a project a year ago with a peer from database administration in another location. They were in frequent communication during the project but have not had contact since the project ended. The infrastructure architect is now working on a project where advice or an introduction to some expert contacts that the database administrator knows would be helpful. But since the two have not talked or seen each other in so long, it may feel awkward to ask for a favor seemingly out of the blue.

It is important to emphasize that the value of investing in good relationships accrues not only to the individual; it also benefits the organization. Most managers understand the value of relationships but do not take the time to invest in them, because they seem to be only for personal gain. In fact, in the example, while the individual may gain from the relationship, the organization benefits as well. Therefore, relationship building is a legitimate activity. Actively encouraging it is a leadership responsibility—one that can be designed, supported, and even measured.

Relationship Mapping A relationship map is a simple tool that helps people map and evaluate the strength and robustness of their network. An example is shown in Figure 4.7. The complete Relationship Map tool is in the Appendix.

When completing a relationship map, a person lists fifteen to twenty people she should have a good working relationship with, maps them on a grid based on organizational relationship, and evaluates each relationship.

FIGURE 4.7 **Sample Relationship Map.**

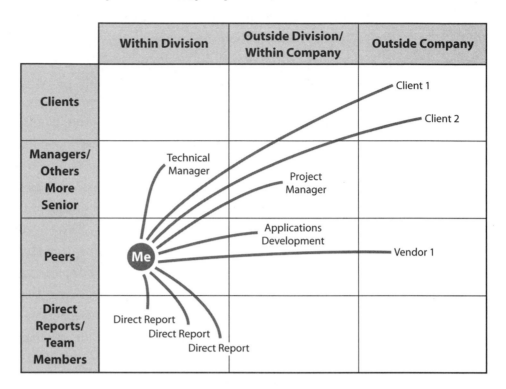

She then can quickly see if there are gaps by function (for example, no one in marketing) or by level (no one more senior than the current manager). Anyone can use this tool to be more strategic about his or her own network. The real payoff, however, comes when it is used as an organizational tool. For example, each matrixed manager in our IT example might sit with both of his lead managers and identify whom he needs to build a relationship with. Those managers then make introductions, create opportunities for interactions, encourage the time spent on fostering the relationship, and check in on how well the manager has done. This transforms relationship building from an activity that is left to chance based on personal comfort and style to a strong fabric helping to knit the organization together.

Organizational Relationship Health Check Another useful tool for fostering organizational relationships is the Relationship Health Check as shown in Figure 4.8 and provided in the Appendix.

The tool assesses the state of a relationship as perceived by an internal customer or peer group. The assessment is given to an internal client or peer group, and they are asked to evaluate the working relationship. Follow-up conversations can focus on where there are lower-than-desired ratings and what actions can be taken to strengthen the relationship. The intent of the tool is twofold. First, it serves as a vehicle to stimulate a structured

FIGURE 4.8 **Relationship Health Check.**

	Stage 1 No partnership/ limited engagement	Stage 2 Coordinating engagements/ encountering frustration	Stage 3 Cooperation	Stage 4 Collaboration	Stage 5 True Partnership
Vision/ identity	"Us" and "them," with little or no middle ground; based on negative	"Us" *and* "them," looking toward a future "we"— building trust	Beginning to think as "we"; some level of personal connection exists	Achieving partnership, based in personal relationships	Us/we, almost transparent— part of the same team
Mindset/ approach	Working together has not come up or is not feasible; sees little or no value in working together	Exploring partnership possibilities; sees other groups as a "necessary evil"	Work together to achieve our individual goals—quid pro quo	Work together to succeed as a team	Shares in both successes and failures
Strategy/ purpose	Plans and decisions are made with complete independence	Plans are made behind the scenes and then discussed	Decision making may involve discussion with and consideration of other groups; when asked, groups share objectives or strategy	Decisions and plans are discussed with other groups; input and feedback is requested regarding objectives or strategy	Decisions and plans are discussed and made together for joint strategy development and execution
Communication	Little to no communication	Infrequent, but with communication modes being developed	Communication is as needed, to gain understanding of other groups' goals—tactically driven	Communication is the norm; both groups clearly understand the common goals; regular meetings with give and take	Communication is frequent, ongoing, honest, and respectful
Trust	Conflicting interests or unawareness of common goals or mutual benefits	Aligning interests or are experiencing conflict in current interests	Still a focus on individual interests, but a degree of trust exists	Desire for mutual benefits; seeks out help and advice	Desire for a long-term partnership that is mutually beneficial; high level of integrity
Results/ value added	Lack of any significant engagement precludes any value added	Value could be added in the future	Value is added for a specific project with limited time frame	Value added for extended period of time	Continually adding value and creating synergy

conversation around the factors behind the low rating and what can be done to improve it. Second, it creates a baseline to measure results against and provides a way to communicate relationship expectations to others in the organization. The tool is useful when the nature of the work requires a high degree of collaboration, positive interaction, and trust—in short, in situations where a stage 5 rating is the desired goal. Not all relationships require such a degree of connection, and in some cases stage 4 may be sufficient.

Strategically Plan Face-to-Face Time

For organizations that are geographically dispersed, face-to-face interactions among staff are rare, and when budgets are tight, travel and retreats are often the first "frills" to be cut. Yet studies have shown that project teams that meet face-to-face at least once at the beginning of their project have a much higher success rate than teams that do not (Duarte and Snyder, 2001).

Teams that come together and create opportunities for members to establish personal connections seem to have many fewer misunderstandings when they then must conduct business remotely using technology. If the employees within the matrix are not co-located, be sure in the beginning of the transition to bring people together, particularly when they are working on setting mutual expectations and operating procedures. Then take opportunities to use training sessions, retreats, town hall meetings, and forums where people will be brought together physically as a way not just to convey information or solve problems but also to strengthen relationships and networks. Assign seating, mix up small groups, create opportunities for communities of interest to meet together, and provide long breaks and lunches and other planned social time.

Make Trust Tangible

When describing a good working relationship, most people use the word *trust* as they paint a picture of what one looks like. But they may have more trouble defining trust; it seems to be one of those things that people know when they see it. In fact, the factors that go into trust can be made tangible. When people understand what these factors are, they can then build trust with others deliberately and even rate the quality of relationships.

One implication of using a matrix is that few individuals have full authority over significant decisions. Numerous people must be involved in decisions both big and small. But if everyone who has an interest in a decision must always be involved (that is, decision making by committee), then the leaders of the organization will soon notice decision making

FIGURE 4.9 **The Components of Trust.**

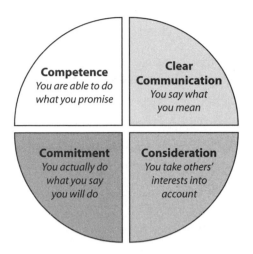

Source: Based on Mayer, Davis, and Schoorman (1995).

slowing down. By building a broad set of relationships based on trust, more people can be assured that others understand their perspective and will take it into account when making decisions that affect them. When this is achieved, fewer people need to be involved in each decision, and overall decisions can be made efficiently without compromising quality.

The four major factors of trust are competence, commitment, communication, and consideration, as illustrated in Figure 4.9.

Any well-functioning organization is strengthened by increased trust levels, but high trust is essential in a matrix. Encounters that occur in the normal flow of business can be explicitly designed to increase trust. Consider a face-to-face meeting between the functional managers and relationship managers in our IT illustration. On the surface, they might be coming together to work on an agenda of current issues and make decisions about them. But if these meetings are well designed, the managers will also take time to educate one another about how they view their piece of the world. This helps others to understand their point of view and take it into account back on the job when making decisions (Consideration, in Figure 4.9). The group might also take a few minutes to assess how well they communicate with one another and what can be improved in terms of clarity and response time (Communication). Highlighting success stories and identifying where unique or desirable talent and capabilities reside in the organization will make the others more aware of resources they can draw on (Competence). Finally, shared agreements and follow-through on action plans demonstrate dedication to common goals (Commitment). Out of this meeting comes not only completion of the day's agenda, but a higher level of trust that facilitates the identification and resolution of future issues. This simple model of trust can be used to quickly assess concerns within a group, identify the root causes, and address them.

Make It Easy to Collaborate, Not Compromise

If relationships are the fabric of the organization, then trust strengthens the threads that help move information and knowledge up, down, and sideways. But good people and good intentions are not enough. People need mechanisms to help resolve the inevitable conflicts that arise in a matrix.

To start, they must understand and accept that there will be conflicts and that these are not an indication of failure in the organization. In fact, a matrix is designed to surface conflict; it is intended to bring different strategic points of view into contact with one another. A common frustration in a matrix, however, is that many conflicts are hard to resolve because the two or three opposing views on the issue are all legitimate, and no one person has the authority to make the call. In our IT example, the lending business that needs a new system truly does need specific functionality and needs it to be delivered within a tight time frame. Meanwhile, the security consultants are genuinely being held accountable for ensuring that all new systems conform to enterprise standards. When some of the functionality desired by the lending business does not conform to the enterprisewide security standards, a conflict will arise.

The creative tension that comes from trying to reconcile these opposing objectives can yield an outcome that is better for the business overall than for either of the individual parties. But the risk is that failure to resolve the conflict will result in a delay in decision making, personal acrimony, or escalation of the decision to a more senior level. Worse than these consequences may be compromise—an outcome that suboptimizes each party's objectives. True collaboration, in which the needs of both parties are met with an outcome that neither party may have conceived of originally, needs to be designed into a matrix organization. Here are some ways to do this:

- *Set criteria for trade-offs.* Senior managers identify and communicate what factors take precedence when trade-offs have to be made. In our IT example, these factors might be time, cost, functionality, and security. These directives cannot anticipate every scenario, but they can provide guidance to lower-level managers when it is impossible to meet all objectives.

- *Establish rules for escalation of conflicts.* Frequent escalation of conflicts is a symptom that managers are unclear about the criteria for decision making or lack the managerial maturity to resolve issues at their level. Policy issues should move up the hierarchy, as senior leaders are often the only people with a broad enough mandate and perspective to set policy. But when midlevel managers do not get along or are unwilling to collaborate on issues that they should be able to resolve, the right leadership move is to push the accountability back down the ladder for resolution.

• *Define parameters for risk.* In a matrix, both the matrix managers and the lead managers frequently find themselves in situations where they have to take personal risk (for example, confronting a manager or colleague) or organizational risk (for example, agreeing to a new process or outcome). Conflicts can end in compromise if people perceive compromise as the safe route—one that will do no immediate apparent harm—although the action may be riskier for the organization in the long run. Many leaders send mixed messages about acceptable risk taking. Failures are quickly circulated through informal communication channels, but opportunities to publicly recognize examples of the behaviors to be encouraged are overlooked or underplayed. Again, not all scenarios can be anticipated, but the more often that senior leaders do communicate and publicly recognize the behaviors they want to see, the better the matrix will function.

• *Make it easy to share information.* Teamwork and collaboration in a matrix are dependent on strong systems for sharing information. All of this organization design discussion assumes that the organization has smoothly functioning project management, customer information, and product development systems, as well as a robust set of technological tools to support collaboration for people who work remotely. Good technology cannot overcome a lack of social capital and lateral capability, but gaps in these systems exacerbate the complexities of working in a matrix. One particularly useful technology tool in a matrix is a searchable directory that contains information on employees' experience, skills, and interests. The directory can help individuals build their network and speed the assembly of teams for project managers.

Efficient and Effective Meetings

Good meeting practice may seem a tired topic. Anyone who has been through a basic management course has learned the value of setting and adhering to an agenda, facilitating group discussions, and capturing and distributing action items after a meeting. And yet organizations continue to suffer from the scourge of holding too many meetings, or conducting poorly planned and run meetings, or having the wrong participants at the table. There is no question that the introduction of a matrix means more meetings. Certainly in the planning and transition process, there will be numerous meetings to bring people together to calibrate expectations and create clarity around the topics we are discussing here. On an ongoing basis, there will be more meetings as well due to the increased points of interface, the number of shared decisions, and the inevitable conflicts, all of which require more participation. Again, the number of meetings, just like the increase in conflicts, is not a failing of the matrix. It should be expected and planned for.

Poorly run meetings can only sometimes be blamed on a lack of individual skill or knowledge. More often, they are a symptom of a lack of overall discipline in the organization. An irony of the matrix is that although it is most often used to drive integration and flexibility, it cannot be run as a loose and informal organization. More thought and care need to be given to creating a common management culture. The more that operating norms are shared, the easier it will be for people to move between teams and units and focus quickly on the work that needs to be done, rather than spend time establishing the mechanics of how they will work together.

If there are no agreed-on and enforced protocols for how meetings are run, information is shared, and decisions are made, the matrix will exacerbate the usual frustrations of organizational life. People will soon blame the matrix for wasting their time. A hard look will likely show that time was being wasted before the matrix in unproductive meetings. Just more of it is being wasted now.

Rewards

Too often, leaders hold the matrix responsible if they fail to meet their objectives, as though it is a living entity in itself. In reality, the real culprits are a lack of desire, incentive, or ability to work together on the part of the management team. The performance measurement and reward systems have to promote and support all of the behaviors described in the lateral connections section above. Otherwise people will act rationally, but solely in their own interest, rather than in that of the broader organization.

Jointly Set Objectives and Manage Performance for Matrixed Managers

A key management process that must be realigned as part of a matrix design is that of objective setting and performance management. The lead managers need to come together and jointly determine what the matrixed managers will be held accountable for and how their performance will be assessed. The conversation this forces regarding expectations for the individual also makes explicit each manager's assumptions about what work is important and communicates their own goals to one another. Among the things to consider when modifying the performance management process are these:

• Both lead managers must have explicit input into the evaluation of the shared matrix manager and must review and agree to the final performance rating. It cannot be delegated to one or the other. Delegation may feel more efficient and less political than a joint evaluation, but it will drive the wrong behaviors. People cannot help but respond more to those who determine their year-end ratings and compensation. The process for who is involved in performance management and the expectations for their participation should be made clear. This is so important that the lead managers' own performance reviews should take into account the quality of how well they execute this process together.

• Although the matrix assumes that some resources are shared, they are not always shared equally, and this should be reflected in the goal-setting and appraisal process. If one manager sets 75 percent of the goals for the year and supervises their attainment, that person should have a proportionate share of the input into the final report or ranking.

• Each manager should focus on areas where they have direct observation and should be responsible for gathering input from project leaders and others who have worked with the matrixed manager over the course of the rating period. In this way, the evaluation process reflects input from all who are dependent on the matrixed manager's performance. When the lead managers come together, joint performance discussions can focus on areas of disagreement, ensuring that the values of the organization are met in addition to the business results, and identifying development and next job moves.

• Do not overlook peer feedback. Some of the most important relationships in the matrix are among peers. Frustration over the need for more involvement, longer decision time frames, additional coordination, and the interdependence that the matrix forces can lead to blame and finger-pointing when things go wrong. Talk of teamwork and collaboration has to be backed by measures and rewards for it. One way is to build some peer feedback into the performance management system. The process can be kept simple. What you want to get at is and answer to, "How easy am I to do business with?" focusing on how peers perceive one's responsiveness, follow-up, and communication.

Align Rewards of the Lead Managers

It may be obvious that the matrixed managers will need to be appraised and rewarded for balancing and meeting two sets of objectives. Less obvious, yet equally important, is the importance of ensuring that that the lead managers are incented to support the goals of the matrix and not just their line-of-business, geographic, project, or functional objectives. A straightforward way to do this is to link their performance rating as well as some part of their variable compensation (if used) to the success of the organization as a whole. If part of their compensation is tied to the success of their counterparts in the other business dimension, you will quickly see the sincere, "How can I help?" behaviors that you desire.

Make Heroes of Those Who Demonstrate the Behaviors

Consider honestly who the heroes are in your organization. Are they the people who exemplify the behaviors we have been discussing? Recognition—outside of compensation—is an inexpensive way to visibly convey the culture and behaviors that you want to encourage. Public thanks, featuring a team on the Web site or newsletter, and selecting individuals for high-profile projects or assignments are all ways to reinforce the message of what personal success in the matrix looks like.

Measure and Minimize Management Rework

The reengineering movement of the 1990s brought focus to the cost of badly designed processes where work and information passed through unnecessary checkpoints and approvals. In the back rooms and operations of most organizations, work now flows efficiently in a streamlined manner. The same cannot be said for most management processes. Organizational assessments and surveys often turn up the complaint that management decisions fail to stick—that, once made, they are revisited in subsequent meetings or challenged behind closed doors or renegotiated one-on-one with the leader.

The matrix creates a host of opportunities for management rework. Anyone who has grown up with two parents knows how to play the game of reopening a decision made by one parent by appealing to the other. Just as a well-functioning family requires both parents to stand firmly together to uphold the family's rules, avoiding this situation in business calls for a well-functioning management team that is clear about the organization's objectives and holds one another accountable for standing by decisions.

One of the best ways to make the problem of management rework visible is to measure the perceptions of the employees in the organization.

Regardless of how the management team believes they are acting, the perceptions of those they manage are the most important reality. A simple survey conducted at six- to twelve-month intervals and focused on these issues can shine a spotlight on where there are gaps in accountability. The survey might ask such questions as, "How well does the management team . . ."

- Address the organization's most important issues?
- Follow up on actions and commitments to ensure they were implemented?
- Make decisions that stick?
- Come to closure when there is disagreement or conflict?
- Engage in productive dialogue?
- Differentiate issues that call for a cross-functional approach?
- Lead change as a cohesive group?

When the results of the survey are seen by the management team, they are more likely to commit to visible actions as a team that will continually improve the scores.

People

In a matrix, the most important set of relationships is among the vertical and horizontal lead managers. In the example we have been using, these would be the relationship and functional managers in Figure 4.2. Their placement in the hierarchy is important, but selecting who will be sharing the matrixed resources is just as critical. The quality of the working relationships among these managers will set the tone and culture of the whole organization. Some design considerations are discussed below.

Carefully Select Lead Managers

Lead managers need to be selected for either demonstrated experience in a collaborative environment or a propensity for the behaviors that support collaboration. For these key positions, selecting people who already demonstrate the ability to work in a complex environment will be easier than trying to train managers and develop these skills. Even better would be to have some of these managers come from organizations where they have experienced working laterally to the degree that the matrix demands. If the lead managers are all in a stretch assignment, the matrix will be much harder to get off the ground. Some of the interpersonal and management competencies that have been shown to be important include the following

(Bartlett and Ghoshal, 1990):

- The ability to manage and resolve conflict
- A level of comfort with ambiguity and change
- Strong project management skills
- The ability to share decision rights and take multiple priorities into account
- The discipline to gather information from multiple sources in order to inform decision making
- Strong communication skills, enabling managers to work with people from other disciplines and backgrounds and to communicate effectively through a wide range of communication technologies
- Skills in negotiation, influence, and building networks
- The ability to align multiple goals
- Cultural sensitivity, enabling managers to build relationships with colleagues who are located in other countries and may have different styles of communication and collaboration
- High levels of emotional intelligence

Actively Build Teams

Lead managers need to have regular face-to-face meetings. A common mistake is to bring these players together (either face-to-face or in a conference call) only when there is a problem or to have them meet so seldom that the agenda is overloaded. This group needs to establish regular meetings to jointly set overall objectives, review and adjust priorities, educate one another about their work programs, and assess and manage talent.

In addition, each of the horizontal and vertical teams needs to come together periodically to create an identity, build intragroup working relationships, and agree on objectives. As we noted, the more that the operating procedures (communication protocols, meeting practices, and decision procedures, for example) are the same from team to team, the easier it will be for individuals to quickly shift their focus from one team to another and contribute equally to each.

Develop Teamwork Skills of the Matrixed Managers

Teamwork is an overused word that has almost lost its meaning. Like *customer focused*, few organizations fail to list teamwork as a desired value and behavior. So what is different about teamwork in a matrix? The head of a business during the transition to a matrix likened it to the difference between the game of football and soccer as a way to help his organization understand how the new organization was different from how they were used to operating. He pointed out that in football, players have well-defined positions, and it is illegal for them to go outside the boundaries of those clearly defined roles (for example, offensive linemen are not allowed to move downfield before a pass is thrown). Likewise, in traditional organizations, job descriptions prescribe the boundaries of one's role. In contrast, soccer positions, although defined, are much more fluid. When one player is in trouble, another can step in and continue moving the ball forward. Sports analogies for business should not be carried too far, but the image can be helpful when trying to convey the culture needed to support a matrix. Since each manager's fate is closely tied to the success of others, the prevailing attitude needs to be, "How can I help?" rather than, "That's not my job."

The introduction of a matrix has profound implications for how work flows. If this is not recognized, you will have hard-working, well-intentioned people struggling over where to make hand-offs, who can make decisions, and where roles begin and end. To extend our soccer analogy a bit further, a soccer team is not just a group of athletes willing to help each other out. Rather, the team goes into the game with a well-defined plan, clear roles, and a set of thoroughly practiced plays. For the majority of situations, there is an agreed-on response that allows each person to play out his role without worrying about conflicts with his own teammates over who goes after the ball. In the same way, the key managers in a matrix are advised to spend time anticipating—practicing, if you will—the most likely scenarios where hand-offs and decisions will need to be made.

We suggest that all employees new to a matrix be given a clear understanding of why the organization is using the matrix, how it is intended to work, and their role in supporting the organization's goals. In addition, make the needed investment in management development programs focused on enhancing interpersonal, influence, meeting, conflict management, and group problem-solving skills. Not only does an investment in such training enhance individual skills, it helps to build the common language and practices that reduce the friction in cross-organization transactions.

•   •   •

Structuring a matrix is fairly straightforward; making it successful is not. Many leaders have found that their experiences with a matrix have not lived up to expectations, and as a result they have abandoned it out of frustration. Typically this is because the matrix has been "installed" instead of implemented. It is best to begin to build the mind-set before undertaking the structural change. What we have learned from observing many organizations that have implemented a matrix is that the principles and tools for success are neither mysterious nor difficult to employ. The suggestions we have put forward in this chapter are good basic practices that are neither new in the literature nor unique to a matrix. Many will be valuable to any organization, however it is configured. The difference in a matrix is that they are not optional. They need to be applied fully and consistently.

The assessment tool available in the Appendix, Are You Ready for a Matrix? will help you determine the maturity of your management structures and the underlying capabilities that will point to success. If your assessment is that you are toward the weak end of the spectrum, especially in the social capital category, we suggest you spend time strengthening these areas before jumping to changing roles and reporting relationships. Then start small and learn from the experience before employing a matrix widely. If you do, you will find yourself in a much better position to reap the benefits of a matrix and minimize the pain of transition.

Chapter 5

Solving the Centralization— Decentralization Dilemma

WHETHER TO CENTRALIZE or decentralize is one of the most vexing questions in organization design. The issue is commonly thought of as an either-or choice: Should we group an activity all together, or should we disperse it out to the regions or business units? The arguments for each can be persuasive. Centralization provides the benefits of cost-saving scale, common processes to drive consistency, and the potential to build deep knowledge and experience in specialized fields for use across the organization. The case for decentralization is equally compelling: it empowers managers by giving them greater control over decisions and resources, thus fostering the speed, creativity, and innovation needed to compete against nimble, highly adaptable competitors.

Each model has its advantages, but when it is taken to an extreme, it begins to undermine the very objectives it was intended to enhance, just as a particular personality strength in an individual, if overused, becomes a weakness. Organizations that swing too far toward centralization often find frustrated managers in their operating units chafing under bureaucratic rules enforced by colleagues sitting far from the reality on the ground. The response is often to swing the pendulum in the opposite direction. Then, after a period of decentralization, the organization finds it has "let a thousand flowers bloom" but is not reaping any of the benefits of its size. Employees come to expect these predictable oscillations and the reorganizations that accompany them. Look at your own organization and where it is on the centralization—decentralization spectrum. More likely than not, its current form is a response to excesses of the previous incarnation. It seems that more than any other organization design change, the oscillation between centralization and decentralization is more often an attempt to correct past abuses than a forward-looking method of implementing a strategic direction.

Centralization versus decentralization is one of the most highly charged issues in organization design, as it gets to the heart of where power lies in a system. Many people have strong feelings about the issue, which pervades many facets of life—from the relationship of one's central government to the states or provinces within the nation to how much power the local school board should have. Words such as *freedom* and *empowerment* are used to extol the virtues of decentralization, while *efficiency*, *fairness*, and *consistency* are often heard when making the case for centralized decision making.

A scan of the business literature shows more calls for decentralization than for centralization. As organizations grow, the natural tendency is for decisions and activities to become centralized as managers add staff and seek to consolidate power. Predictably, after complaints that decision making is too slow or too far removed from the base of operations and customers, the decision to decentralize is put forward.

Do we have a bias toward centralization or decentralization? We can state up front that our bias is toward decentralization where possible, given strategic parity between the two. But it should be clear from the discussion of the many complex forms of organization discussed in this book that few of these approaches work without some strong central guidance. Centralization should be used when such coordination is necessary. Making the appropriate choices of when and where to centralize means gaining the advantages of leveraging the size, assets, and capabilities of an organization. We do not wish to frame this discussion, however, as leading you to choose between centralization and decentralization. Instead, organization designers need to build a coherent system that balances the tensions between these two natural, but rival, forces. We look at the subject as less a choice between centralization and decentralization and more of an imperative to build a rational system for managing the very real, but natural, opposing tensions found in every organization.

This chapter is organized into three sections. We start with a discussion of *corporate center strategy*, since the design of the corporate center can influence and constrain many of the design decisions that are made at lower levels. This section focuses on business portfolio strategy and how to understand the business models within the units that make up a firm. We then discuss the organizational implications of that strategy, examining the amount of value that the corporate center can add depending on the variety of a company's portfolio. Finally, we delineate the three roles of the corporate center: business performance improvement, shared services, and compliance. The next section of the chapter provides a comparison of centralization and decentralization. Although centralization would seem to be the opposite of decentralization, the decision to do either involves different rationales. We discuss the strategic reasons for both centralization and decentralization, and then the predictable potential problems of each. Our goal is to provide a nuanced understanding of why an organization would choose one option or the other. The chapter ends with guidance on how to get the benefits of both centralization and decentralization without the excesses of either.

Corporate Center Strategy

We begin this discussion of centralization and decentralization by looking at the corporate center. By the *corporate center* or *headquarters*, we mean all of the staff and activities that take place outside the operating units. The operating units may be subsidiary businesses, product divisions, market segments, or geographies. These units are where the primary business activities of a firm take place—the profit centers. The corporate center activities generally report to the CEO and provide support for all these business units as well as the overall enterprise. The kinds of activities that might be found in the corporate center include enterprise-level management (CEO/COO), legal, treasury, taxation, financial reporting and control, internal audit, payroll and benefits administration, talent management and career development, executive development, training, government and public relations, corporate planning, strategy, research and development, marketing, sales, procurement and inbound logistics, distribution, supply chain, and information technology.

This is not merely a subject of academic interest, although few readers may be in the position to redesign the corporate center and the headquarters functions of their company. The design of the corporate center influences and constrains the design of activities at every level in the hierarchy. In addition, for a large company, the same analysis that we are applying at the top level of the corporation can apply at the business unit or regional level, where judgments need to be made regarding which decisions and activities to keep at that level and which to devolve further down. Wherever there is a set of operating units, no matter how small or how far down in the organization, there will be decisions to make regarding the design of the center.

Understanding the Business Portfolio

The primary factor that influences the role and design of the corporate center is the diversity of a firm's business portfolio. Low diversity means that the company is essentially a single business with a closely associated set of products. For example, although BMW has different makes, models, and brands, it is in the car and motorcycle business, with only minor interests in other industries. At the other end of the spectrum is a conglomerate or holding company with a high diversity of businesses. General Electric has businesses that range from the manufacture of consumer appliances and industrial equipment, to providing financing and leasing, to the NBC Universal media network.

The value that can be contributed to the operating units by the corporate center is in inverse proportion to the company's portfolio diversity. A company that has a set of closely related businesses and product lines can gain much from a strong and active corporate center. One that has operating units based on different business models, or units that serve different markets and customers through various channels and geographies, will find that the corporate center has much less to contribute.

Figure 5.1 summarizes this spectrum and provides some examples. Business portfolio strategy, the organizational implications of that strategy, and the role of the corporate center are discussed in further detail below.

While a single business and a conglomerate are fairly easy to recognize, it may be harder to distinguish among the states in between. *Integrated,*

FIGURE 5.1 **Value Provided by the Corporate Center.**

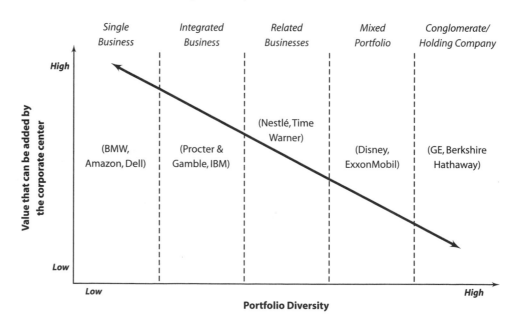

related, and *mixed* portfolios are all composed of a variety of businesses but vary by the degree of similarity among the various business models, as well as by how the company presents its products and services to its customers.

An *integrated* business may offer a variety of products but seeks to sell its products and services as a package to the customer. For example, IBM offers stand-alone servers as well as technology consulting services—very different products—but it provides its products and services as integrated solutions to customers who want IBM to do the integration of complex technology systems rather than doing it themselves. Another example is Procter & Gamble, which offers a wide range of health, beauty, and home care products but works closely with its large retail customers to coordinate supply chain management, marketing, and promotion, again integrating on behalf of the customer.

In a *related* business portfolio, the business units may have strong similarities, but the company does not necessarily seek to sell its products as integrated solutions or bundles. However, there are opportunities to share technologies, knowledge, and resources across the lines of business, which can all be facilitated by the center. For example, while Nestlé sells many products, they are all in the food and beverage sector, consumer based, and sold through the same channels. Brand managers can focus on marketing and product development and adaptations to local markets, while the center can look to leverage what is common in manufacturing and distribution across the various product lines.

In a *mixed* portfolio, there may be a common theme among the businesses, but the units have significantly different underlying business models. Although Disney markets its products in a coordinated way across its business units, the movie studio, theme parks, publishing business, television networks, retail stores, and music business are more different than they are alike in their underlying dynamics. Another example is ExxonMobil, which searches and drills for oil and natural gas, refines oil, runs gas stations and convenience stores, and provides specialty chemicals to other industries, selling to both businesses and consumers. A mixed portfolio may cluster business units into groups of businesses that are more closely related, leaving little relationship between clusters.

Portfolio Diversity

The diversity of a company's business portfolio is not always obvious. The relatedness of the products sold matters less than the similarities in the underlying business models. Different business models require different capabilities, talent, and organizations. Understanding the degree of relationship within the portfolio is essential to determining how much value can be achieved through centralizing activities and decisions at the corporate center. Three examples of seemingly related portfolios—which the acquirers eventually found to be less related than they had expected—follow.

Pepsico bought a number of fast food outlets, including Pizza Hut, Kentucky Fried Chicken, and Taco Bell, in the late 1970s. They appeared to be a good strategic fit that would serve as natural outlets for Pepsi's food and beverage products. On the surface, a fast food chain would seem to be a closely related business to Pepsi's core business, but it was not. Pepsi's core soft drink and snack food businesses are quite similar, as products are sold through other businesses using a highly skilled sales force. Pepsi truck drivers handle sales and customer service as well as make deliveries. Many managers in the company have begun their careers in this way. The fast food restaurant business, however, is a capital-intensive consumer business with a large, low-wage workforce to manage. Rather than running closely related businesses, Pepsico found it was running a mixed portfolio with few transferable capabilities among them. In 1997, it sold and spun off all its food outlets to focus again on its core business. In this way, it could use the strong capabilities it had already developed at the corporate center level—in marketing and distribution, in particular—to create synergy among its beverage and snack food lines.

Another example is UPS's purchase of Mail Boxes Etc. in 2001. Mail Boxes Etc. was a franchise business providing packing and shipping services to individuals and small businesses. UPS already made regular pickups at these locations. The acquisition, which would convert the franchises to UPS stores, seemed like a natural extension of the core shipping business. But trying to integrate a chain of entrepreneurs used to running small franchises their own way into a highly disciplined corporation (where drivers are famously told how to best exit their trucks to save footsteps) resulted in a clash of cultures. UPS's management made decisions that cut into franchisee revenues by mandating discounts and setting nationwide prices and requiring store owners to pay for converting their stores to the UPS model. Even the requirement for the store employees to wear uniforms became a point of contention. The result for UPS was a spate of lawsuits and high turnover among store owners (Gibson, 2006). The company is still struggling with how to transfer its capabilities to a very different business model.

A business with a seemingly related portfolio may also differ in the way in which customers are served. Charles Schwab made its reputation as a discount brokerage serving individual investors. Investments in technology allowed low trading fees and transaction costs. It purchased U.S. Trust, a venerable wealth management advisor, to move the company up-market.

FIGURE 5.2 **Evaluating Portfolio Diversity.**

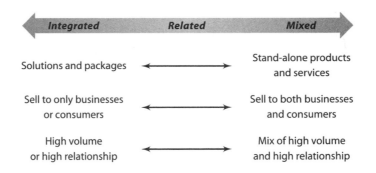

| Integrated | Related | Mixed |

Solutions and packages ⟷ Stand-alone products and services

Sell to only businesses or consumers ⟷ Sell to both businesses and consumers

High volume or high relationship ⟷ Mix of high volume and high relationship

Although U.S. Trust seemed to be a closely related business, it was built on deep personal relationships with high-net-worth clients rather than on high-volume, low-cost transactions. Schwab's technologies, operations, and customer service model provided no synergy. Little value could be added by the corporate center based on the capabilities that Schwab had previously developed. Schwab sold U.S. Trust in 2006, in the company's words, in order to "sharpen ... strategic focus" (Charles Schwab, 2006).

In summary, there are a number of ways to test the diversity of the underlying business models in the portfolio, as shown in Figure 5.2:

- Are products sold as stand-alones or packaged into solutions?
- Does the company sell to both businesses and consumers?
- Do the businesses rely on a high number of transactions or a high level of investment in customer relationships?

The Business Portfolio Strategy tool in the Appendix provides additional guidance in determining how related your business units are.

Organizational Implications of the Business Portfolio Strategy

Once you are clear on your portfolio strategy and the real level of commonality among the business units, a set of complementary organizational options regarding the size and role of the corporate center follows. These are summarized in Figure 5.3.

When the business portfolio strategy changes, the organization should change as well. For example, in the 1990s, in order to support its strategic move from being a product company to a solutions-based company, IBM moved from a related set of businesses organized in a product division structure to an integrated business using a front-back (customer-product) structure. The role of the corporate center was strengthened to facilitate the coordination necessary to execute a strategy that required a high level of

FIGURE 5.3 **Options for the Corporate Center.**

Portfolio Strategy	Single Business	Integrated	Related	Mixed	Conglomerate
Typical structure	Functional	Front-back	Divisional	Cluster	Holding company
Example	Apple computer	IBM	Time Warner	ExxonMobil	GE
Role of the corporate center	Strong	Moderate to strong	Moderate	Low to the cluster; moderate within cluster	Low
Size of corporate staff	Small	Moderate	Large	Low at the corporate level; moderate if clustered	Small
Type of control used by corporate	Operational strategic financial	Operational strategic financial	Strategic financial	Strategic financial	Financial
Business processes	Common	Common	Common	Common within cluster	Different
Compensation system	Company	Company	Company	Cluster	Subsidiary
Bonuses	Company	Company	Company	Cluster	Subsidiary
Careers	Company	Company	Company	Cluster	Subsidiary
Culture	Company-wide	Company-wide	Company-wide	Mix	Unique to subsidiary
Division name or brand	Company name	Company name	Company name	Mix	Differs by subsidiary

interaction among the business units. Much of IBM's success can be seen as a result of matching its organization to its strategy.

Misalignments between organization and strategy can result in missed opportunities. A highly decentralized firm with a strategy in which synergies between business units are supposed to be captured is one such mismatch. For example, Time Warner is constructed as a set of closely related business units. Warner Brothers makes, markets, and distributes films and television shows; New Line Cinema develops and produces independent films; Turner Broadcasting runs a set of cable television stations; Time Inc. in the United States and IPC in Europe are magazine publishers; Time Warner Cable is one of the largest cable providers in the United States; and AOL is an Internet content provider. As media-related businesses, all involved in the production or distribution of news and entertainment, there are apparent opportunities for the businesses to collaborate and for the corporate center to assist in making this happen. Instead, Time Warner is run as a conglomerate, with almost no interaction among units at any level, resulting in frequent calls by investors to break the company into smaller pieces.

General Electric, in contrast, is a conglomerate with a range of businesses from jet engines to finance. Yet it manages talent centrally and is celebrated for its human development and business processes, which are used across all businesses. Even with dissimilar businesses, it finds ways to leverage its size.

Role of the Corporate Center

A good understanding of how related or diverse the business units in your company are is essential to determining the potential value that the corporate center can add. In general, the more tightly focused the portfolio, the more value can be added by the corporate core. The more diverse the portfolio, the harder it is to add value from the center.

The corporate center can be thought of as having three primary roles:

1. *Business performance improvement.* These are activities that provide value to the operating units through the creation and sharing of capabilities. The center determines which capabilities need to be allowed to develop differently across units and which can be shared across the portfolio. Some examples of potentially shared activities include:
   - *Capital.* For many holding companies, and the private equity firms that operate this way, the investment of capital and financial engineering is the primary way in which the corporate center adds value to the acquired units. A corporation with an A credit rating can buy a B-rated company and make money right away by refinancing it.
   - *Strategy and investments.* One of the center's roles is determining how to define the differences between each business unit's focus and make hard choices regarding investment decisions. A challenge for many companies is that the budget is spread too evenly, starving those that can grow and overfeeding those that cannot. The center can provide the strategic focus that creates the rules for making acquisitions and determine where the company's capabilities will best transfer into new markets, new geographies, or new customer bases.
   - *Talent.* Operating units are always reluctant to give up good talent. Managing talent from the center allows the identification,

development, and career management of high performers to benefit not only the individual units but the company overall as well.

- *Sharing knowledge, processes, and resources.* These might include expertise in marketing, manufacturing, channel management, product development, or supply chain management. Even among a mixed portfolio of businesses, the center can identify opportunities for broader uses of innovations developed in the units. For example, Phillips has successfully converted devices produced by its medical division and sold to hospitals into consumer electronics, such as home defibrillators, which are produced and sold by another unit. Staff in the center can see possibilities, make connections between people in units, and encourage and fund new ventures in a way that is unlikely to happen from the bottom up.

- *Management infrastructure.* The center can build the infrastructure to support good decision making at the local level. This could involve creating shared databases, providing training, building systems, streamlining decision processes, collecting external intelligence, and forming alliances with outside groups that will all benefit the operating units.

- *Brand.* When business units share a brand or operate under an umbrella brand (for example, Smith Barney, Primerica, and Citibank are all under the Citigroup brand), development of the brand and brand marketing is usually managed at the corporate level to ensure consistent messages.

- *Government and public relations.* When governments, communities, or health, social, and environmental groups are exerting pressure on a business in the public arena and the company's brand reputation is threatened, the center can provide a coherent response and organize lobbying efforts more effectively than can the units alone.

2. *Shared services.* The center can be the home for support services that can be provided more efficiently and cost-effectively by employing economies of scale (for example, computer help desk or benefits administration services). The center can use size and coordinated action to gain leverage when buying, selling, or partnering. In addition, it can provide specialized services that are too costly for each business unit to house individually, such as legal or acquisition and integration specialists.

3. *Compliance.* These are the obligatory activities regarding governance and regulatory responsibilities that all companies have, which need

to be carried out at an enterprise level. Also in this category are activities that manage risk at an enterprise level and must be independent from the units, such as audit or technology security.

The corporate center is typically organized into functions, and these functions may carry out all three roles. For example, finance may have a business performance role (providing analysis to support investment decisions), a shared services role (accounts receivable and accounts payable processing), and a compliance role (for example, Sarbanes-Oxley reporting). The same is true in the human resource, information technology, and legal functions. The conventional ways of grouping work by function can obscure the fact that each function is carrying out these diverse activities.

Size of Corporate Staff

You may have noticed in Figure 5.3 that many of the dimensions move in a similar pattern across the spectrum from single business to conglomerate. Business processes, compensation, and careers, for instance, all move from being common and companywide to differing by subsidiary in moving to a more diverse business portfolio. Size of the corporate staff, however, does not follow this pattern; it is small at both ends of the portfolio diversity spectrum.

The size of the corporate staff is small in a single business because the business is usually functionally organized, and those functions set the standards that the business uses. In such a company, most corporate roles would be redundant. In an integrated business that is pulling together a range of products and services into bundles and solutions, a larger corporate staff is needed to manage the coordination and conflicts that inevitably arise from trying to execute such a complex strategy. Related businesses have the greatest opportunity to share, so the corporate center is often large and plays an active role in finding commonalities to leverage. As we move to a mixed portfolio, the center becomes smaller again, but for a different reason. The business units have less in common, and there is less value that the center can add. Each unit must build and maintain its own unique set of capabilities. Finally, the conglomerate typically has a small corporate center focused mostly on financial management and selecting the leadership teams for each business unit.

In any organization, the corporate center tends to grow if it is left unchecked. A study by the Conference Board found that 85 percent of surveyed companies had reorganized their headquarters at least once in the past ten years. The most common reason was to reduce head count. But smaller is not necessarily better. For a company that has a related portfolio of businesses, a well-designed corporate center can provide advantage. The key is to put the right decisions and activities at the corporate level and the right ones at the operating unit level.

One of the few studies that has been conducted on the size of the corporate center has found wide variation in the number of staff at headquarters, ranging from fewer than 1 person in headquarters per 1,000 employees to over 890 headquarters staff per 1,000 employees. In general, the study found that the median number of staff in compliance roles was 4.3 per 1,000 employees and 14.4 per 1,000 in the business performance improvement and shared services roles (Collis, Young, and Goold, 2003).

Perhaps of most interest is the finding that there was no apparent correlation, positive or negative, between the number of corporate staff and business performance. This would seem to dispute current conventional wisdom that "lean and mean" is better when it comes to headquarters. Instead, these findings fit with the view that the size and role of the center need to be closely aligned to the business strategy. The more related the portfolio, the larger headquarters can be, the stronger its role, and the more likely that the center will use a combination of direct strategic and operational (in addition to financial) control systems to influence the activities of the business units and actively promote linkages among those business units.

Centralization and Decentralization

In the previous section, we looked at the issue of centralization at the firm level and discussed the role of the corporate center. In this section, we look at centralization and decentralization in more depth—in particular, at the strategic reasons for and potential problems of each. What is critical is to carefully think through the strategic reasons for either centralization or decentralization and to be aware of the predictable potential problems of each.

Definitions

When we speak of an activity or decision as centralized, we mean that it is carried out or made outside the operating unit affected. It does not necessarily mean that the activity or decision takes place only at the corporate level. The decision or activity could instead be centralized in another business unit. In this case, the activity takes place outside all operating units except the one in which it is housed. Centralization also does not automatically

FIGURE 5.4 **Centralization.**

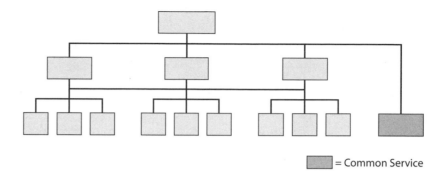

= Common Service

mean that all the people engaged in the decision or activity must be in the same physical location. A call center supporting a number of operating units may report to a central manager at another location who supervises the queue and staff performance and ensures that common processes and standards are used. The call center staff may be at multiple sites to serve different time zones, or they may even work from home. An illustration of what is typically meant by centralization is reflected in Figure 5.4.

Decentralization means that decisions or actions take place in the operating units. Although decentralization implies that decisions are made close to the point of service or where an action must take place, this is a relative term. For example, an operating unit manager may be frustrated that a particular decision must be approved by the regional office. Yet corporate staff from the company may perceive that same decision as being decentralized because it is not reviewed at the corporate level and each region may make the decision as it sees fit. A diagram reflecting what is most commonly meant by decentralization is in Figure 5.5. Notice that the service that was shared in Figure 5.4—the box with the darker shade—is now distributed among the various operating units.

The strategic reasons for—and associated problems of—centralization and decentralization that we discuss here apply when looking at a whole

FIGURE 5.5 **Decentralization.**

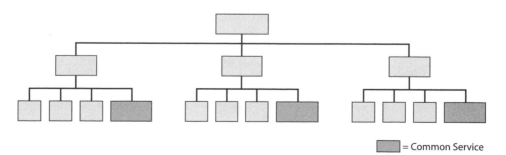

= Common Service

company of twenty thousand employees or a hundred-person unit within that company. The thought process is the same, and the feelings in favor of one option or the other are likely to be just as intense regardless of the level of organization.

Strategic Reasons for Centralization

Paradoxically, centralization makes the most sense for activities that are either tangential and of low value to the core business of the operating unit (for example, common payroll processing) or extremely important and high value (for example, global site selection). The arguments for centralizing an activity or decision are outlined below.

Embed Commonality

When activities are the same or there is some reason to do them the same way, making centralized decisions will support commonality, leverage scale, and reduce costs. If a product that is sold through different channels, business units, or geographies can be supported by the same information technology platform, then doing so will save development costs as well as ongoing maintenance and support expenditures. A decision made from the center can speed the institutionalization of best practices. These best practices do not need to be developed at the center; they may come from units that are innovating close to the customer. The role is for the center to recognize the practice, test or adapt it for broader use, and then embed it throughout the company where it makes sense.

Public Goods Allocation

In any organization, there are initiatives and costs that are not in the immediate interest of all units. These may be regulatory compliance programs, human resource initiatives, or enterprise technology systems that benefit some units over others. Such activities can be thought of as public goods that the business units would not choose to pay for if given the choice. In order to get this work done, the decision to move forward on such expenditures and determine how to allocate the costs has to be done centrally and at a high enough level to compel the business units to comply.

Specialized Knowledge and Experience for High-Value Decisions

Some decisions require deep expertise and experience. They may be high-value decisions, such as the purchase of a major piece of equipment or the selection of a location for a new facility, where the risk of making a mistake will be costly. Or the decision may require a highly specialized type of knowledge, such as securities law, that can be supported only at an enterprise level because the business units cannot afford to attract, develop, or support that level of talent.

Design of Decision Processes

Even for businesses with only loosely related business units, where judgments are best made at the local level, there needs to be a decision framework that has been developed at a higher level. For example, for a company that depends on the frequent introduction of new consumer products, a common challenge is how to phase out older models and discount them in such a way that they do not drag down the price of new products. The center might create a process used by all product management teams to price new products and manage the phase-out and discounting of the replaced product. The goal is not to create commonality for the sake of efficiency, but rather to ensure that the process is effective and the decisions made are well considered (Bright, Kiewell, and Kincheloe, 2006).

For a company making small numbers of large sales to other businesses, negotiating appropriate prices at the point of sale may be critical. The center can determine the criteria for pricing standards and create a pricing model. The center can provide boundaries within which the salespeople are free to use their judgment, with only exceptions outside those boundaries sent upward for evaluation. This leaves the majority of decision making close to the customer (decentralized), but the process and boundaries have been determined centrally.

Leverage

One of the benefits of size is gaining negotiating leverage with suppliers, partners, and even when lobbying the government. A bigger customer is usually a more important customer. And without central coordination, vendors may be charging different prices to different parts of the company. A centralized view of purchasing not only can result in more favorable terms, but can also avoid the problem of an operating unit that is committing to strategic partnerships that benefit the vendor, not the company. The key is to determine which purchasing decisions will benefit from coordination and which will not, and thus can be left to the discretion of the operating units. Centralization allows the firm to speak with one voice and be big when that is an advantage.

Unit Focus

The centralization of support activities and noncore processes allows the business or geographic units to focus on what they do best, whether it is product development, operations, or customer service. The centralized function becomes a form of internal outsourcing for the enterprise, removing the distraction of making decisions about activities that unit managers are not experts in, thus leveraging scale.

Common Culture After Acquisition

Common standards and processes expedite acquisition integration. When everyone is held to the same competency model or uses the same business planning process, then messages about what is important are consistent. After an acquisition, if the strategy is to integrate the new unit quickly, then making key decisions expeditiously and from an enterprise perspective will rapidly communicate and encourage the desired behavior and culture within the new unit. (Conversely, if the acquisition's value is directly tied to the divergence between its culture and practices and those of the acquiring firm, then centralizing decisions about its operations and making them conform to those of the buying company will likely destroy that value.)

Talent Mobility

Common standards and practices around core processes ease the movement of people across organizational boundaries and make rotational assignments easier. The more that basic management, business, and work processes are similar across a company's units, the more easily a manager can assimilate into a new position in a different operating unit and focus on learning what is different and new.

Outsourcing Preparation

An early lesson from the outsourcing experience is that companies with streamlined, efficient processes have had the most success with outsource providers. Those that handed over broken processes found the outsource provider could run them no better than the internal staff. The current practice in many companies is to pull together an activity considered for outsourcing into a centralized, internal shared services unit, reengineer and refine the underlying processes, and then hand it off to an outsource provider in clean condition.

Strategic Reasons for Decentralization

We have enumerated various strategic reasons for centralization: commonality can be cost efficient, allow units to focus, provide a culture that speeds acquisition integration, and make it easy to move talent across an organization. Centralization takes care of public goods issues, including the cost of specialized high-value talent. A top-down view allows intelligent choices about what decisions may need to be guided by a companywide framework, what purchasing decisions or vendor relationships can be centralized, or what processes could be integrated for greater effectiveness and efficiency. There are also strong reasons to leave decision making in the hands of those who are located in individual operating units, as we delineate below. Although we discuss fewer reasons for decentralization than we did for centralization, they are equally legitimate rationales.

Preserve Justifiable Differences

When the business units operate across a true variety of markets, customer sets, or business models and it is important to preserve and exploit these differences, then decentralizing decision making allows managers to respond to these unique conditions. For example, a company that expands into a new geography will be at some disadvantage against local competitors. For all the expertise and superior products it may possess, the expanding company will likely not know the local market and tastes as well as the established local competitor does. These local differences may be subtle but important. Knowing that butter is more often used for cooking in northern Europe than southern Europe is essential to customizing packaging, marketing, and price for different markets. Keeping decision making close to customers in order to pick up and react to this kind of information provides advantage.

Empower and Motivate

By giving employees and managers more control over the decisions that affect their work, using smaller groups with strong identities, and providing a clearer line of sight between actions, outcomes, and rewards, decentralization is considered to create a more motivating environment in which to work. Decentralization clarifies the relationship between individual choices and performance. As a result, it may be easier to measure and track results and create formal incentives linked to individual and team performance in a decentralized environment.

Speed

Not having to coordinate or confer with a centralized location or seek approval from elsewhere in the organization can speed decision making. A manager does not have to spend time influencing people in other parts of the company in order to make sure that decisions go her way. Often when decisions are made centrally, you find, as Caterpillar did, that by the time the forms had been filled out to request permission to discount a tractor in

Botswana and then sent back to Peoria, Illinois, where approval would be given, Komatsu will have come in and made the sale.

Innovation

When units have the authority to act on local information and adapt their practices to better meet their local customers' needs, ideas can be tested without having to conform to corporate standards, and innovations may be more likely to develop. The freedom to use judgment, be creative in finding solutions, and innovate is clearly a need for professionals in areas such as product design, engineering, software development, and law. As more work becomes knowledge centered and employees are expected to make good decisions on behalf of customers, a wider range of employees may benefit from the motivation that is brought by allowing them control over decisions and leeway to act creatively (Malone, 2004). In addition, when multiple teams work in parallel on the same problem, a richer set of alternatives will be generated. The scientific community commonly uses the power of having multiple minds work on the same problem at one time.

Talent Development

An argument for centralization is that common management practices make the movement of staff from unit to unit easier. Nevertheless, managers may gain a greater breadth of experience in a decentralized organization because they have been allowed to make their own decisions on management, business, and work process issues. By keeping decision making localized as much as possible within business units, decentralization can build the judgment and capability of a wider group of people in the company, thus adding to a firm's management bench strength. When managers do move between units, the experience is more like moving between different companies where there are different operating practices and styles. While this may slow assimilation, it can also provide learning opportunities.

Predictable Problems of Centralization

Most of the challenges of centralization that can be anticipated involve questions of control and authority. For operating unit managers, any activity or decision that is centralized represents a loss of control. Complaints about decisions they dislike that were made "back at headquarters" will be heard. Although some of these complaints can be dismissed, there are real dangers when the wrong decisions or activities are centralized. We examine these next.

Uniformity to the Detriment of Differentiation

In order to simplify the task of managing a wide array of businesses, executives tend to seek commonality across those businesses. But when uniformity is applied inappropriately, individual business unit performance can suffer. Competitors that appropriately optimize at the business unit level, as opposed to at the enterprise level, and are not creating unnecessary centralized overhead can gain an advantage. In addition, if management does not clarify what should be standardized throughout the company and what can be customized, conflicts over these issues can take up significant time and attention at all levels.

Uniformity at the Cost of Alternatives and Options

The desire to standardize and find efficiencies through common processes may stifle the generation of alternatives that comes from having multiple units solve the same problem for themselves. For example, a debate is taking place in the legal arena in the United States as to whether the patent courts should remain centralized into one court of appeals, as they have been since 1982. Legal scholars are now making the argument that the benefit of uniformity of application of the law has come at the price of a diminished capacity to adapt to and reflect the innovations in the business and technology issues that come before the court. These scholars believe that even in the court system, where precedent and predictability are honored, the patent court would benefit from a return to a system of multiple courts around the United States, so that more views and perspectives on patent applications could surface, fueling the innovation process and allowing the United States to retain its technological edge (Nard and Duffy, 2007).

Disconnect from Customers

Centralized decision making provides benefits when the decisions in question are so costly and important and require such depth of experience and expertise that they cannot be left to those who do not have a top-down view. But seasoned managers with a top-down view and highly specialized experts are also fallible. They may become disconnected from the needs of constituents and lose touch with real customers. Their business performance improvement role can quickly shift into a compliance role if the center begins to dictate and monitor rules that benefit the center, not the business.

Sclerosis and Delay

An activity may be centralized to save costs, but if so many of the decisions are left at a high level, the result can actually be added expense. A common phenomenon is that the business units become frustrated with the waiting time, inflexibility, or cumbersome processes of dealing with the center. The added time to negotiate all the different needs of the various business units and come up with a solution that satisfies everyone's requirements takes too long. As a result, the business units begin to build their own "stealth" staff units to provide the service in a decentralized manner. For example, a small information technology group is formed to build an application, or a few recruiters are brought on to do local hiring, and soon there is duplication of the activity that senior management had thought they had concentrated in the center on behalf of the business.

Unwieldy Size

The tendency for managers in centralized roles is to accumulate power and staff. Status in many places is still associated with budget size and the number of staff one controls. As a result, managers create work and projects that need resources; when those projects are done, the staff and budget stay if the situation is left unchallenged.

The desire to achieve scale can also create large, unwieldy organizations in both public and private organizations. For example, in the wake of the launch of *Sputnik*—the Soviet Union's unmanned space missions in the late 1950s—Americans were concerned that the Soviets were ahead in math and science education. Small high schools were consolidated in order to create the scale required to provide expensive advanced math and science programs. As a result, in the second half of the twentieth century, when the U.S. school population soared from 25 million to 50 million, the number of school districts decreased from 127,000 to 16,000 (Kleiner, 2006). Now there is a movement to create smaller schools and empower principals to make more decisions at the school level. In New York City, administrative and support services are still managed through regional offices to maintain scale. However, principals in high-performing schools are given autonomy to innovate in such areas as scheduling, single-sex education, and teaching methods.

Predictable Problems of Decentralization

Many of the disadvantages of decentralization are the opposite of the benefits of centralization, just as the dangers of overcentralization are the loss of the benefits of decentralization. Nevertheless, they are worth reviewing as a cautionary example for those occasions when the zeal to decentralize becomes strong, even though the business strategy may point to opportunities for at least some centralization.

Fragmentation and Duplication

Decentralization can result in fragmentation and poor communication within an organization, and may even result in units that work at cross-purposes. Duplication of efforts and resources may be useful to spur innovation, but it only adds cost when applied to commodity activities. For example, if two decentralized units have need for and buy the same software package separately from the same vendor, the opportunity to leverage the organization's buying power is lost.

Variation in Standards

Freedom to run a business in the way the local manager sees fit can yield improved responsiveness and adaptations to prevailing conditions. But if customers buy from more than one business unit, wide variations in standards that are not reflected in price (for example, in customer service) can alienate clients and have a negative impact on brand and reputation.

Limited Ability to Accomplish Enterprisewide Initiatives

Even in a loosely related or mixed portfolio, there may be enterprise management systems such as lean manufacturing, Six Sigma, talent management, or customer relationship management that can be employed across the units. When the business units are strong and there is no role at the center to identify these opportunities or make them happen, they are likely not to get done.

Innovations Stay Local

A corollary of the above point is that the benefits of the innovation that can result from decentralization can be lost if there is no management infrastructure to make it easy to share best practices or reward people for doing so.

The Centralization—Decentralization tool in the Appendix provides a summary of these decision factors.

Making an Explicit Choice

In some organizations, leaders have a strong philosophical bias toward centralization or decentralization regardless of the business strategy, and they are willing to accept the trade-offs of emphasizing one option to an extreme degree. For example, in the five years between 2001 and 2006, Morningstar, an investment research and advisory firm, tripled in size. Joe Mansueto, the CEO, felt that the company—although still a relatively small player in the industry—had slowed in response time and decision making. He decided the company was suffering the disadvantages of centralization without enjoying the advantages of size. He restructured the organization into seven business units focused on individual investors, financial advisors, investment databases, investment research, international, retirement plan advisory, and institutions. Although Morningstar is clearly composed of closely related businesses, each unit operates as a largely self-contained unit and is completely accountable for its own performance. As Mansueto puts it, "You can make the argument on paper that you need to be efficient and save head count, but sometimes it's a trade-off between cost and speed. If innovation is your bread and butter, you cannot fear redundancy" (Le Beau, 2006, p. 10).

Leaders may choose to go to one extreme or another to drive certain behaviors. In the Morningstar case, the decision to decentralize fully is being done with a complete understanding of the trade-offs. It is certainly legitimate to "overdo" it in one direction purposefully in order to get maximum impact, as long as the leader is aware of the likely consequences—both good and bad.

The challenge is that most organizations vacillate between the two extremes of centralization and decentralization, predictably overcorrecting the perceived defects of the previous model by swinging, like a pendulum, too far in the other direction. These changes often accompany a change at the executive level to a new leader who wants to make a rapid imprint on the business. Most organizations really want to gain the advantages of both centralization and decentralization, but that is hard to achieve, and the effort introduces complexity. So they go for the seemingly easier route, and more often than not, they wind up getting the disadvantages of both.

It can happen in the best of companies. In the summer of 2006, Hewlett Packard shut down its central global operations unit and announced it would assign functions like logistics, procurement, and marketing to its three business groups. The stated reasons in the company's press release were to cut costs and make the business units more accountable. When the global operations group was created just three years earlier, a press release at that time said the reasons were to gain annual billion-dollar cost reductions and create end-to-end accountability across the lines of business (Hewlett-Packard Website, accessed January 9, 2007, www.hp.com/hpinfo/newsroom/press/).

Getting the Best of Both: A Balancing Act

One's view on centralization and decentralization will be highly influenced by one's position in the organization. Managers in regional or corporate-level roles tend to see more that is the same than is different. The nature of their role is to find similarities, create common processes, and implement standards. The manager for Europe will have a bias toward synergy and will see opportunities for operating commonly. Conversely, a manager responsible for a country unit within the European region will focus more on how her territory is different from others and how the company's products, processes, and procedures need to be customized. As a result, every country manager in Europe will be able to show how his country is unique. In general, managers want centralization below them, so that they can have control and efficiency. But they also want decentralization above them, so that they can have freedom and autonomy.

Therefore, these design decisions have to be made at a fairly high level so that parochial interests do not overpower what is the best for the company as a whole. We suggest the following thought process for getting the advantages of both centralization and decentralization. This approach can be applied at any level of the organization where there are such choices to be made.

1. Start with the premise of decentralization. Assume that activities and decisions are best made by those who are closest to the situation and affected by the outcome. Determine if the current organizational structure, roles, and power support this premise.

2. Pull out compliance activities and decisions, if dispersed, and centralize them. The compliance activities are best undertaken by the center in order to provide independence (for example, for audit); in cases where an enterprise view and data access are necessary (for example, for regulatory reporting); to pool resources for public goods (for example, legacy system conversions); or to provide necessary oversight and approval to manage risk. This should be a fairly small number of activities and decisions.

3. Identify the shared service opportunities. The shared service work is that which is tangential to the core work of the business units and can be done more efficiently if pooled because of scale, or more effectively through sharing the cost of expertise. These shared services do not necessarily need to be moved to the center. Each could be provided by one business unit on behalf of others in a distributed model of support.

4. Identify the business performance improvement roles that might be played by the center, and ask these questions:
   - What capabilities are essential to our success and need to be guided rather than left to chance? Where will we need to make hard decisions about differentiated investments and resources in order to build capabilities?
   - Where can we benefit from commonality? What are the benefits we would expect to see? (Challenge whether you are seeking commonality for a strategic purpose or just to make the management task easier.)
   - What are the few critical business and management processes that should be designed and maintained by the center? Where do we need to set frameworks and provide decision-guiding data and criteria for the operating units? (Challenge yourself to be sure you are creating the systems and parameters for others to make decisions rather than moving decision making itself to the center.)
   - What information and knowledge needs to be shared? Where are there opportunities to make formal and informal linkages between the operating units?
   - Where are we confusing the need for coordination with the response of centralization? (Challenge whether you are using the lightest touch possible and whether you could accomplish the objective through lateral connections, such as networks, teams, and integrative roles.)

The Star Model™ for gaining the benefits of centralization and decentralization is shown in Figure 5.6 and discussed below.

FIGURE 5.6 **Star Model for Centralization—Decentralization.**

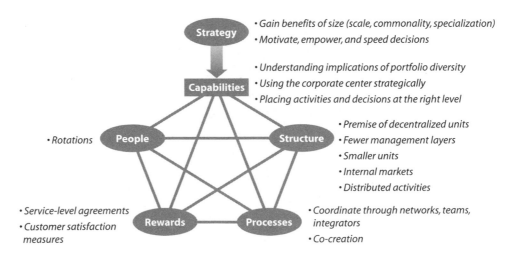

Structure

Once you have determined the role of the center, you can use the organization structure to gain the benefits of decentralization and then use processes and lateral connections to centralize where necessary. Following are a few structural considerations.

Number of Management Layers

One way to decentralize decision making in an organization is to delayer. The more management layers that exist, the more those managers will see it as their role to intervene and participate in decisions at levels below them. The broader the span of control a manager has, the less likely it will be that she has time to become involved in decisions. This is particularly true the more dissimilar the work is that is being managed and the more varied the set of decisions that need to be made. By delayering and increasing the span of control, mangers will be forced to create decision frameworks and focus on exceptions rather than become involved in making or reviewing individual decisions.

Size of Unit

In order to gain the motivational and accountability benefits of decentralization, many large organizations are creating smaller units that provide a clear line of sight between decisions and results. In addition, smaller units increase the surface area that brings employees in closer contact with customers, the business environment, and with other business units.

Internal Markets

In addition to smaller units, another way to get the benefits of decentralization is to create more profit centers in the organization supported by market-based transfer pricing. In many businesses, business units do not sell to external customers and have no natural measures of revenue. While transfer pricing is often derided for taking up a lot of internal negotiation time that can be better spent on other matters or as "trading wooden nickels" (since it is just a movement of money within the organization), it can be a way to create the internal market conditions that drive the levels of accountability, innovation, and motivation commonly found in an empowered, decentralized unit. By using prices based on external markets, such transfer pricing can also surface performance issues that can be overlooked when costs are allocated out. Of course, for such internal units, performance as a profit center is just one measure of success and should be balanced with relevant nonfinancial measures.

Sort Decisions

One way to get the benefits of both centralization and decentralization is to sort an activity into key decisions and determine which are best made close to the ground and which are better made from a perch with a broader view. This is a more refined approach than merely centralizing a whole function, role, or piece of work. For example, in a retail chain, each store can be thought of as an operating unit. Retail chains want to maintain consistency so that shoppers are reassured that they will have a similar experience regardless of the store they shop in. At the same time, stores often face differing demographics and purchasing patterns, and require differing product assortments to meet local differences. In the late 1990s, JCPenney operated in a largely decentralized manner, giving a large amount of discretion to store managers to determine products, promotions, and quantities. Unfortunately, although the store managers were empowered to respond to the local market, they did not have the data to forecast trends and tended to order too conservatively, ending up running out of popular items and having to take deep discounts on slow sellers.

In 2000, Penney began a successful turnaround by reclassifying all of its stores into seven clusters based on an analysis of demand patterns. They then resorted the merchandising decisions and changed the balance between those that were made at the store level and those that were made centrally. Central coordination was used to build relationships with product suppliers and leverage Penney's size. Store design, product mix, buying, and supply chain decisions are now made centrally. Local managers use their local knowledge and relationships with customers to make adaptations and test innovations (Rigby and Vishwanath, 2006).

Distributed Activities

When an activity is ripe to be provided as a shared service, there is often hesitation to make the shift to centralize it. There is a fear, based on experience, that along with cost savings often comes deterioration in service. The queue for new technology systems is longer, training programs are no longer customized, or it takes months to get a vendor paid. Often the problem is not that the activity is centralized; the strategic reasons for pooling resources to gain scale and expertise are still there. The disconnect comes from removing the activity from the operating unit. The managers of the shared service are no longer accountable to real customers, only internal customers.

One option to overcome this phenomenon is to use a distributed model of support in which different operating units house common services on behalf of the others, as shown in Figure 5.7.

FIGURE 5.7 **Distributed Model.**

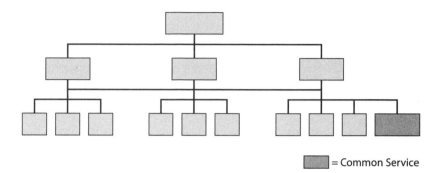

= Common Service

In this case, the activity is located in the unit that is already doing it well. This approach keeps the service close to the external customer, as the employees and managers are providing it for their own customers as well as for their peer units. It also creates interdependence among the operating units and mutual accountability for performance. For activities such as training, technology centers, and back office operations, this can be a viable alternative to moving the activity to the center. Deutsche Bank used this approach for creating management development programs. Rather than have a centralized function, each region took responsibility for developing a set of programs on behalf of the other regions. Each regional team involved colleagues from the other regions in the design and worked to create high-quality programs in order to ensure that the same standard would be upheld globally.

Processes

The frequent response to a legitimate need to centralize an activity or decision is to create a new accountable role and unit. However, this is often too drastic a move when standardization or coordination, rather than centralized control, is needed. The upheaval that accompanies structural reorganizations is rarely necessary to shift the balance between a centralized and decentralized model. Rather than make a structural change, you can use processes to help you dial up or dial down the intensity of lateral connections to gain the desired level of centralized coordination. A number of ways for using processes and lateral connections in this context are discussed below.

Lateral Connections

Lateral connections in the form of networks, teams, and integrator roles can be used to coordinate, standardize, and leverage in order to gain the benefits of centralization. Where coordination and common processes are determined to be beneficial, before moving decision making to a centralized group, consider if formalized networks or teams might not be sufficient to set standards, agree on processes, or review exceptions. This keeps the decision making close to the operating unit. We have used the topic of pricing as an example previously in the chapter as a function that requires centralized coordination combined with local flexibility. Rather than create a separate pricing function, an option could be to create a pricing governance council composed of leaders from brand management, production, sales, channel management, customer service, finance, and operations. This council can serve as a clearinghouse to resolve conflicts, refine and coordinate strategy, review pricing performance, respond to competitor moves, and identify pricing opportunities such as repositioning categories that cut across brands or channels (Bright, Kiewell, and Kincheloe, 2006).

If pricing could benefit from some cross-unit coordination but is not a high-value decision for your company—that is, if, when mistakes or inconsistencies occur, they do not have a big business impact—then the council could be a fairly informal pricing network. It might meet a few times a year or create an intranet site for sharing information. If pricing issues are more important, the council can be constructed as a pricing team, with a regular meeting and agenda, accountability for outcomes, and a charter setting out its scope of authority. Someone from marketing might serve as the team leader, or leadership might rotate. However, if the issues are not only important but also require data that are not easily aggregated or analyzed, or the amount of time that the cross-functional managers must devote to the team becomes onerous, a new role might need to be created. This pricing coordinator role would sit outside the operating units and would be devoted full time to pricing issues. The pricing coordinator might then hire a small team. Thus, a centralized pricing function is born. Figure 5.8 illustrates these examples.

The design challenge is to use the lightest touch possible to get the desired results and move up or down the lateral connections scale as the level of centralized power that is needed changes. There is no need to incur the added cost and tensions that a new central function creates if a network or team will do.

Coordinate Rather Than Dictate

The center's role in business performance improvement is best done through coordination rather than control. The few decisions that require centralized oversight and approval fall under the compliance role and should have already been identified. One of the major arguments against

FIGURE 5.8 **Lateral Connections for Coordination.**

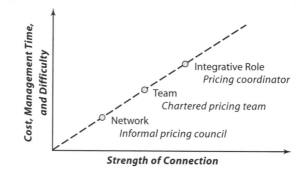

centralizing any activity further is that it stifles innovation. The case for decentralization is that it stimulates creativity and ideas by allowing more freedom for those working closely with customers or directly on problems that affect them. Sometimes it is precisely by not conforming to standard processes that innovations occur. In addition, multiple teams working on a problem in parallel may seem inefficient, but this method will generate more options and insights than one team alone. All of this is true, but by reconceptualizing the center from a locus of decision making and control to one of frameworks, facilitation, and coordination, the right amount of centralization can actually promote innovation. Two examples follow.

When China reported the first deaths in 2002 from what would become known as SARS (severe acute respiratory syndrome), the World Health Organization (WHO) mobilized a response: it asked a dozen or more labs around the world to work on identifying the virus, a common approach in science and medicine. As a central coordinating body, WHO did not direct the work of the labs or tell them what aspect of the disease each should be working on. It left that decision to each lab. However, WHO played an important role by facilitating the sharing of information and tissue samples among the labs. As possibilities were eliminated, this helped to focus the research. When less than a month later, SARS was finally determined to be caused by a coronavirus, it was impossible to say who had made the discovery, as the finding was essentially a decentralized group effort. WHO's role was to create networks among the labs—networks that most likely would not have arisen spontaneously (Surowiecki, 2005). In contrast, the search for the AIDS virus in the early 1980s was characterized by no such coordination and collaboration and resulted in bitter fights over credit between French and U.S. researchers. Such lateral communication and coordination mechanisms have to be designed into the system to work against the go-it-alone nature of organizational units.

In the business world, Procter & Gamble uses a process it calls "connect and develop" to meet the company's goal of having 50 percent of innovations acquired from outside the company. The identification of innovation partners and the actual collaboration occur in the business units. However, at the corporate level is a vice president for innovation and knowledge who has responsibility for building the research and development networks and managing the legal and training resources to support this approach. Research and development is not centralized, but the monitoring of productivity and the creation of the talent networks and mechanisms to support such a level of external collaboration are. It is carried out through a full-time senior executive who has companywide authority and accountability for enabling the program (Huston and Sakkab, 2006). In both of these examples, the innovation process is enabled by a centralized function.

Clear Co-Creation Processes

Most managers appreciate the value of involving the operating units with the center when new shared policies and programs need to be created. Yet many attempts at co-creation end up in frustration, often due to unclear processes and roles in how decisions are made. Trying to reach a consensus that works for all parties can be costly in terms of management time. One of the bitterest fights in the European Union was over whether to allow chocolate to be made with only cocoa butter (as the Belgian and French would have it) or to allow vegetable fats (as other chocolate-producing countries such as Britain and Denmark prefer). The battle to agree on a common standard in order to create a unified market was fought out in the courts, through lobbyists, and in the media, and lasted for over thirty years (CNN.com, 2003).

For the center to successfully involve the business units in co-creating shared programs and processes, a number of questions need to be asked at the beginning of any such undertaking:

- Who will make the final decision? Will it be made by the center?
- What is the role of the representatives from the operating units? Are they merely giving input for consideration? Can they veto the decision?
- If it is a group decision, must everyone reach consensus, or does only a majority need to agree? If consensus is required, how will the group avoid compromise?
- Will the dissenters be allowed to customize the product?

One solution is to gain agreement on core elements that must be the same across units, and then agree on the boundaries within which the local units can make adaptations to suit their own needs and preferences and how these will be paid for.

Rewards

One way to align the goals of an organization that is providing centralized services to the operating units is to have the operating units participate in the development of the centralized unit's plans, or at least agree to them. This brings the internal customer into the planning process of the centralized unit and reduces surprises.

Another way to gain alignment is to use internal market mechanisms. In their business performance and shared services roles, centralized functions are expected to perform like a professional services provider. This is accomplished through service-level agreements that specify such performance indicators as these:

- Response time
- Number and skill set of dedicated resources
- Cost of services and choice in services
- Quality standards
- Frequency of reporting and requests for information

These agreements should be negotiated with the purpose of creating as much transparency as possible between the centralized function and the operating units. The agreement may also spell out the responsibilities of the operating units, such as the format for requests, lead time, and review and decision-making roles.

The benefit of treating the centralized function as an external provider is not simply to hold it to market prices. An internal provider may actually be more expensive, but the company knowledge that the unit possesses or considerations around managing risk and protecting proprietary information may outweigh simple cost considerations. Rather, the benefit of a market approach is the introduction of a balance of power and clarity regarding the role each party has to play in making the relationship work. The service-level agreement can also serve as the basis for measures, particularly around customer satisfaction. The Relationship Health Check tool in the Appendix can be used as a way to measure the health of the working relationship between a service unit and an operating unit.

People

Most friction between centralized staff and the operating unit managers comes from a fundamental difference in perspective. Each sees the benefits of their role in the organization and downplays the inevitable and predictable problems that emerge. These conflicts do not emerge just between functional staff and line managers. They occur within the functions, between the centralized groups, and among the staff dedicated to the various business units. The primary mechanism for building understanding is to have some rotation between the center and the operating units.

To gain the benefits of specialization, an experienced core group of technical staff will always remain in the center. Many functional roles, however, are more general and can be filled using two- or three-year assignments. The benefit is an appreciation for the differing objectives and pressures of the two roles, as well as the creation of the relationships and networks that are so essential for bridging such organizational divides. For example, Marriott has begun to rotate even its specialized human resource managers (talent management, staffing, and organizational capability) into senior generalist roles, not just to expand their individual skill sets through new experiences but also to create a more coherent human resource leadership team. The result has been a noticeable reduction in framing issues as situations that pit headquarters against the field and a marked increase in speed of decision making. Through rotation, the interests of the organization are recreated in microcosm at both the center and the operating unit level, helping to align them.

● ● ●

In this chapter we have provided some guidance to solve the dilemma of having to choose between centralization and decentralization, and have given some suggestions for how to gain the benefits of both by using a range of organization design levers. This approach changes the role of most centralized units from an all-powerful locus of decision making to a coordinating mechanism that fosters knowledge sharing. The central body can still function as the arbiter of disputes and set overall policy direction. However, the shift in its role changes the organizational dynamic and moves the firm closer to the flexible, adaptable system that most managers desire without sacrificing quality and consistency.

Chapter 6

Organizing for Innovation

COMPANIES, PARTICULARLY THOSE that are publicly traded, face an imperative to grow. Wall Street demands yearly profit gains. In 2007, General Electric plans to add $15 billion of new revenue just to meet investor expectations, while Procter & Gamble plans to add $7 billion of revenue—the equivalent of adding a Fortune 500 business to each of their organizations (Colvin, 2006). Growth is also a way to attract and retain talent: good people want to work for an organization that is expanding and creating new opportunities.

An organization can grow in three ways. One is to acquire an existing business. An acquisition is usually made to expand market share or gain a new technology, process, or other competency. However, it is often difficult to realize the synergies that are anticipated from acquisitions, and many companies have found that they have destroyed the value of the acquired company through poor execution of the integration process or that the expected strategic fit was not there in the first place.

The other ways to grow are from the inside out, through what is commonly termed organic growth. One type of organic growth occurs when a company extends its core business by creating product improvements, product line extensions, and new generations of products. We refer to this type of growth as *sustaining* growth. The other type of organic growth depends on a more radical departure from a company's core business, in which wholly new products are launched into new markets. Such *breakthrough* growth is harder to achieve than sustaining growth, as it requires the organization to develop new capabilities while still optimizing its existing business. Breakthrough growth typically results from new ventures that often do not fit easily into the existing business model and may even cannibalize existing products or markets. But successful breakthrough growth also provides the promise of higher returns, and for some companies, it may be a required strategy in order to counter new players that are disrupting the rules of the underlying industry (Christensen, 1997).

Both types of organic growth depend on innovation. We define *innovation* in this context to be the process of turning ideas into commercially viable products and services. The poor success rate of the many mergers and acquisitions of the 1990s means that innovation and organic growth are once again strategies that many companies are pursuing. But continuous organic growth is not easy to achieve. A 2005 study found that 95 percent of corporate CEOs said that organic growth was critical to their success. However, over 20 percent said they were falling short on their objectives, and fewer than half believed that their capability to grow organically was improving (Mercer Delta, 2005).

Innovation is expensive, time-consuming, and risky. Successful innovation sometimes may seem to be somewhat random or dependent on a few big ideas, but it is reliant on neither luck nor strokes of genius. Nor can it be easily bought. A study of a thousand companies found no significant statistical relationships between research and development spending and sales, earnings growth, profitability, market capitalization, or shareholder returns (Jaruzelski, Dehoff, and Bordia, 2006). Rather, it seems that successful innovation comes from a set of complex organizational capabilities that allow companies to generate, assess, and develop ideas and then move those ideas into the marketplace. These are capabilities that are not easily developed or copied. As P&G's CEO, A. G. Lafley, sees it, "We have to grow market shares and move into adjacencies and create new categories of business. So the name of the game is innovation. We work really hard to try to turn innovation into a strategy and a process that's a little more consistent, a little more reliable, so that we can build a portfolio of innovations" (Colvin, 2006, p. 10).

This chapter is about the organization design issues involved in building innovation capabilities that can fuel organic growth. We focus particularly on the challenge of launching and developing new business opportunities alongside the core business and how to design the organization to support new success formulas, even when they are threatening to the old way of doing business.

The chapter is organized into three sections. The first focuses on strategies for innovation, from sustaining growth to breakthrough results, and describes how the organizational response differs depending on the strategy. Following that is a discussion of the capabilities that innovating organizations need to have. The third section, and the primary focus of the chapter, is a summary of organization design considerations to ensure that the organization is a facilitator of innovation instead of an obstacle.

Innovation Strategies

Innovation is typically thought of as something that applies only to products and services. However, innovations can also occur in one's business model or business processes. For example, Dell's innovation was to create a new process for manufacturing and distributing personal computers, not a new kind of computer. By providing direct sales over the Internet, the company circumvented middleman retailers and saved customers the costs of that channel. For commodity products, where developing new features or functionality is not possible or is not valued by customers, production innovation is important to increase supply chain efficiency and reduce manufacturing costs. For simplicity, in this chapter we discuss the creation of new products, but our discussion can also apply to process or business model innovation.

Types of innovation can be arrayed along a continuum, as shown in Figure 6.1. Regardless of the type of innovation undertaken, the organization is affected to a greater or lesser degree depending on where on the spectrum the innovation lies in relation to the core business. The farther to the right an innovation falls in Figure 6.1, the greater the innovation's distance is from the core business. Different organizational responses are required for each type of innovation.

FIGURE 6.1 **Innovation Spectrum.**

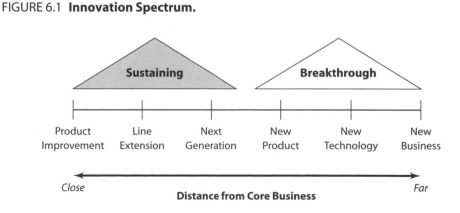

Sustaining Innovation

At one end of the spectrum are sustaining innovations. These build on and extend existing assets and competencies, such as manufacturing capacity, distribution channels, established customer bases and supply networks, brands, technology expertise, and industry knowledge.

Product improvements and *product line extensions* typically involve new features or new formulations of existing products. For instance, in packaged food, an example of a product improvement might be blended yogurt instead of yogurt with fruit at the bottom. A product line extension might be putting yogurt into tubed packaging so that no spoon is necessary. These types of innovations are usually carried out by the core business unit responsible for the product, and they grow out of customer insights and feedback.

Next-generation product innovation is typically found in technology-driven industries. The new product is fundamentally the same as the original product, but more advanced technology is integrated into the new product, upgrading it. The consumer then replaces the older product with the newer one. For example, as digital camera technology improves, cameras with more pixels replace those with fewer. As most computer users know, each new generation of Microsoft Windows upgrades the one before, eventually replacing it completely. Within a company that pursues this form of innovation, a discrete team may work on the next-generation product, but the work takes place within the core business and is closely linked with the marketing and sales functions that will sell the product, primarily to existing customers.

Breakthrough Innovation

At the other end of the spectrum are breakthrough innovations resulting in new products, new technologies, and new business models. These tend to have high-growth potential but carry more risk, as the markets for these new products are less established and the company has less experience in these markets. Most important, such innovations depart from the corporation's proven business model and its assumptions about what makes a business successful. Breakthrough innovations require the development of entirely new knowledge and capabilities.

Truly *new products* are built from new uses and combinations of existing technology. For example, nytimes.com is not just the *New York Times* newspaper on the Web. Internet technology is used to create a wholly new product that not only has different features but also an audience that is different (although it overlaps) from that for the print version. In firms that are pursuing a strategy of new product development, teams are usually pulled out of the core business. When the new products are launched, they are usually separated from the existing product and owned by a different product manager, although the new venture may remain in the same division among related products if the company is large. While drawing on the core capabilities of the existing business—for example, on the brand and content of the *New York Times*—the new product is managed separately, with a new set of goals and measures.

New technology innovation begins to require even more separation from the core business. This type of innovation tends to make the old technology obsolete. Unlike next-generation product development, which is planned for and managed internally, new technology may also come from outside the company. It disrupts the dynamics of the industry, often by radically changing existing pricing and distribution models. For example, high-definition liquid crystal display and plasma televisions will eventually destroy the market for cathode-ray-tube televisions. Similarly, light-emitting diode (LED) lighting is expected to essentially replace tungsten light bulb technology, and Internet downloads are threatening the traditional music business. To respond to threats from start-ups or competitors with such disruptive technology, a company may need to defensively launch its own new technology business alongside its existing core business.

A *new business* is one that is built on a totally different model from the core business. It may grow out of a disruptive technology. It may be a new business for the company, or it may even create an entirely new area of business in an existing industry, such as social networking sites have on the Internet. The new business may be related to the core business, but it is based on a fundamentally different set of business assumptions, practices, and metrics. The launch of low-cost airlines by the established carriers, such as Ted by United Airlines, represents such a move. A new business still has some strategic link to the core business and can make use of some of its expertise or assets, but in large part it represents a wholly new way of delivering a product or service.

At the breakthrough end of the innovation spectrum in Figure 6.1, the development and launch of new products and businesses are typically kept quite separate from the existing core business. Managing innovation in this realm is about creating the links that leverage the assets and capabilities of the core business—no matter how seemingly distant—while giving the new business enough freedom to compete with start-ups that are unencumbered by corporate parents (Govindarajan and Trimble, 2005). The right links are important not only during the creation of the new business but also as it matures, so that it can transfer capabilities back to the core. As General Motors found with its Saturn division, the company was able to achieve a fairly high level of success in starting up something new. But it was less effective in creating mechanisms to transfer back new capabilities to the old business to make it stronger.

Innovation Capabilities

Innovation requires a company to maintain a dual focus: optimizing products and processes to serve existing markets efficiently while at the same time building new capabilities. These two activities have been referred to, respectively, as *exploiting* and *exploring* (March, 1991). To survive, companies need to be able to recognize the need for new directions and begin heading toward those goals well before the current business goes into decline. This is easier to achieve if the business is in a relatively stable environment and can succeed by employing a series of sustaining innovations that can be carried out using its current capabilities. It is much more difficult and complex if the competitive environment forces a breakthrough innovation strategy that requires the continual development of new products, technologies, and business models.

Breakthrough innovation requires a number of capabilities. One is an end-to-end process, from idea generation to commercialization, which can turn inspiration into profitable products. Another key capability is portfolio management. Tough decisions must be made about which opportunities to invest in and which not to pursue. Finally, successful innovation requires the ability to balance protecting new ventures from the core business while finding the right linkages to leverage.

Innovation Process

Both sustaining and breakthrough innovations pass through five basic steps. The scope of effort and resources involved, of course, varies depending on where one falls on the innovation spectrum:

1. *Idea generation.* Ideas can come from customer requests, market research, or applied research, but not every idea comes from marketing or the lab. Innovative companies encourage and recognize insights that come from all parts of the organization.
2. *Concept definition.* This is the work of taking an idea and assessing the potential market and the resources required to develop it into a new product or service. The farther the idea is toward the breakthrough end of the spectrum, the more difficult it is to determine market potential.
3. *Project selection.* For many organizations, this is perhaps one of the most difficult steps. New ideas have to rise to an appropriate level

in the organization to be assessed strategically, and then funding commitments need to be made. Sometimes the screening and selection process is insufficiently rigorous, and the organization is overwhelmed by the activity generated by too many projects. For other companies, possibilities outside the established core are not recognized. Developing good criteria and evaluation processes that are neither too tight nor too loose and having the discipline to say no or to stop pet or political projects are essential but difficult aspects of the innovation process.

4. *Development*. At this stage, prototypes are created, tested, and refined. The output of this stage is a business case that must be evaluated and approved before the project moves into commercialization. The discussion of project teams in the section on structure below addresses some considerations for configuring and staffing teams for the development phase.

5. *Commercialization*. The launch of a new product or business comes at the end of the innovation process and raises many organization design challenges. The relationship that is established between the new venture and the core business should be determined by where the product falls on the innovation spectrum. Much of this chapter focuses on how to design the relationship between the two.

Having strong innovation capability means being good at all five of these steps. This is not to imply that innovation is a linear process. The idea generation phase alone is dependent on an iterative process of identifying problems to be solved and finding potential solutions. Rarely is innovation simply a "market-back" process, where marketing hands off a specification to engineering. Nor is it likely to be simply a "technology-forward" process, where research and development comes up with solutions, and marketing goes out to create customer demand. In addition, it is rare that one person is capable of both defining a need and creating the solution. Therefore, the innovating organization has to be able to encourage the interaction of divergent perspectives in the organization (and even beyond) in order to mesh the ideas and skills that will result in workable ideas (Galbraith, 1982).

Even when workable innovations are produced, many get stuck in the development phase. Management time and company resources may not be directed toward the most promising ideas because of unfocused and scattered efforts. Sometimes organizational inertia or a reluctance to look beyond the success of the current business blocks ideas from turning into profitable ventures. For example, although Kodak essentially invented the digital camera in 1975 and amassed a thousand patents for the technology, it did not aggressively enter the market until it was forced to by competitors in 2001. In the meantime, it tried not to undermine its flagship film business by promoting hybrid cameras. Innovations that are developed as defensive moves rarely gain the same organizational momentum as those that are seen as winning plays.

Portfolio Management

Few organizations suffer from a lack of ideas and possibilities for future ventures and expansions. More often the challenge lies in sorting the ideas and choosing which ones to focus on, and then allocating resources to those with the most promise. Successful companies may try many ideas that will ultimately fail, but this does not mean that they employ a scattershot approach. Rather, they are clear on the criteria for strategic fit and focus time and resources on generating possibilities within those boundaries. Procter & Gamble centers its efforts on eight to ten core technologies in which it wants to be world class, and it continually pares down the number of new initiatives to focus on those that are likely to be most successful (Colvin, 2006). Innovations that are promising but fall outside these boundaries may be developed but then sold or licensed to other companies.

Portfolio management is not simply a stage-gate process to sign off on projects once they meet predetermined criteria. It is a leadership team activity that depends on the team's skill in risk assessment. The team has to find a threshold of confidence that will likely result in success, yet is not so onerous that speed to market for innovations is compromised. This requires a senior team that is knowledgeable about the whole business, comfortable with challenging one another regarding assumptions and attachments to projects, and yet willing to trust colleagues who feel strongly that an investment is warranted.

Balancing Separation and Linkage

For many businesses, the 1990s were characterized by a focus on efficiency, quality, cost cutting, and process improvement. Reengineering efforts yielded these improvements, but such efforts focused on exploitation of the current business, not necessarily exploration for the future. As process reengineering has expanded beyond manufacturing and operations into product design and development, sales, and service in an effort to bring the same level of discipline to these realms, some observers express concern that too much of a focus on driving out variation may reduce an organization's capacity for innovation (Benner and Tushman, 2003). Because exploration is fed by experimentation and variation, process improvements that direct resources and attention to the needs of existing customers may come at the expense of uncovering new opportunities and serving the needs of emerging segments or new customers.

It becomes senior management's role to balance this duality of optimizing the current business while fostering the innovation required for the future. O'Reilly and Tushman (1996) use the evocative term *ambidextrous* to describe an organization that is equally adept at both aspects. But just as important as being able to do both activities well is the ability to know when to separate and buffer new ventures and where to create linkages back to the core business. Like portfolio management, managing this tension is an executive task. It requires answering hard questions such as:

- Where should control be applied?
- Where should autonomy be allowed?
- When should short-term metrics be applied?
- When is it wise to have patience for the long term?

 The tool, Assessing Your Innovation Capabilities, can be found in the Appendix.

Designing for Breakthrough Innovation

The Star Model™ shown in Figure 6.2 summarizes the design considerations for successful innovation at the breakthrough end of the innovation

FIGURE 6.2 **Star Model for Innovation.**

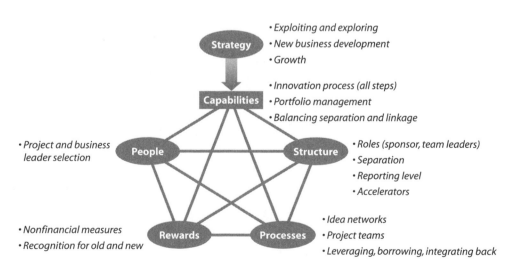

spectrum. We will illustrate the design considerations related to innovation with the story of MeadWestvaco's Specialty Chemicals Division, an organization that employed many of these ideas to build its innovation capability in the early 2000s.

MeadWestvaco Specialty Chemicals Division

MeadWestvaco is a $6 billion dollar U.S.-based paper and packaging company formed from a merger of Mead and Westvaco in 2002. A variety of by-products are produced from the paper milling process, including tree resin, lignin, and sawdust. A small division in the company that was originally part of Westvaco, Specialty Chemicals, is charged with turning these organic residues into viable products. Examples of such products include additives to improve the performance of asphalt, dyes, and inks and carbon filters formed from the sawdust and used extensively by the auto industry in pollution control devices. Specialty chemicals is a highly competitive industry, and products rapidly commoditize. Success is dependent on continually finding new ways to enhance the performance of current products. Ideas come from customer requests as well as from applied research in the laboratory.

The Specialty Chemicals Division (SCD) consists of approximately eight hundred people based in the southeastern United States, which is where most of MeadWestvaco's paper mills are located. After rapid growth in the 1980s, SCD's annual revenues leveled off between 1995 and 2003, which created a number of problems. With the merger, SCD became a very small part of MeadWestvaco and faced corporate pressure to contribute more. In addition, it needed to grow in order to become a larger player in the industry and attract new clients. Finally, its stagnation was hurting career and development opportunities for staff, many of them highly trained chemists and engineers.

In 2003, in order to underscore the need for breakthrough rather than incremental growth, new SCD leadership set an ambitious revenue goal for the division. It set a strategy of strengthening the division's core markets and managing its commodity products for cost, but it also set a goal to grow by building new product platforms in selected high-potential markets. An assessment at the time concluded that the barrier to growth was not a lack of talent, ideas, or potential markets. Rather, the division's leadership concluded that the organization was the obstacle. It was designed to optimize the current business and lacked a way to turn exploratory activities into profitable products.

FIGURE 6.3 **Historic Structure of Specialty Chemicals Division.**

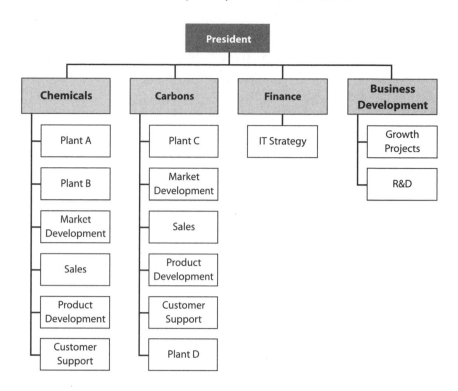

The SCD organization reflected a historical product structure with two businesses—chemicals and carbons—each run by a strong general manager with end-to-end control over the business, which encompassed market development, refining, operations, sales, and customer support. A small business development unit was responsible for long-term growth activities but had just a handful of permanent staff and was dependent on the business units to fund new projects. The 2003 structure is shown in Figure 6.3.

The assessment highlighted five common organizational barriers to innovation and growth.

1. Almost all SCD employees were located in one of the two business units. This classic product division structure created enormous focus on business unit activities but left few resources available to pursue SCD-wide initiatives. As a result, even when a project was started in the separate business development unit that reported directly to the president, it struggled to get funding and frequently ended up with whoever was assigned to work on it.

2. A result of having strong general managers for both chemicals and carbons was that the SCD operated like a holding company. Each business line had complete autonomy. The leadership team, composed of the heads

of each unit and the president, operated on the assumption that the business unit general managers had the best and most complete knowledge of their businesses and that others would have little to offer. The dominant relationships were between the leaders of each area—carbons, chemicals, finance, business development—and the president of SCD rather than laterally across the leadership team. The prevailing attitude was, "You stay out of my business, and I'll stay out of yours." As a result, there was little to talk about at leadership team meetings and little dialogue about the overall direction of the division.

3. The metrics in place failed to reward patience. Each of the two business units was under pressure to produce quarterly results, encouraging them to put resources into satisfying current customers rather than pursuing new markets. As a result, although each of SCD's business units was profitable, the division overall was not growing.

4. The four plants and the operations associated with them were embedded in the business units. Priority was given to current customer orders, reducing capacity for long-term projects, small runs, and experiments. No one except for the two general business managers had authority to change these priorities or push for their reexamination.

5. The research function, although nominally located in Business Development, was controlled by funding from the business units. Like the employees working in the plants, these Ph.D. chemists in research were frequently tied up working on incrementally new formulations of existing products rather than on the type of applied research that might lead to true innovations.

Using the framework of the Star Model, we discuss how SCD addressed these barriers through organization redesign.

Structure

Different innovation strategies require different structures. Figure 6.4 shows the range of options that correlate to the strategies. Innovations that we have characterized as sustaining tend to be managed in the product's business unit. Even when a new product team is formed to extend the product line or develop next-generation features, the activities are typically under the purview of the existing product manager, and activities are highly integrated with those of the existing product line. Marketing, sales, and brand management for the existing product plan the market positioning of the new initiative and the repositioning or phase-out of the old.

Breakthrough strategies require a higher degree of separation from the core business during both the development of the new product and the

FIGURE 6.4 **Matching Structure to Innovation Strategy.**

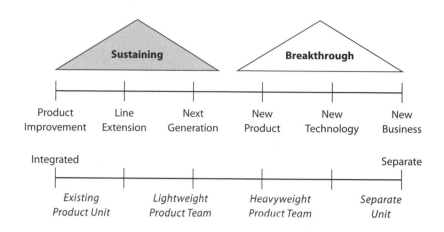

commercialization and launch phases. This can be accomplished through "heavyweight teams," which are described in the section on Processes below, or through the creation of separate units or even divisions.

SCD is typical of many other organizations in that it was quite successful in developing and bringing to market sustaining innovations developed in the business units. The staff frequently came up with new formulations and new applications for existing products, and these were sufficient to maintain market share. However, ideas that did not fit neatly into an existing product line, or would require a diversion of resources, or had no readily identifiable customer were generally put aside.

Structure by itself does not create innovation. However, the right structure creates the organizational conditions for innovations to succeed. Following are some structural considerations for achieving the right amount of separation and linkage.

Err on the Side of Separation

To foster breakthrough innovation and protect start-up ventures from the inertia of a core business, organizations should lean toward providing more separation during development and in the initial stages of commercialization, and possibly longer (Burgelman, 1985). By "separation," we mean creating a new business unit, with a product or business manager dedicated to the new venture, rather than having the new business housed within an existing business unit. Physical separation is also a possibility if there is a need to further detach the new venture from the dictates and culture of the core business. There are a number of reasons that organizational separation is prudent.

Not only is it unlikely that the same cooks will come up with a new recipe, but often the cooks need to put out of their mind the very recipes that made them successful in the past. Govindarajan and Trimble (2005) call this the organizational need to forget. Ironically, it is the organizations that have strong cultures and are disciplined and consistent in their use of common processes, both generally positive attributes, that can create the kind of managerial mind-sets that inhibit innovative thinking.

It is hard to be ambidextrous. Managing both exploitation and exploration is best left at the leadership team level rather than imposing the task on midlevel managers. The pressures on core business managers to meet current customer needs, optimize processes, and meet short-term financial expectations make it almost impossible for them to fully engage in exploring new opportunities at the same time. It may even be that the effort required to meet the needs of the company's most advanced and demanding customers blinds managers to making investments in potentially breakthrough opportunities that would appeal to an even wider set of customers (Christensen, 1997).

Separation allows development of a new business model when it is needed. For example, in the lighting business, tungsten and halogen products are typically on a three-year development cycle. The new LED technology evolves every six months. In order to accomplish this, most lighting companies have set up separate units for the LED business, allowing them to build the necessary concurrent engineering capabilities and partnerships with the semiconductor suppliers that are required by the new business model to meet these faster cycle times.

Initial separation provides options when the time comes to determine what to do with a new venture. If the launch is successful and the new product or business is related to an existing product line, it may be integrated back into a division. Or if the underlying business model is dramatically different from the existing product lines, it may be put into its own division. Other options are to form a joint venture, sell the new business, spin it off as a separate business, or even shut it down. All of these options are easier if the venture does not have to be disentangled from the core business.

Separation also brings visibility. While internal start-ups require patience and investment, they also need to be carefully scrutinized. As they are competing against independent start-ups and venture capital, the question needs to be asked repeatedly: Can they succeed in the open market? By pulling new business opportunities out of the existing structure, a greater degree of oversight and accountability can be applied. In addition, a tailored set of metrics that reflects differences in the business model can be used.

Often the initial market for an innovation is small. If left in the core business, the new venture will likely be overlooked by sales and marketing staff. Organizational separation and measures to reward "small wins" make worthwhile the pursuit and promotion of smaller opportunities that have the potential to grow.

Leverage Assets

If the unit is allowed to be too separate from the core business, however, the company may miss some opportunities. First, the new venture will fail to benefit from the advantages of the existing business. Entrepreneurial activity needs its own space in order to flourish, but it can be augmented and supported by the knowledge and resources that the company has built up in its existing businesses. Leveraging existing assets is the incumbent's advantage over the start-up. These assets may be brand name, sales force and relationships, manufacturing capacity, financial resources, or industry experience. Some analysts of innovation call this phenomenon "borrowing," and stress the need to be selective in choosing the few assets from the core that will confer advantage without overpowering the new venture (Govindarajan and Trimble, 2005).

The second reason to create linkages is to preserve the possibility that the new venture can be integrated back into the portfolio of an existing division, an approach that is more efficient for management. In this way, every new venture does not result in a new division, with the attendant increased management overhead cost. Reintegration also offers the possibility that the new venture can transfer its capabilities and technology back to the core and invigorate it. If the new venture is too isolated and is allowed to diverge too much from the parent company's processes, practices, and culture, then the task of fitting it back into the business will be considerably harder. Essentially, the company will have created a problem similar to that of integrating an acquisition.

The more the new venture is different from the core business's processes and assumptions, the more separate it should be. A business based on a disruptive technology or a business that will significantly cannibalize the core business may need to be completely separate. If it is related to the core but involves the use of new technology, entry into a new market, or a new process—qualities that can potentially feed back to the existing business—then more links are appropriate. Some questions to consider follow:

- Will the innovation enhance the existing competence or destroy or replace it?
- Will the new business cannibalize the sales of the existing business?
- How big is the opportunity? Does it need to be separate from the core business in order to be protected or made visible?

The tool, How Separate Does the New Venture Need to Be? in the Appendix provides further guidance in making this decision.

Accelerators

Rather than separate out new ventures on an ad hoc basis, some companies set up separate divisions to house and nurture these new products and opportunities. These divisions serve to accelerate the growth of the new business by giving it the advantages of separation. In addition, the manager of the accelerator unit (they are also sometimes called "incubators") can identify the appropriate links, if any, for each of the internal start-ups. For example, Nokia has a ventures organization in addition to its handset and network business units. It is used to test and develop ideas that are beyond the scope of Nokia's current businesses but within the overall company vision. The division takes ideas that involve new technologies generated in the businesses or new markets that have been identified and gives them a home. After the new venture is established, it is integrated back into the core business, becomes a new business unit, or is sold (Day, Mang, Richter, and Roberts, 2001). Cisco launched the emerging markets technology group to jump-start new growth outside its maturing network equipment business. The purpose of the Cisco accelerator is not only to develop and launch new products, but to create a playbook, which can be replicated, on how to bring ideas to market. An added benefit is that the internal ventures group may keep talent from leaving for Silicon Valley start-ups (White, 2007).

Reporting Level

One of the most important design considerations when pursuing innovation at the breakthrough end of the innovation strategy spectrum is the reporting level for the new venture. The unit, whether separate or housed in an accelerator, needs to report to the same level in the hierarchy as do other business units—or even to a higher level—regardless of its size. This ensures that the new venture is given the same consideration in resource allocation as the current businesses. If it is buried deep in the organization

FIGURE 6.5 **SCD Breakthrough Growth Structure.**

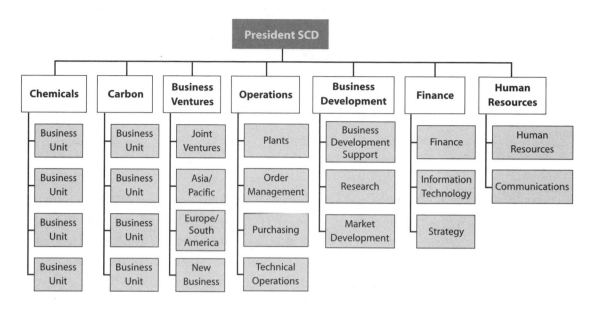

and is not under the direct purview of the executive level, the success of the venture is more likely to be hampered by lack of attention and resources.

SCD Structure Change

Our case example of MeadWestvaco SCD illustrates a number of these structural guidelines. After identifying the barriers to growth in the current organization, the SCD leadership team generated a set of design criteria to guide their organization design process. They identified these capabilities as critical to supporting innovation:

- Matching business talent with technical talent to bring new products and processes to market
- Leveraging multiplant capacity
- Managing the portfolio of initiatives at the leadership level

After considering a number of design options and testing them against the criteria, the leadership team restructured the organization as shown in Figure 6.5.

The new SCD structure, in response to the design criteria, had these key elements:

- Creation of a separate growth accelerator unit, called Business Ventures, for breakthrough-level innovations. This unit would include start-ups and joint ventures as well as exploration teams dedicated to business development opportunities in Europe, South America, and the Asia/Pacific region.

- Placement of the Business Ventures group at the same organizational level as the core chemical and carbon businesses (that is, as a peer to them).
- Creation of an Operations unit to manage all plant capacity and expansion on behalf of both the core and new venture businesses.
- Consolidation of all research staff and funding into Business Development so that research and development talent could be managed as a shared division resource.

An example of a new business launched by SCD is the development of a chemical process that gives inexpensive soft woods (such as pine or fir) the properties of exotic hardwoods (such as ebony and mahogany). This idea came out of the laboratory and provides the building industry with the cost advantage of allowing common wood to mimic expensive decorative wood; it may also have the benefit of potentially relieving pressure on the harvest of hardwoods in environmentally sensitive areas. SCD provides the technology for the process, but has created a joint venture with a small external firm that has commercial connections in the decorative wood business to manage marketing and sales. The Business Ventures group provides needed separation for this new business, which represents a completely new technology platform for SCD. In addition, the organizational changes made to Operations and Research now allow the Business Ventures manager to leverage these division assets on behalf of the new business, giving it all the advantages of SCD's technical expertise and plant capacity.

Processes

Process elements of innovation include the networks that serve to connect different perspectives in the organization and spark the insights that lead to new ideas; the project selection process that is an essential part of portfolio management; the cross-functional teams that are used to develop and launch new products; and the executive sponsor roles that serve to link and integrate the work of the teams into the broader organization's objectives.

Networks to Generate Ideas

The unit of innovation is not the individual genius working alone but rather the network that connects research and development, marketing, and production within the company, as well as the larger connections that employees maintain to customers and partners outside the company. These networks are built on a foundation of cross-organization relationships and social capital. (Techniques for building networks are discussed in Chapter Four.) Ideas often occur at the intersections of disciplines. A dispersed organization needs good tools and processes to support virtual collaboration in order to facilitate these networks and connections.

One of the primary obstacles to the generation of new ideas is the high cost of research and development. In many companies, research budgets are climbing faster than sales (Howe, 2006). As a result, leaders are looking not only for new ideas internally but also for new sources of ideas. Procter & Gamble has set a goal of having 50 percent of its innovations acquired from outside the company. The process of "connect and develop," as it is called at P&G, relies on finding partners directly, as well as using intermediaries (Huston & Sakkab, 2006). This technique, also called "crowdsourcing," links independent individuals who are in fields related or adjacent to the company's business in order to work on specific technical problems. Firms such as NineSigma, YourEncore, and InnoCentive serve as intermediaries, sending out technical challenges to independent scientists. For example, when Colgate faced the challenge of how to inject fluoride powder into a toothpaste tube without dispersing it into the air, it posted the need in this way. An underemployed engineer with a background in physics came up with the solution within hours. He was paid twenty-five thousand dollars for his efforts (Howe, 2006).

This emerging trend to broadcast problems when searching for innovation draws on norms developed in the open source software community, which is characterized by transparency, permeable access, and collaboration (Lakhani, Jeppesen, Lohse, and Panetta, 2007). Outsiders on the periphery of a problem often bring a new perspective to the issue. A problem may occur in one knowledge domain (for example, where the company has expertise), but the solution may be found in another (where the company does not). Many companies are large enough to begin applying such network approaches internally to find both insights and solutions at the intersections of their own functions or businesses.

The idea of crowdsourcing and informal partnering is made possible by the level of global connectedness provided by the Internet. One might assume that companies would be reluctant to share their research challenges externally and might fear that in employing such openness, companies would lose control over their intellectual property. However, consistent with our contention that innovation is a complex organizational capability, emerging research into this approach has found that exposing problems, and even solutions, does not give away the organizational knowledge needed to turn such information into profitable products (Lakhani, Jeppesen, Lohse, and Panetta, 2007). Generating initial ideas is only the start of the innovation process. The capability to turn such inspirations into profitable businesses is not easily imitated.

Project Selection

Innovation is characterized by high unknowns, occurring in business environments typically striving for predictability. One way to ensure that nascent ideas are not screened out too early in the process is to generate many ideas, knowing that many will fail, investing only enough to gain sufficient data to make further investment decisions. In this way, more alternatives can be seen relatively cheaply. An additional part of the project selection process is determining who will lead the project through to the next phase. Sometimes the person generating the idea and business plan may not be the best one to see it through. Part of the process is then matching talent to ideas.

Project Teams

Once a firm has gotten past the concept definition and project selection steps, cross-functional teams are often used to develop the new product or business initiative. Studies of successful innovation teams distinguish between two types, referred to as lightweight and heavyweight.

On a lightweight development team, staff remain connected to their functional areas while working on the project. Their functional manager continues to serve as the primary supervisor. If a number of people from each function are participating on the project, one person from each area may serve as a representative on a project coordinating committee, led by a project manager. The role of the project manager for the initiative is to coordinate the staff involved, inform the corporate leadership of progress, schedule key milestones, manage the project plan, and facilitate communication among the team. The project manager does not, however, have power to reassign people in the functional areas and has only minor input into the performance management process for them.

A lightweight team is often used at the sustaining end of the innovation spectrum. The product line improvement or product extension team may be drawn from the core group involved with the ongoing support of the product. Therefore, a large investment of resources is not required to refocus efforts on a new project. The team is familiar with the product and what is needed and is working within a familiar framework. The project is usually led by a midlevel project manager who works part time on the task.

A heavyweight project team is used for innovations that diverge further from the core product and business (Clark and Wheelwright, 1992). In comparison with a lightweight project team, the project manager is more senior, has more influence, and usually supervises the work of the team directly. In heavyweight teams, people may be pulled out of their functional units for the time span of the project and may even be co-located for a time. Typically there is a core team dedicated to the project for at least three-quarters of their time. Other team members may contribute part of their time or may be pulled in during specific project phases. Although dedicated and focused on the project, a heavyweight team is still working within the framework and practices of the larger business.

In the popular imagination, innovations are often brought about by a highly independent, skunk works team that goes off on its own, breaks all the rules, and comes up with a revolutionary concept. Some companies have found that they do need completely autonomous teams when attempting to come up with breakthrough products and businesses. Usually this occurs in companies that have such a strong culture of adherence to current process that any attempt to locate a team within the existing environment would constrain it too much. For example, Motorola's development of the popular RAZR mobile phone was conducted by a tightly knit team that worked largely in secret in a secondary facility. Their complete freedom from Motorola's process-oriented culture allowed them to use materials and techniques that Motorola had never tried before.

A danger of using completely autonomous teams, freed from usual organizational procedures, is that they are less likely to come up with ideas that can be folded back into the core business. Therefore, such teams should be used only when the strategy requires innovation that lies at the far end of the breakthrough spectrum. The reality is that most innovation development work takes place through lightweight and heavyweight teams, which are an unglamorous but effective way to get the work done.

Members of heavyweight and autonomous project teams often develop a strong team identity and commitment to project success. A strong internal team identity can sometimes lead to frustration with the rest of the organization if the company's norms and practices are perceived as constraints. Clear project team charters specifying operating boundaries and expectations are helpful to forestall any surprises. For example, the teams need to have clear make-or-buy guidelines, so that they do not unnecessarily bypass the firm's shared service and functional groups to expedite work. The teams should use the strengths of the existing organization (for example, IT platforms, purchasing agreements, or manufacturing protocols) where possible for consistency.

Executive Sponsor Roles

Each innovation project, once it passes the concept definition phase and is funded for development, requires an executive sponsor (Galbraith, 1982; Dougherty and Hardy, 1996). For sustaining innovations, the sponsor may be part of the product unit or division. For breakthrough innovations, the sponsor needs to be at the top leadership team level.

The executive sponsor serves as a link to the leadership team and champions the innovation. Executive support is needed because a truly innovative idea is never politically neutral. It may destroy the value of previous capital investments or undermine the decisions and products on which people have staked their careers. Even in companies where innovation is part of the mission and value statements, the actual process is often a political struggle—one biased toward those in the established business who already have control of resources and authority. Therefore, a sponsor is needed to defend and champion the team. The sponsor's role is to secure extra resources when needed, resolve boundary and turf issues, and manage the transition plans from development project to commercial launch. Just as important as defending the innovation is the executive sponsor's role in holding the team accountable for results and ensuring that they are working within the strategic framework. He or she is often in the best position to know when an initiative is not working out and can bring that information to the leadership team's portfolio discussions.

SCD Process Changes

In addition to the organization structure change, SCD employed a number of new processes to build the division's innovation capability: improved portfolio management processes, new guidelines for forming development teams, established linkages of development teams to the core business, and the enterprise management of research and development resources.

Portfolio management is a major focus of attention for the SCD leadership team. Growth is centered on eight platforms that represent the business and technical competencies of the division, as well as two geographic areas where the company is exploring how to expand its business. These platforms are used as a screen to ensure that innovation activities are directed and to avoid pursuing opportunities that are outside SCD's strategic boundaries. Over the course of three years, the team has built a culture of open discussion. Unlike before, any leader can now comment on any other leader's business unit or project. This comes from the understanding that any one of their products or businesses could become obsolete because of technical improvements made by SCD or its competitors. It has become a joint responsibility within the leadership team to make decisions about enterprise investments.

Heavyweight development teams are used for growth initiatives on SCD's ten platforms (lightweight teams in the business units handle product extensions). The leadership team chooses the staff of the heavyweight teams, which SCD calls "growth teams." This helps ensure that the right talent is allocated to the opportunity and that people can no longer be hoarded by business units. A business development director serves as the project manager, and a core group of functional staff (from operations, marketing, technical, and research) is dedicated to the project at least half-time. If the initiative moves toward commercialization, part of the team is formally pulled out of their functional roles and moves into the Business Ventures accelerator. They now become the core business team for the product. SCD may hire resources from outside at this point if it lacks people with the necessary commercial expertise. If the new venture is successful and is to be integrated into one of the primary business units, the whole team joins the business unit.

Growth teams are given wide latitude to pursue solutions that will produce results. However, they use the company's SAP and PeopleSoft IT systems, abide by the performance management processes used throughout the division, comply with MeadWestvaco's financial and accounting practices, and are expected to use SCD's manufacturing work processes. The executive sponsor has to agree to any deviation from these standards.

SCD made the structural change of pulling all research out of the business units and consolidating it under Business Development in order to ensure that research would be managed as an enterprise resource. In addition, this change allowed better development of technical talent through the broader variety of assignments that became available. However, when a researcher is placed on a growth team, he or she is directly managed by the project manager for the length of the assignment. SCD calls this a "temporal hard line," and it avoids the complexities of a matrixed relationship. When the assignment is over, the researcher returns to the Business Development unit, where the director of research retains responsibility for skill development and career management.

SCD also employs executive sponsors. While a project is in the development phase, the head of Business Development serves this role. If a project moves into commercialization, the head of Business Ventures assumes this responsibility.

Rewards

Metrics and rewards need to be aligned with the innovation strategy that is being pursued. They should also be calibrated to match the balance that the organization strives for between running and optimizing the current business and fostering innovation. The metrics and rewards to cultivate innovation should be crafted to provide the appropriate incentives for new ideas and new products.

Tolerating Failures

Many organizations list innovation as a core value, but many that tout innovation as a value do not tolerate failure, which is an unavoidable by-product of the risk inherent in innovation. In any industry, the ratio of failures to successes is high. The organization has to be willing to accept more failures in order to get more winners. Successful companies focus on measuring and rewarding the activities that result in ideas and collaboration across disciplines in the idea generation, concept definition, and development stages of innovation. Although they do not encourage unnecessary risk, these companies make sure that they do not create a culture where people fear that they will be punished for working on a project that fails. In addition, they not only allow but actively encourage the networking that so often brings together the perspectives that lead to new thinking.

Invention is not enough. If a company measures and rewards new patents, it will secure a lot of new patents, but they will not necessarily translate into viable products. Rather than waiting for ideas to emerge and then rewarding them, some companies make explicit the expectation that employees will spend time contributing to the innovation networks that spark insights. As a vivid example, Google requires that employees spend 70 percent of their time on the core business, 20 percent of their time working on related projects, and 10 percent on projects and activities completely of their choosing that could benefit the company. Google News, Google Finance, and Gmail are innovations initially developed by employees pursuing their own projects (Jaruzelski, Dehoff, and Bordia, 2006).

Measuring Results

In the early stages of commercialization, it is often counterproductive to use the same finance-based metrics that are applied to more mature business units. At best, financial projections can be treated as informed estimates rather than budgets to be met. In the existing business, managers are rewarded for delivering on commitments. In new businesses, they need to be rewarded for learning and making the right adjustments. This is one of the reasons to keep the new venture separate from the core business. The focus on making adjustments rather than meeting imprecise goals leads to frequent planning for new ventures, sometimes on a monthly or quarterly basis. In this planning process, the focus is on analyzing trend lines and rates of change rather than on simple comparisons of actual to predicted results.

Patience is vitally important, as is the use of customized measures. At the same time, the new venture has to be held accountable for real results in the marketplace as a profit center. The role of the executive sponsor is to help formulate the metrics that the business will be judged by, balancing the opposing tensions of patience and rigor.

Motivation and Compensation

A challenge for firms pursuing innovation is how to motivate employees who are not working on new ventures. It can sometimes feel that one set of employees is responsible for business-as-usual and bringing in the money, while another group is working on exciting, high-visibility, glamorous initiatives.

This tension can be exacerbated if different compensation systems are used for the two groups. There are opposing views regarding how best to compensate those working on innovation-related projects. One view is that the company has to reward managers differently if they are taking the risk of launching new businesses. One reason for this is that the company may need to attract different talent. For example, internal Internet start-ups have to attract the same people who could work for firms with potentially lucrative stock options, so an established company has to pay in a way that neutralizes the difference.

The other view is that unless the new business is so different from the core that there will be no relationship between the two, different compensation schemes (including phantom stock option plans) serve only to divide the organization in an unhealthy manner. Divergent expectations, different cultures, and the resentment that different compensation plans can spawn make it that much harder to move people between the core and new businesses and increase the difficulty of successfully reintegrating the new venture. For example, Nokia pays people working on projects in the New Ventures accelerator the same as it does people in the core businesses of mobile phones and networks.

A further consideration is that when people join a start-up, they accept a lower salary and take a career risk in the hopes of a later payoff in stock. Internal staff working on new businesses are taking less personal risk in terms of pay or career. Therefore, there is little reason to pay them differently. Most internals are motivated by the opportunity to pursue an idea and see it through to realization. In general, it appears that compensation criteria should remain consistent unless the new business brings the company into a new industry where there is an external market pressure to compensate differently. In that case, there may be a need for some type of stock options for purposes of retention. However, these should not be confused with compensation for rewarding or motivating staff, for which the criteria across the firm should remain consistent.

SCD Reward Mechanisms

SCD uses the same approach as Nokia and employs a standard performance evaluation and compensation system across the division whether people are working in the Chemicals and Carbons business units or in the Business Ventures accelerator. The highest performers in the division, whether they are squeezing cost savings out of commoditized products or working on new endeavors, are managed as a group by the leadership team in terms of salary, performance, and career development. New venture managers are given no special rewards beyond the incentive of the experience of being able to follow an idea through from concept to commercialization. However, the leadership team is aware that working on growth projects is perceived by many as being a high-status assignment. They deal with potential tensions by publicly recognizing the important and real contributions of managers who lead the ongoing businesses. In addition, they have committed to honest career development conversations that make clear that not everyone will work on growth projects. Those who are best at running the day-to-day business are not given false expectations.

New ventures are given a profit-and-loss statement and are held accountable to a financial pro forma. The leadership team frequently reviews progress and makes the determination of whether to pull the plug on an initiative or to be patient and reinvest.

People

The primary question in designing people practices to support innovation is how best to staff development teams and new initiatives. Except for those in research and development roles, the other staff members on these cross-functional teams are typically pulled from their functional or operating units. Each team will need a unique mix, and getting the mix right is a management art.

Insiders or Outsiders?

Those who study innovative organizations disagree on whether breakthrough innovations should be led by insiders or by new talent recruited from outside the company. One line of thinking is that an insider, albeit one who is able to challenge the status quo and has an entrepreneurial streak, is the best choice. He or she will already have the internal relationships that can be used to build support for the new venture and negotiate for resources. An insider will also be able to identify which assets to use and which to bypass. One study found that unit leaders from the inside were more successful than outsiders because they could better understand the opportunities for leveraging assets (Markides and Charitou, 2004).

But others suggest that if the company really wants to create something new, only an outsider can challenge the institutional memory and inertia that come with having participated in the success of the core business (Govindarajan and Trimble, 2005). For companies that have firmly established ways of working, the task of "forgetting" may be larger than the task of "borrowing," and it is best to bring in a fresh perspective to lead the new venture. In general, the nearer the breakthrough end of the innovation spectrum a new venture lies, the more likely it is that an outsider may be needed at some point to lead it.

A related question is whether to depend on volunteers or assign people to these new teams and business units. The advantage of volunteers is that they are motivated and can sell the idea to others. Especially if they were part of the early phases, their passion will keep a high level of momentum. Nevertheless, the leadership team has to be realistic about matching talent to the project. Those who are best at generating and championing new ideas may not be the best to see them through. Some mix is usually necessary.

Competencies

Regardless of whether the team leader or new business manager is an internal transfer or hired from the outside, researchers in the field of innovation agree that more than technical skills are needed for success (Kanter, 2006). Some of the essential competencies for innovation leadership include:

- Good relationship skills to make the links back to internal groups to leverage knowledge and assets and to gain acceptance for improvements generated by the new venture that might be integrated back
- Ability to lead in an ambiguous environment without clear measures or known outcomes
- Sufficient motivational skills to guide and inspire teams through difficult periods
- Ability to facilitate communication among scientists, business development, marketing, engineers, and other participating functions; ability to help specialists see the intersections of their work with others
- Quick to learn and make adjustments; able to plan, project, and analyze the root causes of trends

Building capabilities around innovation process, portfolio management, and determining the level of separation and linkage requires focus at every level of the organization. For example, in order to support its primary initiative of organic growth, General Electric has reoriented its famed executive development programs to focus on the key factors that the company believes support successful innovation: external focus, decisiveness, inclusiveness, risk taking, domain expertise, and team training (Colvin, 2006).

SCD People Practices

SCD makes staffing decisions for its development and commercialization teams based primarily on who has the best skills and most relevant experience. New venture managers may be drawn from an internal pool, or if the competence is new and not resident in the organization, they may be brought in from the outside. For example, on the softwood-into-hardwood project, two people were two hired externally: the general manager of the project was brought in from the joint venture partner, and a sales director was hired from the outside. Internal SCD research and technical staff rounded out the team.

The SCD leadership team recognizes that the division has stronger skills in R&D and technical areas than in commercialization, so it is willing to hire in business talent. At the same time, in order to develop commercialization skills, the teams are mentored by a steering committee of managers with strong commercial experience beginning in the development phase. In this way, more input is available on the business decisions at each step of the innovation process, and the team develops analytical business skills as they follow the project through from development to commercial launch.

Another way in which the commercialization phase is supported is through the use of an integration project manager. For the first ninety days of the commercial launch, the new venture business manager and team are assisted by a full-time project manager who works alongside them to provide added focus on building the new organization and accelerating the start-up activities. Borrowing from best practices used in integrating acquisitions, the integration manager works with the division's functional areas such as purchasing, finance, customer service, and safety to make the right linkages and ensure the support mechanisms are in place to get the new business off the ground.

• • •

The discussion in this chapter has focused on design considerations for the breakthrough innovations that fuel organic growth. Organizations pursuing an organic growth strategy need to be strong at all five steps of the innovation process and have a willing leadership team capable of making the hard investment choices required to manage a portfolio of new ventures in various stages of development. A further capability is the ability to balance the tensions between separating new ventures and finding the linkages that will leverage the core business assets. These capabilities are not easily developed or copied, giving advantage not to those companies that come up with the best ideas but to those that can turn ideas into profitable new products, services, and businesses.

Chapter 7

Conclusion

THE CHAPTERS of this book have focused on the concepts of organization design and how they apply to specific design challenges. But organization design is just as much a process by which to make decisions as it is a set of concepts or a body of knowledge. We close with a brief overview of some key points to keep in mind on how best to move toward implementing the organizational forms we have described.

An organization design change is not a decision. It is a *project*—a project to build organizational infrastructure, one that needs the same thought and discipline that would be put into a capital infrastructure or technology infrastructure project. Making good design decisions is important, of course, but the quality of the implementation often determines whether the desired change is realized. When thought of as a project, a number of implications become important for leaders undertaking a design process. In our work, we have found four areas that can have a significant impact on how an organization design project is implemented.

• *Using a decision framework.* Changes resulting from an organization design initiative will affect jobs, power bases, and careers—often those of the very people who are charged with making decisions about what now should be different, each of whom brings a distinct perspective to the project. Using a disciplined process and a clear framework helps to ensure that debates and decisions are based on comparisons of options against criteria rather than who wins a battle based on reputation, power, or persuasion. A clearly defined decision framework also sets a common language that decision makers can use, helping them to more quickly identify underlying assumptions and true areas of disagreement and allowing clearer communication of decisions to the larger organization.

- *Goals, measures, and milestones.* If an organization design change is to be a successful project, then it will need a set of goals and milestones. Often the large goals are clear—increase sales, market share, or profit margin, or reduce costs or time to market—but these outcomes are in many ways lagging indicators. While the strategy determines the overall goal of the project, the design criteria shape those broad goals into tangible and measurable milestones. Leaders can create qualitative and quantitative metrics from the design criteria as a way to measure and communicate how well the organization is doing in progressing toward its goal. How well the organization is building organizational capabilities then becomes a leading indicator of strategy achievement.

- *Project management.* Design is the fun part, but implementation is the real work. Many organization design projects fall short in sustaining energy and focus through implementation, as managers return to concentrating on pressing business issues. The danger is that as people fall back into old ways of working, the organization is stuck at an in-between stage, only halfway to the desired final state, as leadership attention gradually is drawn away from implementation. One way to avoid this problem is the use of a transition manager. Typically this role is given to a mid- to senior-level manager with good knowledge of the organization and the credibility to drive forward all of the work required for implementation. It is a time-limited role (six to eighteen months), usually with a seat on the leadership team, that is responsible for ensuring that momentum is sustained through the implementation process.

- *Change management.* In addition to a project plan, with all of the activities and milestones clearly identified, a successful change also depends on a well-thought-out and executed engagement plan, which focuses on managing the natural human reaction to change. When an organization is in a crisis, it is fairly easy to get people to see the benefit of doing things differently. But many of the organizational forms we discuss in this book will be undertaken by healthy and successful companies that are anticipating need for a new direction. This presents a more difficult environment in which to convince employees of the value of the change. We prefer using a participative process whenever possible to build engagement, an approach that has several key elements. First, communication is open and frequent. Leaders are clear at every stage about what has been decided, and they communicate the full story behind decisions rather than simply announcing them. Second, a range of employees at different levels from the affected units are involved in the process at different points in order to share their ideas and concerns. Such involvement helps build understanding and commitment to the eventual changes, but we also find that powerful and overlooked ideas often emerge from these conversations. Third, communication does not move in only one direction. At each major step in the change process, there is a clarification and feedback component so that employees understand how leaders arrived at key decisions. Particularly during implementation, these feedback loops provide vital early warning if changes are not working as expected or if the project is off track.

Keeping these four areas in mind when planning an organization design project can go a long way toward building understanding and acceptance. Creating broad understanding of and support for a change can begin at the start of an organization design project rather than being left as an implementation task.

One of the most common questions that we are asked is whether, once decisions have been made, they should be implemented slowly or all at once. Any number of factors can drive the need for an organization design project. In general, an organization needs to have an internal rate of response equal to the rate of change in the surrounding environment. Therefore, if the driver for change is a crisis of performance or a significant change in the competitive landscape, design changes should be put in place quickly. In these circumstances, with the right communication, employees will be generally understanding and open to the need for speed.

It is more difficult to make change when the organization is performing well and the change is intended to move a company from solid to exceptional performance. Although the design decisions, once made, may be compelling, and leaders want to move quickly to implement them, they may be better off evolving slowly toward the future state to ensure that capabilities are built and that employees and managers build the capacity to work effectively in the desired organization. One of the most overlooked factors in determining how fast to implement is the maturity of the management cadre. Many of the organizational forms we have discussed in the book require experience working together on projects, managing change, and working in collaborative structures.

However you decide to make changes in your organization—quickly or gradually—all of the design options we have discussed in this book require a skilled and seasoned leadership team in order to achieve success. As we have stressed throughout this book, organization design is a responsibility of top leadership. If you believe—as we do—that the quality of your organization is a strategic lever that can give you an advantage in the marketplace, it is imperative that the leadership involve themselves in and take ownership of decisions that may change how the organization is designed. Every organization faces unique challenges, depending on its size, industry, location, and maturity, among other factors. The challenges that we have addressed in this book, however, recur frequently and across all contexts. The tools that we have provided can serve as a starting point for you to tailor a design process that fits your organization's needs.

Appendix

Decision Tools

THIS APPENDIX CONTAINS the decision tools that are referenced throughout the book. Since a number of these tools are applicable to some or all of the design topics addressed in the book, we have organized them here according to how you might use them in practice. Figure A.1 illustrates the basic organization design process. The tools are grouped into four categories to reflect the major steps in the process: Strategy, Capabilities Assessment, Design Options, and Implementation. These tools are not intended to be comprehensive for each step, but rather represent some of the key decision enablers that we use in our work.

FIGURE A.1 **Organization Design Process.**

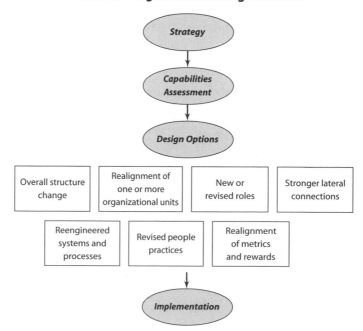

These tools are also contained on the accompanying CD-ROM in Microsoft Word format. Please feel free to use them and modify them in your organization design work. We ask only that you provide appropriate credit to this book. We would be happy to receive feedback on the book and the tools and to answer any questions you might have about using them. Please contact Amy Kates at AKates@DowneyKates.com with any comments and questions.

Tools in the Appendix

Strategy
    Customer-Centric Strategy
    Strategy Locator
    International Strategy
    Business Portfolio Strategy
Capabilities Assessment
    Developing Design Criteria
    Customer-Centric Capabilities
    Assessing Your Innovation Capabilities
    Are You Ready for a Matrix?
Design Options
    Structural Options
    Selecting Lateral Connections
    Country Autonomy
    Region Configuration
    Centralization—Decentralization
    Multidimensional Structure
    How Separate Does the New Venture Need to Be?
Implementation
    Responsibility Charting
    Relationship Map
    Relationship Health Check
    Spreadsheet Planning

Customer-Centric Strategy (Strategy)

Before embarking on a journey to organize around your customers, it is useful to test if your strategy is, or needs to be, truly customer-centric. Talk of customer-centricity may be confused with customer focus. Use this tool with the leadership team to test how strong the case is for a customer-centric strategy and how ready the team is to take on this change.

Rate your organization for each factor below: 1 = never/disagree, 5 = always/agree	1	2	3	4	5
Customer Readiness					
Customers buy multiple products.					
Customers buy/want to buy complex, customized products from our company.					
Customers complain about dealing with multiple salespeople or points of contact for service.					
Customers ask for presales advice.					
Customers ask for postsale service support.					
Customers have complex needs that require in-depth understanding and dedicated resources to uncover and respond to those needs.					
Customers are willing to pay a premium for advice, service, or integration, or some combination of all three.					
Organization Readiness					
We have strong relationships with many of our customers and understand their purchasing behavior.					
We have an understanding of why we retain customers and why we lose them.					
We work with our customers to design solutions to meet their needs.					
We know which of our customers are profitable.					
We have created/can create discrete customer segments.					
We have created products that are flexible enough to be customized for specific markets.					
We are experienced at configuring and reconfiguring teams to meet opportunities and service customers.					
We do/are willing to integrate external resources in our solutions when they are superior to internal products/services.					

Leadership Readiness					
The executive team has articulated a compelling strategic rationale for customer-centricity.					
There is leadership tolerance for and ability to manage complexity.					
There is leadership tolerance for the "overhead" cost of coordination and collaboration.					

Strategy Locator (Strategy)

The strategy locator is used to determine the level of customer-centricity that your organization will need based on your customer strategy. Use this tool with the leadership team to clarify what type of customer-centric organization you need to build.

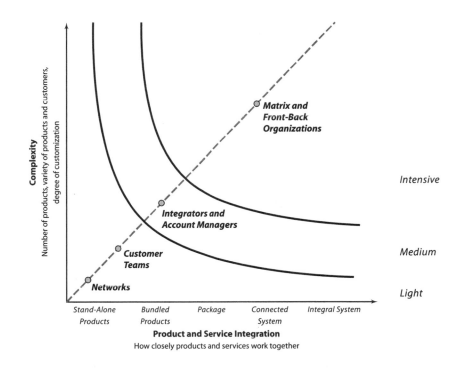

Process

1. *Determine the level of integration.* The horizontal axis measures the intention of your strategy regarding how your business will be offering products and services to customers.

Level of Integration	Examples	Where you are today	Where you aspire to be
Very low or none at all	Stand-alone products (perhaps sold under a common invoice)		
Low	Bundled products (all retirement products)		
Some	Package (investment banking services for an acquisition)		
Moderate	Connected system that allows substitutions (computer system)		
High	Integral system (car interior)		

Integration determines how customer-centric your strategy is. If you are low on integration and intend to stay that way, you can remain with a largely product-centered organization. As you move toward the right—that is, toward higher levels of integration—the more the internal organizational units will have to work together. They will likely have to be reconfigured in order to do so.

2. *Determine the level of complexity.* The vertical axis indicates how much your organization will have to change in order to implement a customer-centric strategy. The more complex the business, the more difficult it will be to manage the internal interactions. Therefore, if the business is complex and the strategy is customer-centric, new organizational forms and capabilities will be required. Use the table below as a guide to determine how complex your business is from this perspective.

LOWER COMPLEXITY   HIGHER COMPLEXITY

⬅————————————————————————————————➡

Number of products that will be integrated into an offering or solution

Fewer than 4	5 to 11	More than 12

Variety of underlying business models in the offering

Same business model (for example, all products)	Mostly the same (for example, all products with some post-sale service)	Mixed (for example, consulting, products, services)

3. *Determine the level of customer-centric organization.* Plot the two dimensions on the strategy locator. It is useful to determine where you are today and where you intend to be given your strategy.

Since the strategy locator is not an exact tool, the quality of the conversation among the leadership team is important. This is the time to be sure that assumptions are clear and articulated.

Remember to begin with the lightest touch. If you do not need a more intensive level of customer-centric strategy than customer teams, then do not jump to reorganize into a front-back structure. Even if you do determine the need for a medium or intensive level of application, you may want to conduct pilot projects with a light level of application to build and assess your organization's capabilities.

International Strategy (Strategy)

The international strategy tool helps to confirm your strategic direction and identify the capabilities needed to achieve it.

Strategy	Description	Organizational Characteristics	Capabilities Required	Current Capability Assessment			
				Absent	Weak	Moderate	Strong
Level 1: Export	Sell products and services abroad that are manufactured in home country	Sales units	□ Modify products for different markets □ Modify advertising and promotion for different markets				
Level 2: Partner	Create partnerships or joint ventures with local firms Increased level of assets outside home country Partnering is used as a means to gain market access in foreign country—may be required by government Usually a stepping-stone or learning platform	Varies depending on the partnering model used	All level 1 capabilities, plus □ Select partners/suppliers □ Negotiate with partners/suppliers □ Maintain multilevel contacts □ See situation through partner/supplier's lens □ Achieve mutually beneficial outcomes for firm and partner/supplier □ Manage change □ Manage endings				
Level 3: Geographic	Expand business by setting up complete operations Full-fledged business in one or more geographies Competitive advantages transferred from home country Integration achieved through home country functional units	Geographic division appended to home country structure	All level 2 capabilities, plus □ Transfer and modification of advantages from home country □ Integrate acquisitions □ Start-up operations □ Manage remotely □ Build and maintain local government and community relationships				
Level 4: Multidimensional network	Higher level of integration across geographies through global product lines or global customers Significant portion of assets outside home country, but home country still dominates and transfers advantage	Organized along multiple dimensions: geography, product, business, function, and/or customer	All level 3 capabilities, plus □ Integrate work across geographic, product, and/or customer units □ Balance power among multiple dimensions □ Measure and reward cooperation				
Level 5: Transnational	Significant portion of assets outside home country International units play leading and contributing role in generating advantages Home country is no longer the center or most important location	Peer model with a distributed power structure Multiple centers of capability based on where activity can be done best	All level 4 capabilities, plus □ Manage a distributed organization □ Communicate transparently across boundaries □ Measure and reward reciprocity and collaboration □ Build a team-based culture				

Process

1. *Confirm your international strategy.* Based on the table and the description in Chapter Three, determine what international strategy your business has. You may use different strategies in different parts of the world, so be clear about what part of the business you are referring to.

2. *Assess your current international capabilities.* Honestly appraise the current level of capabilities in your business using the table.

- Where are there gaps?
- Where are the strategic aspirations ahead of the organization?

Business Portfolio Strategy (Strategy)

The degree of relatedness among the business units in the business portfolio determines the role and strength of the corporate center, as described in Chapter Five.

Use this tool to analyze your business portfolio. It can be used at any level of the organization: business unit, division, region, or corporate.

	Business Portfolio	General Characteristics	Our Company's Characteristics
Very Related	Single business (Amazon, IBM, Dell)	One product line or very closely related product lines One business model is dominant	
	Integrated business (Procter & Gamble, IBM)	Solutions and packages Sell to only one type of customer (for example, consumers or other businesses) Either high-volume or high-relationship business	
	Related business (Nestlé, Time Warner)	Products and business models may differ across units but opportunity to share common technology, knowledge, and resources	
Not at all Related	Mixed portfolio (Disney, Exxon)	Common theme across units, but largely separate Stand-alone products and services—not integrated across units Some units sell to businesses, some to consumers Some units high volume, others high relationship	
	Conglomerate/holding company (General Electric, Berkshire Hathaway)	Little or no relationship across business units Different business models	

Developing Design Criteria (Capabilities Assessment)

Organization design is a set of decisions. You cannot make a good decision or guide others through the decision process without a set of clearly defined criteria. This tool will help you translate your strategy into specific criteria that can inform how you design your organization.

Design criteria allow you to:

- Translate the strategy into actionable, tangible statements
- Focus your organization's leadership on what is most important
- Make more objective decisions
- Document and communicate rationale
- Create a framework for making trade-offs
- Provide measures of success
- Focus on fulfilling the strategy—not just solving today's problems

Definition

We use the following definition of *design criteria:* the organizational capabilities that your business or unit needs to have in order to deliver on the strategy.

Organizational capabilities are the integrated and internal set of skills, processes, technologies, and human abilities created and managed by the organization that provide competitive advantage.

Design criteria allow your organization to do something; therefore, they should start with a *verb.*

To determine your design criteria, complete the following sentence: "In order to achieve our business strategy, our organization needs to be able to _____ better than the competition." Here are some examples:

- Create new products faster than our competitors
- Build depth of expertise, particularly in research and development
- Produce leading-edge products
- Offer a diverse product line
- Manage all steps of the innovation process
- Create common standards
- Become a low-cost producer
- Continually increase process efficiency
- Build long relationships with customers and increase our repeat business
- Deliver high levels of customer satisfaction

- Customize products at a customer's request
- Cross-sell and bundle products
- Create preferred sourcing relationships with customers
- Exploit multiple distribution channels
- Create alliances with other organizations in order to deliver comprehensive solutions

Guidelines: Writing Good Design Criteria

Guideline	Poor Criteria...	Better Criteria...
1. **Specific**: not too broad, measurable	Make the best products	Design products that meet the needs of our target accounts
2. **Differentiating**: not simply table stakes	Use technology effectively	Create technology solutions that support our clients in servicing their customers
3. **Actionable**: start with a verb	Be a good organization to work for	Build a reputation as a good community citizen in our key communities
4. **Future oriented**: aspirational	Reduce cost	Operate state-of-the art, cost-effective customer service centers
5. About **Capability**: not activity	Select the best people	Create a leadership pipeline to support global growth

Process

Design criteria are developed by the leadership team of the organizational unit. The discussion, debate, and surfacing of assumptions are important to ensure the criteria represent the most important goals to work toward during the design process. Since the leadership team is accountable for the organization's strategy and overall effectiveness, this activity cannot be delegated downward.

Design criteria are best generated over the course of two meetings. A facilitator is helpful to guide the activity and to sort and summarize the criteria. We suggest following these steps:

1. *Review and clarify strategy.* Even if the strategy has not changed, it is useful to review it before generating criteria. One group member should present the strategy, and then the group can discuss it. Test for clarity and agreement. As a way to begin generating capabilities, ask the

group such questions as, "What are the underlying assumptions in the strategy? Where are there gray areas? What do we have to do so that we can be better than everyone else in order to achieve this strategy?" This discussion may take a few hours and should not be rushed. The group needs to get to the point where the strategy is clear and agreed on.

2. *Generate design criteria.* Review the definition of design criteria, examples, and guidelines. Then break the group into pairs, and give each pair a stack of index cards. Each pair brainstorms criteria, putting each one on an index card. The criteria represent the capabilities the organization needs to have to deliver on the strategy. They should be written according to the guidelines. Each pair should generate as many criteria as they can, without making judgments as to which are most important. This is the end of the first meeting.

3. *Summarize and prioritize.* Before the next meeting, the facilitator or a group member sorts the cards into categories, combines similar ones, and then rewrites them as a list for review. There may be twenty or more options. At the next meeting of the leadership team, the group reviews the items on the list and then votes to select those that are most important. The goal is to narrow the list to no more than five. This will be difficult. The tendency will be to want to include more in order to capture all that the organization has to be able to do. The group needs to continually refocus on those capabilities that are differentiating. Be sure that the criteria are precise and clear. These will be the basis of the organization design process.

Customer-Centric Capabilities (Capabilities Assessment)

Each organization needs a unique set of organizational capabilities. The table lists many of the capabilities that customer-centric organizations need.

Process

First, identify the capabilities listed in the table that are most important for your organization—those that will be differentiating and will provide competitive advantage. Then rate how strong that capability is today. This will provide you guidance in where to focus your design efforts.

Light, medium, and intensive refer to the level of customer-centric organization that you are trying to achieve. Use the Strategy Locator tool first to determine which level of application your strategy requires.

	Customer-Centric Capabilities	Most Important for Us	Current Strength (from weak to strong)
Light	Analyze sales and profit data by customer		
	Understand the needs of target market groups, and establish strong relationships based on fulfilling those needs		
	Convert customer information and knowledge into market-leading products and services		
	Develop core products that are flexible enough to be customized to specific market segments		
	Deliver end-to-end (pre- and postsale) customer service that enhances the value of products		
	Build a sales support infrastructure that enables relationship selling		
	Manage matrixed customer teams		
	Collaborate at all levels across organizational boundaries to make profitable decisions		
	Offer and integrate outside products or services when asked		
	Create a cross-organizational planning system		

Medium	Use information and accounting systems that allow customer relationship management at all touch points		
	Manage complexity		
	Collaborate and share market and customer information across marketing and sales		
	Assemble and disassemble multiple teams against opportunities as they arise		
	Use and maintain a robust customer relationship management system		
	Select and develop account managers who can both collaborate internally and advocate for their customers		
Intensive	Create decision-making and conflict-resolution processes and governance structures to manage complexity and conflict		
	Manage the product portfolio and pricing to create profitable solutions		
	Deliver project management support throughout the organization to support team projects		
	Create pricing rules and market mechanisms for front-back interaction		

Assessing Your Innovation Capabilities
(Capabilities Assessment)

Successful innovation requires three primary capabilities. Use this assessment to determine where your organization's strengths and weaknesses are.

Capabilities	Current State		
Innovation Process	**Weak**	**Developing**	**Strong**
Encourage and recognize insights that come from all parts of the organization			
Assess the potential market and the resources required to develop an idea into a new product or service			
Select projects and ideas for investment using a rigorous set of criteria and an evaluation screen that is neither too tight nor too loose			
Say no, and stop pet or political projects			
Evaluate a business case on a range of qualitative and quantitative factors			
Create, test, and refine prototypes cheaply enough for evaluation			
Commercialize new products or businesses			
Portfolio management			
Sort ideas for strategic fit, and allocate resources as a leadership team			
Make adequate risk assessments as a leadership team			
Make investment decisions as a leadership team			

Balancing separation and linkage			
Make good decisions regarding when controls should be applied and when autonomy should be allowed			
Identify the key core assets to leverage for the new business			
Create the right level of separation to protect and shield the new business from the core			

Are You Ready for a Matrix? (Capabilities Assessment)

A matrix will be most successful if it is deployed in an organization with strong interpersonal networks and clear and disciplined work and management processes. Use this assessment to determine where your organization needs to build underlying capabilities that will help a matrix succeed.

	Weak ➡ Strong				
Interpersonal Skills					
○ **Opportunities to build networks and relationships:** — People are introduced to others in the organization and there are directories of skills, knowledge, experience — Forums bring people together across business and functions (training, meetings, seminars, intranet sites, etc.) — People are encouraged by their managers to spend time to build networks and relationships					
○ **Staff can use the tension created by the matrix to collaborate rather than compromise because:** — They understand from senior management the criteria for trade-offs — There are established rules for escalation — Parameters for acceptable risk have been defined and illustrated by example					
○ **Managers who share resources work well together:** — Expectations, objectives, and priorities are jointly set — Managers make the time to align their agendas and create clarity for the people who report to them — When priorities change, the managers resolve conflicts so that they neither "drop" onto the matrixed manager or have to be escalated up					
○ **A culture of teamwork, demonstrated by:** — Joint accountability, both when things go well and when they go wrong — Frequent giving of credit to others — Recognition of those who demonstrate collaborative behaviors — Sharing of information					
Work Processes					
○ **Clarity around how work flows across the organization:** — New work processes have been mapped with the actual people in the matrixed positions to anticipate and clarify gray areas and new ways of working					

	Weak ⟶ Strong				

	Weak				Strong
○ **Clarity around how information flows across the organization:** – There are formalized processes for how decisions are made, conflicts are resolved or escalated, problems are solved, and information is communicated					

○ **Clarity around roles and responsibilities:**
  – Everyone understands the expectations of their role and others' roles, the boundaries between roles, the purpose and expectations of the various new coordinating roles
  – Overlaps among roles are minimized
  – Gaps are minimized; all work is accounted for					

Management Processes

	Weak				Strong
○ **Governance mechanisms resolve issues quickly and at the right level:** – Councils, committees, and steering committees have been chartered and operate effectively to cut across the normal hierarchy and get the right people talking to one another about customers, objectives, conflicts, resources, and performance on a regular basis					

○ **Efficient and effective meetings:**
  – The right people are invited to ensure that perspectives along all dimensions of the matrix are represented when needed
  – Meetings are structured and facilitated to result in outcomes that meet both enterprise and LOB needs					

○ **There is minimum management "rework":**
  – When decisions are made they "stick," and are not reopened or revisited
  – Decisions are communicated and supported consistently by managers
  – Managers have built a high enough level of trust that decisions can be made by the minimum number of people necessary
  – There are upward feedback mechanisms that inform managers of how well they are doing					

○ **There is a clear process for objective setting and performance management:**
  – Performance appraisal that gathers relevant input and makes clear the weight of each manager's input
  – Peer feedback mechanisms that promote a culture of collaboration and measure "How easy am I to work with?"
  – The reward systems make "heroes" of those who demonstrate the values, and give incentives for team and collaborative behavior					

Structural Options (Design Options)

When designing an organization, you have a wide number of options to choose from to use as the structural building blocks. The table outlines some advantages and disadvantages of various options. Depending on your organization's strategy, the ability of the management team to deal with complexity, the makeup the your team, and other variables, some of these advantages or disadvantages may be more significant than others.

Option	Advantages	Disadvantages
1. Function Organized around major activity groups such as research and development, operations, marketing, finance, human resources	• Increased knowledge sharing within functions • Ability to build depth and specialization—attracts and develops experts who "speak the same language" • Leverage with vendors • Economies of scale • Standardization of processes and procedures	• Difficult to manage diverse product and service lines • Cross-functional processes cause contention • Different departments have different priorities; the customer's interest can get overlooked • Integration tends to occur only at the leadership team level
2. Geography Organized around physical locations such as states, countries, or regions	• Local focus and customization • Relationships with active local governments • Reduces transportation costs	• Difficult to mobilize and share resources across regional boundaries
3. Product Organized into product divisions, each with its own functional structure to support product lines	• Rapid product development cycles • Focus allows for "state of the art" research • Profit and loss responsibility for each product is located at the division level with a general manager • Positive team identity develops around product lines—clear line of sight between decisions and success of business	• Divergence among product lines in focus and standards • Loyalty to product division may make it hard to recognize when a product should be changed or dropped • Duplication of resources and functions • Lost economies of scale when functions are spread out • Multiple points of contact for the customer
4. Customer Organized around major market segments such as client groups, industries, or population groups	• Customize for customers • Build in-depth relationships and customer loyalty • Create more value-added product and service bundles and solutions • Avoid commoditized products and competition on price alone	• Divergence among customer/market segments in focus and standards • Duplication of resources and functions • Challenge of measuring customer profitability and identifying appropriate segments

Selecting Lateral Connections (Design Options)

No matter what type of structure is chosen, many activities require lateral coordination across departments. The amount of cross-functional coordination needed must match the level of collaboration that the company's strategy demands. Lateral processes broaden involvement in decision making and can yield better decisions, but they also have costs in time and effort. This diagram outlines the basic types of lateral processes and shows the relative amount of management involvement that each one requires.

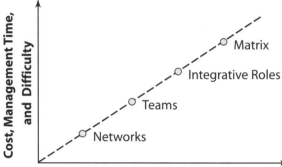

Type	Benefits	Drawbacks
Matrix	• Mirrors the reality and complexity of the client world • Enables more flexible utilization of technical depth • Forces employees to adopt a multi-functional perspective • Enhances communication and information transfer by creating multiple channels	• Dual reporting relationships can cause conflict • Decision strangulation—severe "group-itis" • Increased need for complex communication due to ambiguity • Employees may feel lost without a permanent "home"
Integrative Roles	• Creates an "account manager" to resolve conflict through mediation and negotiation instead of escalation • Creates formal point of responsibility for communication • Creates one point of contact for coordination	• Cost associated with hiring individuals for newly created roles • Adds a management layer • Difficult to find people with the right level of technical, influence, and relationship skills • High-stress position
Teams	• Utilize multiple organizational perspectives and resources for real-time problem solving • Pushes decision making downward • Can be a permanent or ad hoc part of the organization structure • Uses existing staff—does not increase headcount	• Requires investment of internally-focused time to build team skills and develop operating agreements • May waste resources if there is no clear charge or charter • Relies on healthy networks • Can be overused and diffuse focus
Networks	• Tend to occur naturally • People are eager to form them—provide personal as well as organizational benefit • Relatively inexpensive to foster • Relies on simple communication • Does not add levels or meetings	• Dependent on spontaneous interactions—may not be used consistently • Too informal to rely on for critical processes • Difficult to capture learning across the organization

Hard ↑ Easy

Country Autonomy (Design Options)

A key design decision for a geographic international structure is to determine how much autonomy each country unit should be given.

More autonomy allows each unit to make locally responsive decisions. It also may result in divergence from the practices of the corporate headquarters or home country and other geographic units.

Less autonomy will make it easier to integrate the country unit into a multidimensional network if that is desired. Too much control from the home country or corporate center can hamper the country unit from competing effectively against unencumbered local businesses.

Use the following guide to determine how much autonomy your country units need.

	Less Autonomy		**More Autonomy**	
Cross-border Integration				
	Yes			No
Is there intention/opportunity to coordinate operational activities across geographic units?				
Is there a strategic intent to manage products or customers across geographic borders?				
Activism of local host government				
	No			Yes
Is the local government active in managing the economy? Are there many specific local regulations?				
Does the geographic unit do business with the local government?				
Business portfolio of subsidiary				
	Diverse			Narrow
Is the range of products offered in the geographic unit by the business diverse or narrow?				
Cultural distance				
	Culturally similar			Culturally different
Is the geography culturally similar to the firm's home country or very different?				

Region Configuration (Design Options)

In a geographic international structure, the company adds country units. After there are about six units, they will become too numerous to manage as one group. At this time, the countries are typically clustered into regions for easier management. This tool will help make clear your logic behind these clustering decisions.

Process

1. *Confirm the rationale for how you are clustering countries.* Use the table to assess your current or proposed clusters to test the underlying logic for your choice.

Option	Description	General Benefits	Our Rationale
Proximity	Physically adjacent countries	Reduces travel time for the regional manager Shared market or cultural commonalities Ability to leverage manufacturing or distribution with reduced transportation time and cost	
Common market	Political and economic commonality	Reduced importance of country boundaries Ease of trade	
Development level	Same economic development level (per capita GDP)	Common management practices Common investments Sharing of learning	
Customer profile	Common customers or buying patterns	Shared market characteristics Learning and leverage across common customers	
Business life cycle stage	Development stage of business	Share learning Leverage common investments	

2. *Identify a possible secondary clustering logic.* You can cluster countries along more than one dimension by using networks, communities of practice, and teams.
   - What would be a logical secondary way to cluster for your business?
   - What are some of the ways in which you could link these countries together to gain the benefits of this dimension also?

Centralization—Decentralization (Design Options)

For each decision or activity that you propose to centralize (whether at a business unit, regional, or corporate level), be sure that the rationale is clear and the potential consequences have been anticipated and accounted for.

Use the following guide to test your thinking. This tool may also be useful when communicating the logic behind decisions made. Check all items that apply.

Rationale for Centralization

We are proposing to centralize this decision/activity because it will:

- ☐ Build shared culture and values and drive and maintain common standards (for systems, risk, behavior, and so on)
- ☐ Force cross-functional behavior between otherwise insular groups
- ☐ Allow economies of scale and more efficient resource allocation of the organization's "public goods" (such as IT services, purchasing, HR, marketing, finance, operations)
- ☐ Build specialized knowledge and allow efficient use of those resources with specific skills or deep expertise (for example, for high-value, high-volume, or complex vendor relationships)
- ☐ Aid in the institutionalization of best practices
- ☐ Leverage our size when buying or negotiating with partners, suppliers, or customers
- ☐ Remove infrastructure concerns so that the business units can focus on the business
- ☐ Allow common metrics
- ☐ Provide a way to bring together business units that have a lot of variety into more common ways of working (for instance, after an acquisition)
- ☐ Provide easier movement of top talent across business lines (through common business and management processes)
- ☐ Streamline processes in anticipation of outsourcing

Anticipated Consequences of Centralization

These are some of the likely consequences of centralization if it is not managed well, and this is what we propose to do from the very beginning to mitigate them:

- ☐ The center will lose touch with customers and begin to dictate rather than respond.
  What we will do: _____

☐ The business units will become frustrated with the waiting time, inflexibility, or cumbersome process of dealing with the center and will begin to rebuild their own "stealth" units, adding expense.
What we will do: _____

☐ We will have conflicts over customizing for the business unit and standardization at the corporate level.
What we will do: _____

☐ Decisions will be slow; added time will be needed to negotiate all of the requirements and come up with a solution that meets everyone's needs.
What we will do: _____

☐ "One size fits all" may satisfy no one; the result is a less-than-optimal compromise.
What we will do: _____

☐ The leader of the centralized function begins to build an empire (staff, budget, power) without accountability.
What we will do: _____

☐ In the name of efficiency, we force-fit units with different business models into the same mold.
What we will do: _____

☐ We limit the variety of experience that managers gain, since all units work the same way.
What we will do: _____

Rationale for Decentralization

We are proposing to decentralize this decision/activity because it will:

☐ Allow units to stay close to customers and markets

☐ Foster a culture of responsiveness, agility, and empowerment

☐ Increase the speed of decision making by reducing the need for involvement and approval from the center

☐ Allow more focus on innovation, because ideas can be tested without having to conform to corporate standards

☐ Foster better, more responsive customer service

☐ Increase motivation and creativity by keeping units smaller and the line of sight to results clearer for employees

☐ Preserve legitimate differences among the business units

☐ Allow multiple units to work in parallel on similar problems and experiment with solutions

☐ Provide managers with a wide variety of experiences in markets and environments as they move through the organization

Anticipated Consequences of Decentralization

These are some of the likely consequences of leaving this decision/activity decentralized, and this is what we propose to do from the very beginning to mitigate them:

☐ We will have fragmentation and poor communication within the organization, which may result in units working at cross-purposes.
What we will do: _____

☐ There will be variance in standards that will be costly or can alienate clients.
What we will do: _____

☐ We will have costly duplication of efforts and resources (for purchasing, program development, training, and so on).
What we will do: _____

☐ Important enterprisewide initiatives may slip through the organizational cracks because they are not clearly the responsibility of one unit.
What we will do: _____

☐ The benefits of innovation that can result from decentralization will be lost without a structure for sharing best practices.
What we will do: _____

☐ We will foster a "cowboy culture" of undisciplined decision making.
What we will do: _____

☐ If conditions in individual units differ widely, managers may not be prepared to take on other roles in the enterprise.
What we will do: _____

Getting the Best of Centralization and Decentralization

Start with the premise of decentralization. Then for those decisions and activities that are proposed for centralization, ask the following questions:

• Is this a high-risk decision? If it is made incorrectly at the local level, what is the risk?

• Is this a high-cost decision? Do the savings and other benefits of standardization outweigh the trade-offs in reducing local autonomy?

• Is corporate or regional involvement in this decision important for control purposes or for informational purposes? If it is for informational purposes, is there a way to gather the information without being part of the decision-making process?

- Is there a way to set the boundaries and criteria for decisions and then let the local managers determine their own course within those parameters?
- Can you use a lateral connection (informal network or community of practice, formal team, or integrative role) to achieve coordination without centralization?

Multidimensional Structure (Design Options)

In a multidimensional, multinational network, a key decision is the balance of power among the various dimensions. One of the most common networks used is one composed of geographic and business/product dimensions. This tool can aid in making these decisions and communicating the rationale behind them.

Process

1. Consider each factor and where your business is on the scale.

Factors \ Structure	Geographic Units (Cemex)	Geography Dominant (Black & Decker)	Geography and Business Matrix (IBM)	Business Units Dominant (Hewlett-Packard)	Global Businesses (DuPont)
Portfolio Diversity	Low	Low	Moderate to High	Moderate to High	High
Consistency of Markets (amount of adaptation needed)	Local adaptation	Local Adaptation	Local Adaptation	More standardization of products	More standardization of products
Customers (buying patterns)	Local	Local	Global and Local	Global and Local	Mostly Global
Product Transportability (opportunity to make in one place and sell in another)	Very low	Moderate	High	High	High
Host Government Role (as buyer and regulator)	High	Moderate	Moderate to Low	Low	Low

Opportunity for cross-border coordination (bracket spanning Consistency of Markets, Customers, and Product Transportability rows)

What is your dominant dimension?

_____

What is your secondary dimension?

_____

2. Determine how you will coordinate the nondominant dimension.
    *   What level of coordination is needed? Remember to use the lightest touch possible.

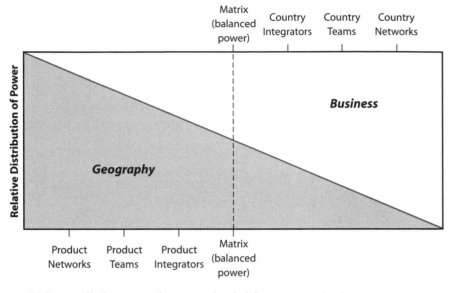

*   What will this coordination look like in practice?

_____

_____

_____

_____

How Separate Does the New Venture Need to Be? (Design Options)

Breakthrough innovations for organic growth often result in the creation of new business units. As discussed in Chapter Six, an important decision is how much to separate the new venture from the core business. This is not an either-or choice. In addition to separation and integration, there are the options of leveraging assets first and then separating the venture out, or separating it out first with the intention of later integration.

There are two sets of considerations (Markides and Charitou, 2004).

Likelihood of Conflicts

The possibility for conflicts is greater if the new business:

- May undermine the value of the existing business (for example, become a low-cost competitor or represent a replacement technology)
- Take away customers or change the service level
- Defocus employees or confuse customers with conflicting activities and priorities
- Move customers from high-value to low-margin products

Divergence in Business Models

Business models diverge when there is marked difference in:

- Customers and markets served
- Cost structures and revenue sources
- Distribution channels and supply networks
- Talent profiles needed

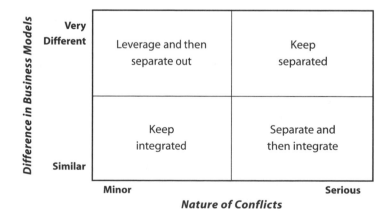

Responsibility Charting (Implementation)

After completing the design and staffing process, you need to ensure that employees understand the new expectations of how work will flow and how the various roles will work together. Use this tool to clarify levels of responsibility for key decisions. It is best used with the actual staff members who are working in the affected roles.

Process

1. List the key decisions in the numbered left column.
2. List the roles in the organization across the top row.
3. For each decision, assign a code as shown below.

R = Responsibility	Responsible for making and/or carrying out the decision. If more than one person is responsible, all have to agree to the decision.
A = Accountability	May not make the decision, but will be ultimately held accountable
V = Veto	Can veto the decision because it will significantly affect their role or work; different from the normal veto a boss has based upon position
C = Consult	Must be consulted and give input before the decision is made
I = Informed	Needs to be informed about the decision after it is made

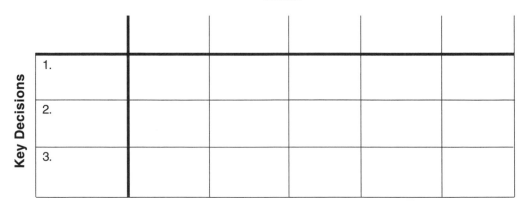

Roles

Key Decisions

1.

2.

3.

Guidelines

1. Avoid obvious or generic activities—for instance, "attend meetings."
2. Each decision should begin with a good action verb: for example, *evaluate, approve, publish, schedule, conduct, report, write, develop, review, record, update, inspect, determine, collect, train, determine.*

3. When the action verb implies a judgment or a decision (such as *evaluate, monitor, inspect,* or *review*), add a phrase to indicate the primary outcome. Example: "Analyze data to identify source of delay."
4. Place accountability (A) and responsibility (R) at the level closest to the action or knowledge.
5. There can be only one "accountability" per activity, except in a matrix, where two managers may share accountability.
6. Vetoes should be used rarely. They are often found in legal, compliance, or standard-setting roles.

Horizontal Analysis

If you find:	Then ask:
No R's	Will the job get done? Some roles may be waiting to approve, be consulted, or informed. No one sees it as their role to take the initiative.
Too many R's	This is decision-making by committee and will slow the process.
No A's	Why not? There must be an A. Accountability should be pushed down to the most appropriate level.
More than one A	Only in a matrix. And, even then, it is better to have only one. It will create confusion, because every person with an A has a different view of how it is or should be done.
Lots of C's	Do all the functional roles really need to be consulted? Are there ways to build trust so that fewer people need to be involved?
Lots of I's	Do all the roles need to be routinely informed, or only in exceptional circumstances?
Every box filled in	They should not be. If they are, too many people are involved—usually too many C's and I's.

	R		A		C			I	C	
	A			R	V	C	I			I
	C	C	R		C	C			R	A
	←								→	
	I	A		R				C		R
				C	R	A				C

Vertical Analysis

If you find:	Then ask:
Lots of R's	Can the individual(s) stay on top of so much? Can the decision or activity be broken down into smaller, more manageable functions?
No empty spaces	Does the individual need to be involved in so many activities? Is he or she a gatekeeper, or could management by exception principles be used? Can C's be demoted to I's, or left to the individual's discretion when something needs attention?
No R's or A's	Should this functional role be eliminated? Have processes changed to a point where resources should be redeployed?
Too many A's	Does a proper segregation of duties exist? Should other groups be accountable for some of these activities to ensure checks and balances and accurate decision making throughout the process? Is this a bottleneck in the process (is everyone waiting for decisions or direction)?

R		A		C			I	C
A			R	V	C	I		I
C		R		C	C		R	A
C		A			R		R	
I			R			C		R
				C	R	A		C

Relationship Map (Implementation)

Relationship mapping is a tool for identifying whom you need to build relationships with—upward, downward, laterally, and externally—in order to do your job.

A relationship map shows the most significant people in your work life—those whom you:

- Rely on to get work done
- Deliver work to
- Depend on for resources
- Depend on for support
- Go to for advice and counsel
- Rely on for information

A relationship map also helps to analyze your networks. A network is an invisible web of trusted connections. The challenge is to detect them, render them visible, understand their underlying structure, and leverage them to increase productivity.

In each organization, there are multiple layers of networks. An organization needs all of these networks to be healthy. Successful managers cultivate relationships within each type of network:

Work network	With whom do you exchange information as part of your daily work routines?
Social network	With whom do you "check in," inside and outside the office, to find out what is going on?
Innovation network	With whom do you collaborate or explore new ideas?
Expert knowledge network	To whom do you turn for expertise or advice about your work?
Career guidance network	To whom do you go for advice about the future?

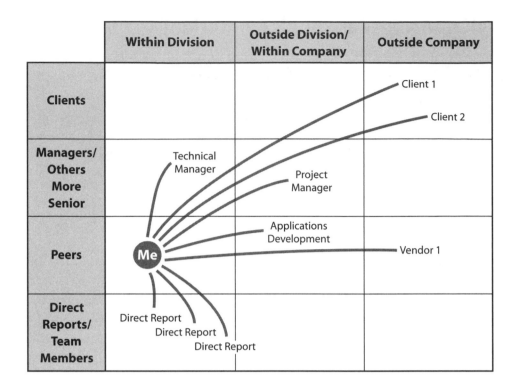

	Within Division	Outside Division/ Within Company	Outside Company
Clients			Client 1
			Client 2
Managers/ Others More Senior	Technical Manager	Project Manager	
Peers	Me	Applications Development	Vendor 1
Direct Reports/ Team Members	Direct Report / Direct Report / Direct Report		

Directions for Building a Relationship Map

1. Write the names of ten to twelve people with whom you should have or do have a relationship. Indicate, if you can, the type of network each is in for you (work, social, innovation, expert knowledge, or career guidance).

Name	**Type of Network**
1.	
2.	
3.	
4.	
5.	
6.	
7.	
8.	
9.	
10.	
11.	
12.	

2. Transfer the names and roles you identified in the previous step to the appropriate section of the relationship map that follows:

- Clients
- Manager

- Peer
- Direct report or team member (those you manage directly or indirectly)

3. Draw a line from the center circle in the relationship map ("Me") to each name.

4. Evaluate the strength of the relationship:

- Place a circle around the names of the people with whom you have a strong, solid relationship.
- Place a box around the names of the people with whom you need to build a stronger relationship.

Relationship Map

	Within Division	Outside Division/Within Company	Outside Company
Clients			
Managers/Others More Senior			
Peers	Me		
Direct Reports/Team Members			

Relationship Health Check (Implementation)

Individuals need to have healthy relationships. So do organizational units that are interdependent and rely on one another to get work accomplished. However, it is often difficult to initiate and structure candid conversations about the state of the relationship. Use this tool to determine what stage of cooperation the two units need to achieve in order to work well together. Stage 3 or stage 4 may be adequate. Then rate where the relationship is today. Use the rating to have a discussion around these questions:

- What would shared success look like? What would each unit experience in terms of results and behaviors from the other?
- What is going well? What needs to be communicated, celebrated, and reinforced?
- What needs to change? What specific actions will each unit take to ensure that these changes occur?

This discussion is best done jointly by the leadership teams of the two units.

	Stage 1	Stage 2	Stage 3	Stage 4	Stage 5
	No partnership/limited engagement	Coordinating engagements/ encountering frustration	Cooperation	Collaboration	True partnership
Vision/ Identity	"Us" and "Them," with little or no middle ground; based on negative	"Us" and "Them," looking toward a future "we"— building trust	Beginning to think as "we"; some level of personal connection exists	Achieving partnership, based in personal relationships	Us/we, almost transparent— part of the same team
Mindset/ Approach	Working together has not come up or is not feasible; sees little or no value in working together	Exploring partnership possibilities; sees other groups as a "necessary evil"	Work together to achieve our individual goals – quid pro quo	Work together to succeed as a team	Shares in both successes and failures
Strategy/ Purpose	Plans and decisions are made with complete independence	Plans are made behind the scenes and then discussed	Decision making may involve discussion with and consideration of other groups; when asked, groups share objectives or strategy	Decisions and plans are discussed with other groups; input and feedback is requested regarding objectives or strategy	Decisions and plans are discussed and made together – joint strategy development and execution
Communication	Little to no communication	Infrequent, but with communication modes being developed	Communication is as needed, to gain understanding of other groups' goals – tactically driven	Communication is the norm; both groups clearly understand the common goals; regular meetings with give and take	Communication is frequent, on-going, honest, and respectful
Trust	Conflicting interests or unawareness of common goals or mutual benefits	Aligning interests or are experiencing conflict in current interests	Still a focus on individual interests, but a degree of trust exists	Desire for mutual benefits; seeks out help and advice	Desire for a long-term partnership that is mutually beneficial; high level of integrity
Results/ Value Added	Lack of any significant engagement precludes any value added	Value could be added in the future	Value is added for a specific project with limited time frame	Value added for extended period of time	Continually adding value and "creating synergy"

Spreadsheet Planning (Implementation)

Whenever collaboration is desired across organizational boundaries, there are bound to be conflicts. Each of the units has its own set of priorities and measures of success. When they come together to solve problems, make decisions, or execute plans, there are likely to be disagreements.

Many of these conflicts can be anticipated and addressed as part of the planning process. But even when all scenarios cannot be planned for, the act of discussing how the organization will handle a situation ahead of time eases tensions when conflicts do arise.

Process

Spreadsheet planning is a simple tool. Any two dimensions of the organization can be arrayed along each side of the spreadsheet, such as product/geography, customer/product, geography/function, or customer/function.

Planning can be focused on revenue—"How much do we forecast for this customer in this geography?"—or customer service standards—"How quickly will we respond to particular service issues?"—or any other topic where there is likely to be disagreement or misunderstanding regarding goals.

The key to using this tool is to employ it as part of the planning process rather than wait until conflicts arise. It should be negotiated among the leaders of the units involved, and the agreements reached should be communicated to those who will interact and implement the agreements.

Ideally, each stakeholder fills in his or her own grid with suggested allocation of resources. Then the group comes together to compare, negotiate, and agree.

An example is shown below. In this case, the tool would be used to clarify the allocation of resources in a marketing function against customer segments.

	Direct Marketing	New Media Advertising	Promotions	Traditional Media Advertising
Customer segment 1				
Customer segment 1				
Customer segment 1				

Bibliography

Ashby, W. R. 1952. *Design for a Brain*. London: Chapman and Hall.

Avoiding the Cost of Inefficiency: Coordination and Collaboration in Supply Chain Management. 2006. Knowledge@Wharton. September 6. Available at http://knowledge.wharton.upenn.edu.

Bartlett, C., and S. Ghoshal. 1990. Matrix Management: Not a Structure, a Frame of Mind. *Harvard Business Review* 68(4):138–145.

Bartlett, C., and S. Ghoshal. 1998. *Managing Across Borders: The Transnational Solution*. (2nd ed.) Boston: Harvard Business School Press.

Bartlett, C., and S. Ghoshal. 2003. What Is a Global Manager? *Harvard Business Review* 8:101–108.

Benner, M. J., and M. L. Tushman. 2003. Exploitation, Exploration, and Process Management: The Productivity Dilemma Revisited. *Academy of Management Review* (April): 238–256.

Bright, J. K.; D. Kiewell; and A. H. Kincheloe. 2006. Pricing in a Proliferating World. *McKinsey Quarterly* (August). Available at http://www.mckinseyquarterly.com/article_page.aspx?ar=1841.

Burgelman, R. A. 1985. Managing the New Venture Division: Research Findings and Implications for Strategic Management. *Strategic Management Journal* 6(1):39–54.

Burrows, K. 2003. Presentation at the Duke University Fuqua School of Business, Durham, N.C., March 29.

Charles Schwab. 2006. Schwab Announces Agreement to Sell U.S. Trust. Press release. November 20. Available at http://www.aboutschwab.com/press/press-release.cgi?release_id=932940.

Christensen, C. M. 1997. *The Innovator's Dilemma: When New Technologies Cause Great Firms to Fail*. Boston: Harvard Business School Press.

Clark, K. B., and S. C. Wheelwright. 1992. Organizing and Leading "Heavyweight" Development Teams. *California Management Review* 3:9–28.

CNN.com. 2003. Britain Wins EU Chocolate Battle. January 16. Available at http://www.cnn.com/2003/WORLD/europe/01/16/chocolate.war/index.html.

Cohen, M. A.; N. Agrawal; and V. Agrawal. 2006. Winning in the Aftermarket. *Harvard Business Review* (May): 129–138.

Collis, D. J.; D. Young; and M. Goold. 2003. The Size, Structure, and Performance of Corporate Headquarters. Harvard Business School Strategy Working Paper 03-096. Available at http://papers.ssrn.com/sol3/papers.cfm?abstract_id=475162.

Colvin, G. 2006. On the Hot Seat. *Fortune*. (November 12):75–82.

Davis, S., and P. Lawrence. 1978. Problems of Matrix Organizations. *Harvard Business Review* (May–June): 131–142.

Day, G. S. 2006. Aligning the Organization with the Market. Unpublished paper. Available at http://knowledge.wharton.upenn.edu/papers/1315.pdf.

Day, J. D.; P. Y. Mang; A. Richter; and J. Roberts. 2001. The Innovative Organization: Why New Ventures Need More than a Room of Their Own. *McKinsey Quarterly* 2:21–31.

Dougherty, D., and C. Hardy. 1996. Sustained Product Innovation in Large, Mature Organizations: Overcoming Innovation-to-Organization Problems. *Academy of Management Journal* 39(5):1120–1153.

Duarte, D. L., and N. T. Snyder. 2001. *Managing Virtual Teams*. San Francisco: Jossey-Bass.

Forteza, J. H., and G. L. Neilson. 1999. Multinationals in the Next Decade: Blueprint, Flow and Soul. *Strategy + Business* 16(Third Quarter):13–27.

Galbraith, J. R. 1982. Designing the Innovating Organization. *Organizational Dynamics* (Winter): 5–25.

Galbraith, J. R. 2000. *Designing the Global Corporation*. San Francisco: Jossey-Bass.

Galbraith, J. R. 2002. *Designing Organizations: An Executive Guide to Strategy, Structure, and Process*. (Rev. ed.) San Francisco: Jossey-Bass.

Galbraith, J. R. 2005. *Designing the Customer-Centric Organization*. San Francisco: Jossey-Bass.

Galbraith, J. R.; D. Downey; and A. Kates. 2002. *Designing Dynamic Organizations*. New York: Amacom.

Ghemawat, P., and J. L. Matthews. 2004. The Globalization of CEMEX. Harvard Business School Case 9-701-017. Boston: Harvard Business School.

Gibson, R. 2006. Small Business (A Special Report); Package Deal: UPS's Purchase of Mail Boxes Etc. Looked Great on Paper; Then Came the Culture Clash. *Wall Street Journal*, May 8.

Govindarajan, V., and A. K. Gupta. 1999. Taking Wal-Mart Global: Lessons from Retailing's Giant. *Strategy + Business* 17(Fourth Quarter): 14–25.

Govindarajan, V., and C. Trimble. 2005. Building Breakthrough Businesses Within Established Organizations. *Harvard Business Review* 83(5):58–68.

Howe, J. 2006. The Rise of Crowdsourcing. *Wired* (June): 176–183.

Huston, L., and N. Sakkab. 2006. Connect and Develop: Inside Procter and Gamble's New Model for Innovation. *Harvard Business Review* (March): 58–66.

IBM. 1998. *Annual Report*. Armonk, N.Y.: IBM.

Iyengar, S., and M. Lepper. 2000. When Choice Is Demotivating: Can One Desire Too Much of a Good Thing? *Journal of Personality and Social Psychology* 6:995–1006.

Jaruzelski, B.; K. Dehoff; and R. Bordia. 2006. Smart Spenders: The Global Innovation 1000. *Strategy + Business* 45(Winter):46–61.

Kanter, R. M. 1995. The New Business Cosmopolitans. *Strategy + Business* 1(Fourth Quarter):66–77.

Kanter, R. M. 2006. Innovation: The Classic Traps. *Harvard Business Review* 84(11):72–83.

Kates, A. 2006. (Re)Designing the HR Organization. *Human Resource Planning* 2:22–30.

Kates, A., and D. Downey. 2005. The Challenges of General Manager Transitions. In *Filling the Leadership Pipeline*, edited by R. B. Kaiser. Greensboro, N.C.: Center for Creative Leadership.

Kim, J. J. 2006. Big Banks on Campus: Looking to Lure Lifelong Clients, Firms Dangle Plane Tickets, iPods; Worry over Credit-Card Debt. *Wall Street Journal*, September 6. Available at http://online.wsj.com/article/SB115749726344454406.html.

Kleiner, A. 2006. William G. Ouchi: The Thought Leader Interview. *Strategy + Business* 43 (Summer):125–133.

Kranhold, K. 2006. The Immelt Era, Five Years Old, Transforms GE. *Wall Street Journal* (September 11):B1–B3.

Lakhani, K. R.; L. B. Jeppesen; P. A. Lohse; and J. A. Panetta. 2007. The Value of Openness in Scientific Problem Solving. Harvard Business School Working Paper, No. 07-050. Boston: Harvard Business School Press.

Lawler, E. E., III, and C. G. Worley. 2006. *Built to Change: How to Achieve Sustained Organizational Effectiveness*. San Francisco: Jossey-Bass.

Lawrence, P. R., and J. W. Lorsch. 1967. *Organization and Environment*. Cambridge, Mass.: Harvard University Press.

Le Beau, C. 2006. Separate and Equal. *Crains* (June 12). Available at http://chicagobusiness.com/cgi-bin/article.pl?portal_id=47&mpid=47&article_id=25984.

Learning How to Profit When Customers Rule. 2006. *Strategy + Business* 44(Autumn): SS2–SS5. Available at http://www.strategy-business.com/sas-article/06318?pg=0.

Lin, N. 2001. *Social Capital: A Theory of Social Structure and Action.* Cambridge: Cambridge University Press.

Malone, T. W. 2004. *The Future of Work: How the New Order of Business Will Shape Your Organization, Your Management Style, and Your Life.* Boston: Harvard Business School Press.

Mann, M. 1998. After 25 Years, British Chocolate Nears Victory. *Independent* (London), May 31. Available at http://findarticles.com/p/articles/mi_qn4158/is_19980531/ai_n14157542.

March, J. G. 1991. Exploration and Exploitation in Organizational Learning. *Organization Science* 2(1):71–87.

Markides, C., and C. D. Charitou. 2004. Competing with Dual Business Models: A Contingency Approach. *Academy of Management Executive* (August): 22–36.

Mayer, R. C.; J. H. Davis; and F. D. Schoorman. 1995. An Integrative Model of Organizational Trust. *Academy of Management Review* 20(3):709–734.

Mercer Delta Organizational Consulting. 2005. In Search of Growth: Ten Practices That Create Organic Growth Champions: Executive Summary. Available at http://www.mercerdelta.com/organizational_consulting/mercer_download/MD_Growth_Survey_exec.pdf.

Milgrom, P., and J. Roberts. 1995. Complementarities and Fit: Strategy, Structure, and Organizational Change in Manufacturing. *Journal of Accounting and Economics* 19(2):179–208.

Nard, C. A., and J. F. Duffy. 2007. Rethinking Patent Law's Uniformity Principle. *Northwestern Law Review* 101 (forthcoming).

Neilson, G. L. and B. A. Pasternack. 2005. The Cat That Came Back. *Strategy + Business* 40(Fall):32–45.

"The New Organisation." 2006. *Economist* (January 21):Special Report.

Nohria, N., and S. Ghoshal. 1997. *The Differentiated Network: Organizing Multinational Corporations for Value Creation.* San Francisco: Jossey-Bass.

O'Reilly, C., III, and M. L. Tushman. 1997. *Winning Through Innovation: A Practical Guide to Leading Organizational Change and Renewal.* Boston: Harvard Business School Press.

Peters, T. H., and R. H. Waterman, Jr. 1982. *In Search of Excellence.* New York: Warner Books.

Pink, D. 2005. *A Whole New Mind.* New York: Riverhead Books.

Porter, M. E. 1998. *Competitive Advantage: Creating and Sustaining Superior Performance.* New York: Free Press.

Quelch, J. A., and H. Bloom. 1999. Ten Steps to a Global Human Resource Strategy. *Strategy + Business* 14(First Quarter):18–29.

Rifkin, G. 2006. Building Better Global Managers. *Harvard Management Update* (March):3–6.

Rigby, D. K., and V. Vishwanath. 2006. Localization: The Revolution in Consumer Markets. *Harvard Business Review* (April):82–92.

Roberts, J. 2004. *The Modern Firm: Organizational Design for Performance and Growth.* New York: Oxford University Press.

Rossotti, C. O. 2001. Customer-izing the IRS. *Strategy + Business* 23 (Second Quarter): Special Report. Available at http://www.strategy-business.com/press/article/17382?pg=0.

Selden, L., and G. Colvin. 2003. *Angel Customers and Demon Customers: Discover Which Is Which and Turbo-Charge Your Stock.* New York: Portfolio.

Shapiro, B. 2002. Want a Happy Customer? Coordinate Sales and Marketing. Harvard Business School Working Knowledge, October 28. http://hbswk.hbs.edu/item/3154.html.

Stopford, J. M., and L. T. Wells, Jr. 1972. *Managing the Multinational Enterprise: Organization of the Firm and Ownership of the Subsidiaries.* New York: Basic Books.

Surowiecki J. 2005. *The Wisdom of Crowds.* New York: Anchor Books.

Sy, T., and L. S. D'Annunzio. 2005. Challenges and Strategies of Matrix Organizations. *Human Resource Planning* 28(1):39–48.

Thorne, M. 2002. Leadership in International Organizations: Global Leadership Competencies. James MacGregor Burns Academy of Leadership Publications. January 11. Available at http://www.academy.umd.edu/publications/global_leadership/marlene_thorn.htm.

Tushman, M. L., and C. A. O'Reilly III. 1996. Ambidextrous Organizations: Managing Evolutionary and Revolutionary Change. *California Management Review* 38(4):8–30.

Vandermerwe, S. 1999. *Customer Capitalism: The New Business Model of Increasing Returns in New Market Spaces*. Naperville, Ill.: Nicholas Brealey Publishing.

White, B. 2007. Cisco's Homegrown Experiment; Slower Growth Forces Networking Company to Be Its Own Start-Up. *Wall Street Journal*, (January 23):A14.

Whittington, R.; A. Pettigrew; S. Peck; E. Fenton; and M. Conyon. 1999. Change and Complementarities in the New Competitive Landscape: A European Panel Study, 1992–1996. *Organization Science* 10(5):583–600.

Wilke, J. R. 1994. Digital Equipment Speeds Plans to Cut 20,000 Jobs, Takes $1.2 Billion Charge. *Wall Street Journal* (July 15).

Index

How to Use the CD-ROM

System Requirements

PC with Microsoft Windows 98SE or later
Mac with Apple OS version 8.6 or later

Using the CD with Windows

To view the items located on the CD, follow these steps:

1. Insert the CD into your computer's CD-ROM drive.
2. A window appears with the following options:

   Contents: Allows you to view the files included on the CD-ROM.
   Software: Allows you to install useful software from the CD-ROM.
   Links: Displays a hyperlinked page of websites.
   Author: Displays a page with information about the author(s).
   Contact Us: Displays a page with information on contacting the pub-
     lisher or author.
   Help: Displays a page with information on using the CD.
   Exit: Closes the interface window.

If you do not have autorun enabled, or if the autorun window does not appear, follow these steps to access the CD:

1. Click Start → Run.
2. In the dialog box that appears, type d:\start.exe, where d is the let-
   ter of your CD-ROM drive. This brings up the autorun window
   described in the preceding set of steps.
3. Choose the desired option from the menu. (See Step 2 in the preceding
   list for a description of these options.)

In Case of Trouble

If you experience difficulty using the CD-ROM, please follow these steps:

1. Make sure your hardware and systems configurations conform to the systems requirements noted under "System Requirements" above.

2. Review the installation procedure for your type of hardware and operating system. It is possible to reinstall the software if necessary.

To speak with someone in Product Technical Support, call 800-762-2974 or 317-572-3994 Monday through Friday from 8:30 a.m. to 5:00 p.m. EST. You can also contact Product Technical Support and get support information through our website at www.wiley.com/techsupport.

Before calling or writing, please have the following information available:

- Type of computer and operating system.
- Any error messages displayed.
- Complete description of the problem.

It is best if you are sitting at your computer when making the call.